THE
LANGUAGE
OF THE
CAVE

THE
LANGUAGE
OF THE
CAVE

Edited by

ANDREW BARKER
Department of Classics, University of Chicago

MARTIN WARNER
Centre for Research in Philosophy and Literature
University of Warwick

ACADEMIC PRINTING & PUBLISHING
P.O. BOX 4218
EDMONTON, ALBERTA
CANADA T6E 4T2

APEIRON: a journal for ancient philosophy and science
Volume XXV, no. 4 (December 1992)
ISSN 0003-6390

Canadian Cataloguing in Publishing Data

Main entry under title:

The Language of the Cave

Includes bibliographical references and index.
ISBN 0-920980-52-X (bound). — ISBN 0-920980-53-2 (pbk.)

1. Plato.   2. Plato— Language.   3. Meaning (Philosophy)
I. Barker, Andrew, 1943-   II. Warner, Martin.
B385.L35 1993   184   C93-091309-4

Cover Design by Ottilie Sanderson
Printed by Art Design Printing Inc., Edmonton, Alberta, Canada

Contents

Introduction

Andrew Barker and Martin Warner

I

Plato's writings display a vivid sense of the tensions that exist between the ideals of philosophical enquiry and the nature of the language through which such enquiries must be conducted, expressed and stimulated in the minds of others. These tensions form the shared focus of the papers in this collection, which originated in a series of papers presented and discussed during 1991-92 at the University of Warwick's Centre for Research in Philosophy and Literature.

The dialogues contain acute and troubling reflections on the ways in which language achieves meaning, on the powers and epistemic credentials of discourse in its various forms, and on the uses and abuses of special linguistic devices and strategies. But these explicit remarks are by no means the dialogues' only contibutions to the debate. They leave us in no doubt that their author had thought long and hard about the roles of language in the pursuit of truth and the encouragement of enquiry, about what is involved in a word's 'signifying' something, about the strengths and defects of poetic, rhetorical and argumentative discourse, about relations between analysis, analogy and example, about allegory, myth, symbol, imagery and much else. At the same time, however, the dialogues are themselves striking exemplifications of this complex of phenomena, intricate verbal tapestries woven from strands of every linguistic sort. To reach any genuine understanding of the ideas and puzzles about language embedded in Plato's dialogues, we must seek to establish a dialogue of another sort, one in which ideas expressed in his works are made to engage with the literary and linguistic practices of the writings in which they find expression.

> Understand, then, that in speaking of the other segment of the intelligible I mean that which argument (*logos*) itself grasps through the

> power of dialectic, treating the hypotheses not as principles but really as hypotheses, as steps and springboards, so to speak, so that it may come to the first principle of everything, and having grasped it, may hold on, in turn, to the things that depend on that principle, and thus come back down to an ending, making no use whatever of anything perceptible, but using Forms themselves, going through Forms and ending at Forms.
>
> (*Republic* 511b-c)

At the highest level of understanding, for Plato's Socrates, the philosopher's dialectical skills enable him to review the whole realm of truth, and to establish his grasp on it as knowledge. His knowledge depends on his recognition of the 'unhypothetical first principle', the Form of good, to which dialectic has led him and in whose light it demonstrates to him all other truths. Nothing counts as knowledge unless it is established and confirmed through dialectic, and this applies as much to knowledge of the first principle as to any other (*Rep* 534b-c).

But in what language will the philosopher represent these truths, and submit his arguments to the critical scrutiny of his own mind and those of others? According to the view found commonly in dialogues of Plato's middle period, words possess meanings in so far as they are signs or 'images' of things beyond themselves (eg. *Cra* 422d-4a, 430a-1d). Any utterance or set of written symbols that does not represent something that there is, as it really is, must be either meaningless (since it is an image of nothing) or at best false (if we can resolve the problems that Plato notoriously encounters in elucidating the notion of falsehood: see *Cra* 429b-31a, *Tht* 187dff., *Sph* 236dff.). The ideal language of dialectic must therefore contain only terms that are perfect images of realities; and the relations between these terms, relations embedded in the logic of this form of discourse, must precisely mirror those that hold between the elements of reality itself. The *Republic*'s dialectic will make manifest to the mind the structure of what there is, and the nature of its elements, by constructing in words a perfect image or symbolic representation of truth.

No image, however, is identical with that whose image it is (*Cra* 432a-d). In contemplating the philosopher's discourse, whether the philosopher is oneself or another, we are not looking directly at the reality it purports to represent. But if image and original are inevitably different, might not the differences be such as to undermine the capacity of any system of images to reflect 'perfectly' the nature and interrelations of its originals? Can we know whether they do so or not? Have we the right to be confident that the rules of language that create 'logical' relations between words or propositions are exact formal counterparts of 'real' relations between the items that our language seeks to portray? Perhaps the notion of a 'perfect' image is ultimately devoid of sense.

Plato's difficulties with the notion of an ideal language do not end here. The terms deployed in dialectic must have determinate meanings if their use is to have any definite significance. They acquire their meanings, as we have said already, by being images of other things; and these things must therefore be fully determinate themselves. Whatever they are, they must *be* without qualification (*Rep* 476e-7a). This is why the ideal dialectical discourse envisaged at *Rep* 511b-c refers only to Forms, since only they have the characteristic of unqualified 'being'. But it appears that we have no direct access to the nature of these Forms, none that is independent of the linguistic manoeuvres of the very dialectic whose credentials are in doubt. We cannot demonstrate the perfection of our discourse by pointing to the perfection of its correspondence with the reality it claims to describe, since our knowledge of the reality, if knowledge it be, is wholly contained in our mental engagement with statements in the language. We cannot see beyond the discourse. How, then, can we know what our words mean, or indeed that they mean anything at all (cf *Prm* 133a-4e)?

Further complexities arise as soon as we consider the task that Plato assigns in the *Republic* to the true philosopher, or the role that he himself assumes in writing philosophical works. Even if we concede the possibility of a perfect dialectic, its exponent is not merely to spin for his own delectation a symbolic tapestry of truth: he is to speak to others less enlightened than himself, and guide them towards an understanding equal to his own. A perfect understanding might see reality perfectly mirrored in the philosopher's discourse, but his words nevertheless miss their aim unless they achieve appropriate signification in the minds of the hearers or readers to whom they are actually addressed. Given the very variable emotional and conceptual standpoints of human individuals, and their differing intellectual powers, what the philosopher's audience makes of his discourse may be seriously adrift from its objective meaning. Plato's acute sense of the fragility of the bridge formed by words between mind and mind is a major factor underlying his familiar strictures on the written word (*Phdr* 274b-8b; *Ep* 7, 341a-4d). Live speech and discussion are no doubt preferable from this perspective, but even so the risks cannot be eliminated; and in any case we must not lose sight of the fact that Plato himself wrote prolifically, and apparently with serious intent.

If Plato's speech, or his written dialogues, or the educational discourses of the *Republic*'s philosophers are to have any value, they must address their audience in a language to whose significance they have access. Language will be meaningful to them, pointing beyond its own sounds and symbols to things that they represent, only in so far as they are capable of recognising what is represented. Its words must be 'images' of things within the domain of which their minds conceive. But all members of this audience, all of us, are inhabitants of the Cave (*Rep* 515a). So long as we are sitting in chains, facing the Cave wall, the only 'realities' we recognize and the only things that words can designate to us, are mere shadows of things that are themselves unreal. The mountebanks who foist these illusions on us, the puppeteers and showmen of Plato's allegory, would seem to be the orators, poets, politicians and sophists who provide the community with its values and goals, and mould the citizens' conceptions of the world. The paraphernalia they display in the firelight, so the allegory suggests, are quite artificial constructions, the merest fictions, unrelated to the truths outside our dusky prison to whose existence the philosopher seeks to alert us. What we take to be real are not even these figments themselves, only their shadowy images, products of seductive language, rhetoric and propaganda. How then can the philosopher say anything that is both a true representation of the reality he recognizes and appropriately significant to us? Our minds, as Socrates says, must be turned in a new and unfamiliar direction (*Rep* 518b-d); but how can this conversion be achieved through language that we can understand?

The language of the Cave must in fact be defective even when it is restricted to its own immediate domain. Such meaning as it has derives from its capacity to designate, to be an 'image' of things beyond itself. If a statement in a language is to mean something that could be true or false, its terms must have determinate significance; but in so far as these terms are grasped by us as images or symbols of things in the world we perceive, there is no such significance for them to have. These things are radically indeterminate in their natures. They are and are not what they are said to be, in equal measure (*Rep* 479b); and in that they are perpetually changing, they can never correspond to any single description for two instants together (*Tht* 182b-d). Either our language is as indeterminate in its meaning as they are in their being, or it must invariably fail to have significance of the sort we attribute to it. Whichever view we take, we must concede that what we say, and the way we understand what is said, are nonsensical: yet it is to us, in our language, that the philosopher must speak.

This way of putting the problem, however, seems to contain the seeds of its own solution. The conundrums spun by Socrates in the *Republic* are ones whose force we can recognize, despite the limitations imposed by our 'unreal' frame of reference. Even in the earlier dialogues, Socrates argues compellingly that the meaning of terms in our languages cannot be understood merely through their reference to concrete items in the world of our direct experience, and that this is as true of simple-looking words such as 'shape' or 'bee' (*Men* 72a-b, 73e-5a) as it is of those like 'virtue', 'knowledge' and the rest whose complexity and obscurity are more immediately evident. Such reflections may lead us to understand that the source of meaning, even in our own imperfect language, lies beyond the realm of the items superficially designated by its words. If our words are images, most directly, of things in the domain of our experience, we can assign them intelligible significance only if we construe those things, in their turn, as images of realities not contained in that domain.

This brings us to a point from which we can get a clear view both of the powers wielded by the sophisticated language-user and of the risks he runs. A poet, for example, may tell us the tale of Achilles. At one level the content of his story is trivial. It is a mere trace of deeds done long ago, or never. It has significance in our world in so far as Achilles and his actions stand as images of something else, of courage and heroism, perhaps, which we may admire and seek to emulate. Plato never underestimates the power of poetry to mould character and disposition: the entire educational programme of Books 2 and 3 of the *Republic* is premissed on it. But it is a maverick power, randomly exercised. The poet persuades us to admire one image and despise another not because his words reveal to us the truth about what is good or bad, but because of the emotional appeal of his surface play of imagery. To be an effective poet or orator, shaping his hearers' characters or sensibilities, a speaker need have no knowledge of virtue or goodness, only the knack of charming, terrifying or disgusting us with the shadowy pictures conjured up in his words,

But the philosopher, it may be argued, is in a privileged position. He knows the truth: hence in speaking to us in language we understand, deploying all the powers of imagery, narrative and rhetoric, he can be relied on to use them in the right way, and to turn our minds towards what is real and good (cf *Phdr* 277b-c). Hence, perhaps, we might seek to explain away the tensions in Plato's own writings, the fact that while he idealises an inaccessible dialectic and roundly condemns rhetoric, poetry, myth, dramatic representation and their kin, his writings nevertheless exploit these despised resources to the full. But this suggestion has its own problems. In the first place the philosopher's poetry and rhetoric will work on us only as those of other clever speakers do. What we become convinced of may be the truth, but we shall not know that it is so. Secondly, if the arts of philosophical persuasion can indeed initiate our ascent from the illusory world of the Cave, we have still to face the problems we touched on earlier, those that lurk at the heart of the notion of an ideal dialectic, a language in which truth can be perfectly represented. Finally, we must surely pause to wonder whether, in purging language of its cloudy images and forging it into a shining mirror of eternal truth, we may have lost as much as we have gained. We live as shadows among shadows, and the fact is reflected in the elusive ambiguities of the language we speak. In the logic of pure dialectic, that of which we currently speak is strictly unspeakable. Through commitment to that logic we may gain access to truth, but we risk losing the power to speak or think of our own world, or even of ourselves. Does any vantage point exist from which Plato, and the *Republic*'s philosophers, can speak credibly and meaningfully inside the Cave?

II

The account provided by the first contributor to this volume puts in serious doubt the possibility of any such perspective. The tension between the language of the Cave — with its imagery, myth, poetry and rhetoric — and the ideals of dialectic may be irresoluble. The 'literary' language of the Cave-dwellers articulates a reality of contradiction and conflict which is incompatible with that of the world of dialectic; as John Gould puts it: 'if the fictional worlds of literature, of epic poetry and drama, present a true image of the real, then Plato's image of reality is quite simply false.'

For Gould there is 'a war in progress'; Plato, like Tolstoy, is at war with his culture's 'greatest achievements', and in his assault on the traditions of Homer and the Tragedians uses 'any weapons' to enforce a picture of reality from which 'almost every recognizable and defining trait of both divinity and humanity as they appear in ancient Greek literature has been excluded'. For virtually all such literature is 'performance literature' with polyphonic voices, subverting the Platonic aspiration to a 'simple univocality of meaning' in favour of an 'incorrigible plurality' whose paradoxes are presented with 'sophisticated and ironical detachment' by his arch-enemy Homer.

But this compounds the problem, for Plato is at least equally capable of sophistication and irony, and here the parallel with Tolstoy weakens; the writings in which Plato addresses art and literature are themselves among his most achieved works of literary art, but the same can hardly be maintained in the case of Tolstoy. Plato's strategy, one might say, is the pursuit of analogous objectives to those of Tolstoy by means other than that of the warlike diatribe — seeking to be 'winning' in the sense of 'persuasive' rather than 'coercive'.

But open contradiction is less than persuasive, and Penelope Murray is concerned to explore the apparent incompatibility between Plato's exaltation of the poets as inspired interpreters of the gods in the *Ion* and the *Phaedrus* with the hostile account of the poet as imitator in the *Republic*. Both accounts turn out to be ambiguous: the notion of *mimēsis* in Book 3 of the *Republic* relates to mimicry or impersonation applying only to certain forms of poetry, whereas in Book 10 the analogy is with visual representation and now all poetry comes under condemnation. Again, the eulogies of the poets as divinely inspired are ironically equivocal. The two accounts are brought together in the *Laws* where the notion of inspiration enables Plato to generalise *Republic* 3's use of *mimēsis*, for on both accounts 'the poet does not know what he is doing, and is therefore incapable of judging his productions'. By emphasizing the passivity of the poet and the irrational nature of the poetic process Plato turns the traditional concept of poetic inspiration as a guarantee of truth upside down. So persuasive was this strategy that 'the image of the frenzied poet', hardly known before the fifth century, became a commonplace even among poets themselves, being taken up in the notion of the *furor poeticus*.

Mary McCabe focusses on the tension between Plato's use of myth, allegory and image and his stricter argumentation. The significance of the former turns in part on Plato's conceptions of argumentation and understanding. The ambiguities of the world of our senses make nonsense of all forms of explanation save the strictest — such as the 'simple-minded' account of the *Phaedo* — yet such strict accounts are too 'thin' to give full understanding. Full understanding is systematic, requiring connectedness within a complete and teleologically ordered system — but neither observation nor argument will yield it. Thus two ideals are in conflict. The 'scientific theorising' of the 'simple-minded' procedures is governed by principles of simplicity and economy. But it is a fuller understanding that is sought : 'an entirely systematic and exhaustive account of the universe' of the sort sketched — though with intellectual 'health warnings' — in the teleological myth of the *Timaeus*. The myth of the Cave, one notes, provides a perspective in terms of which this conflict is readily understandable.

The role of such myths, McCabe argues, is in an important sense argumentative. Understanding is a cognitive state, 'an active character of the mind', and the characteristic mode of activity is that of argumentation; at its best this is dialectical, 'a dialogue within the soul' which has an innate drive towards consistency. But 'the only real live souls involved in the Platonic dialogues are the souls of his readers', and Plato is concerned to move each of us from passive reader to 'active dialectician'. Part of his method is to juxtapose argumentation with images, allegories and myths which are significantly discordant with the argument and obey radically different principles of explanation — teleological comprehensiveness contrasting with argumentative reductionism. 'The combination of myth and argument is itself an argument — of the dialectical sort. It is left to the reader to untie the knot.'

For Manuela Tecuşan the role of imagery and metaphor in Plato is less argumentative than didactic. She considers some of the characteristic ways Plato seeks to go beyond 'scientific theorising' by interconnected uses of image and example. These are characteristically introduced with McCabe's intellectual 'health warnings'; the form of presentation through images and myths 'allows us to abbreviate matters considerably, but one should not expect from it real explanations about the nature of things' — for this we need to turn to dialectic. The functions of such forms are didactic, persuasive and clarificatory; Plato uses images 'to reach subjects or modes of thought which have no images' and thereby to overcome states of mind which impede the proper working of that dialectic.

The status of 'real explanations' remains, however, problematic. Christopher Rowe focusses on that 'simple-minded' account of explanation described in the *Phaedo* which provides the model for McCabe's account of Platonic 'scientific theorising'. The direct route to what McCabe terms 'full understanding' is blocked, but there remains Socrates' 'simple-minded' route 'which will take him, and us, at least somewhere'. To look directly at reality is like looking directly at the sun in eclipse; if blindness is to be avoided one is better advised to look at its reflections — here, in propositions (*logoi*) — and to examine the truth of things in them. But such a procedure will not give full teleological explanation; it leads at best merely to a 'hypothesis worthy of acceptance' — which is very different from the full vision of the Sun aspired to in the *Republic*. We are still in the Cave, and 'in the language of the Cave, we can get to the entrance, perhaps, but no further'.

The final papers consider what may be learnt from the dialogue form itself — Plato's subversive use of polyphonic voices from the Cave to undermine the vision of 'incorrigible plurality' itself. They address in detail ways in which dramatic context in three of the 'middle period' dialogues may properly influence, even transform, our understanding of what is said by the participants.

In the early dialogues Socrates standardly takes his premises from his interlocutors and draws unwelcome conclusions from them by means of *elenchus* (refutation through cross-examination); he should not be taken to endorse the conclusions themselves. Michael Stokes argues that such procedures play a significant role in the final argument of *Republic* 5, which separates — in sharp contrast to the *Meno* — the provinces of belief and knowledge; this separation, he argues, 'need not be accepted as an item in Plato's own stock of philosophical beliefs', at least on the basis of this argument. The latter has been fiercely attacked, but the edge of much of the criticism can be turned once it is recognized that the passage represents genuine dialogue with the 'sightlovers' in which Socrates argues for his views in accordance with 'the Queensberry rules of dialectic' — soon to be codified by Aristotle — according to which 'the argument should use only claims acceptable to the respondent'. The whole strategy is elenctic, designed to bring out the internal incoherence of a position that at once admits the reality of sights and sounds and yet denies '"beauty by itself" and the like — what we now call the Forms'. Since the argument is based on non-Platonic premises, 'we should not saddle Plato himself with any other than the *literary* responsibility for either the course or the conclusions of the argument'.

Analogous considerations are at play in Richard Rutherford's exploration of the unity of the *Protagoras*. Both the lack of obvious conceptual coherence in the development of the dialogue and its concluding defence of the hedonic calculus — apparently so opposed to what we find elsewhere in Plato — have long puzzled the commentators. Rutherford takes these two features together and relates them to the overall context. The argument of the dialogue is contaminated by motives and methods other than the dialectical, such as the competitive spirit of the sophists and the desire of the spectators for 'a good show rather than a philosophically correct solution'. The undisciplined development of the argument is dictated by Protagoras himself, and the defence of the hedonic calculus demonstrates 'the inadequacy of Protagoras' thinking about his profession and its intellectual basis' — the doctrine does not represent Socrates' own view; Protagoras and his fellow sophists 'in the end fall short of the dialectical ideals which Socrates offers'. The true conclusion of the dialogue is a matter for the reader, who 'is left to evaluate Protagoras' performance for himself'. Taken as a unified whole, the *Protagoras* turns out to be an object lesson in the dialectician's difficulties in turning the Cave-dwellers' eyes towards the light.

In the instances discussed by Stokes and Rutherford, identification of the elenctic nature of the discussions points to a negative evaluation of the conclusions drawn. Martin Warner's exploration of the *Symposium* as 'dialectical drama' considers analogous features in an instance where the theses developed by Socrates cannot be so readily dismissed — providing, indeed, a counterpart in terms of psychology and sensibility of the more austerely intellectual ascent from Cave to Sun of the *Republic*. The counter-narrative of Alcibiades serves to confirm, not undermine, the account Socrates attributes to Diotima, while the latter takes up into itself what for Plato were the most defensible relevant considerations available to contemporary non-philosophical culture. The ascent to the vision of 'the beautiful itself' develops out of elenctic dialogue with Agathon, and many of the apparent argumentative weaknesses are a function of the latter's own presentation; but these features themselves arise out of what the preceding speakers have maintained, so that Socrates may be seen as 'weaving together and transforming what the others have said in terms of a coherent sensibility'. At least for those of us in the Cave, there may be no forms of demonstration available which are 'independent of our subjectivities'; what Plato does enact, here and elsewhere, is a form of

> philosophical activity which, though according to method, is not probative; its aim is rational persuasiveness, but ultimately the only test of this is the actual persuasion of those who are fitted to judge and have argued rationally.

On this reading of the *Symposium* Plato uses the ambiguities of our experience and language to point beyond them, encouraging us to open our eyes 'toward the light', to that which can only be grasped (if at all) in a transformed form of life. It runs counter to David Halperin's recent suggestion that such ambiguities are set against each other, with certain elements of the dialogue setting up an 'erotics of narrativity' which others subvert, an account which reads Plato as 'a kind of deconstructionist *avant la lettre'* (Halperin 1992: 118) — a remarkable modern instance of the ancient narcissistic practice of seeing in Platonic texts reflections of one's own era. It is more productive to attempt to learn from these texts by refusing premature syntheses, which can then be deconstructed, but treating them as the sort of coherent wholes recommended in the dialogues themselves — and hence as capable of challenging our own preconceptions. Reading them, that is, as the language of one who would remain accessible to those who dwell in the Cave while endeavouring to lead them from it.

If we set aside as premature Halperin's conclusion that 'Plato says one thing and does another', at least two possibilities open. If the recognition of an unhypothetical first principle which alone can ground knowledge of reality is indeed a possibility, as Plato appears to have believed, it is of that which is strictly unspeakable in terms of the language of the Cave — within which most of us live. Such language can at best be used to show that the source of meaning lies beyond the world of direct experience, in that which transcends it; thus there is at least as much point to the Patristic understanding of Plato as an integral part of the *praeparatio evangelica* as to contemporary attempts to claim him as a deconstructionist *avant la lettre*. But if the aspiration is senseless or otherwise ill-founded, the Platonic procedures may nevertheless help to show both the scope and the limitations of language and argument; the objects of the dialectical search for the true nature of virtue, knowledge, beauty and the rest may be chimerical, but the procedures used may help us to extend and deepen our grasp of the concepts available to us and the extent of their grounding in experience.

In this there is some irony. One of the great opponents of the whole Platonic enterprise is Nietzsche, who attacks the ideal of 'a cold, pure, divinely unconcerned dialectic', insisting that we find other ways of sifting good from bad 'modes of interpretation' (Nietzsche 1966: paras. 5 & 22). It may be that a careful reading of his dialogues will show that we can learn from Plato's own practice — whether or not we are prepared to credit any reality other than that which for him is Cave-like — in our attempts to develop such procedures for testing and improving our representations of reality.

Plato and Performance[1]

John Gould

It seems undangerous to say that Plato has a problem with art and literature. Not only does he come back again and again to the central questions of the creative process, the nature of the created work of art and the quality of its audience's response to the art-work, but what he has to say of these things both gives the impression, at least, of being self-contradictory and succeeds in leaving large issues of his meaning veiled in ambiguity. Moreover the extremity of the conclusions to which more than once his argument leads him is itself an index that these are not questions with which he engages in any wholly dispassionate mood of critical enquiry.

And yet of course from another perspective Plato is doing no more than returning to issues seen as raised by the work of art, above all the work of literary art, already in the imagined world of Homeric epic. The Homeric epics, especially the *Odyssey*, present their audience with a whole host of problematical, sometimes even paradoxical, issues that are triggered self-referentially by the part played by the art-work, in almost all cases by the narrative art-work, within the primary fictional narrative of the poems. The episode of Phemius' first narrative, for example, in the opening book of the *Odyssey* (1. 328-64) raises both the question of the differing emotional responses of different audiences to the same work of art, but also the crucial issue of authorial responsibility: is the singer responsible for the painful or morally disturbing

---

1 The text of this paper is presented here very much as it was delivered to the Warwick seminar. The argument of the final pages draws on an unpublished paper, delivered as the Corbett lecture at Cambridge in May 1991 under the title: '... and tell sad stories of the deaths of kings: tragic drama as narrative'.

quality of the experiences he presents to his audience or do those experiences themselves belong in another realm of discourse, outside the song and the singer's control, and hence outside his responsibility?

The problematic nature of the audience's response is taken up again in Book 8 with Demodocus' three narratives: the Phaeacian audience listens to all three with equal pleasure but Odysseus' response to the first and third, the Trojan tales of Odysseus' quarrel with Agamemnon and of the horse made by Epeios that Odysseus 'brought to the acropolis', is the socially inappropriate one of tears and groans. It is only saved from causing acute and general embarrassment by the tact and social sensitivity of Alcinoos. It is only with the middle tale of the three, that of Ares and Aphrodite, that Odysseus' response is in line with that of his hosts. Nothing is made explicitly of these happenings but it is clear that for Odysseus, as for Penelope in Book 1 (but not, tellingly, for the Phaeacians), the narratives of Troy are of experiences too close to home to be received without pain. By contrast, with the tale of Ares and Aphrodite, for Odysseus as for the Phaeacians, the subject of the tale is distanced so far as to be the source of pure pleasure. Moreover, Odysseus' explicit comments on Demodocus' first narrative, the story of the quarrel at Troy, already touch on one of the problems that Plato was to address first in *Ion*, that is, the epistemological and psychological issues raised by the story-feller's ability to persuade his audience that they are being taken into a world of happenings far distant from their own experience by one who speaks as if he had been there, in that other world, himself.

Questions as to the relationship between fiction and reality and between pain and entertainment are again implicit in Alcinoos' intervention in Odysseus' own narrative on Phaeacia in *Odyssey* 11. 362ff., while the puzzling and problematic issue of the source of the story-teller's ability to create the world of his narrative is present both in Odysseus' false tale in the nineteenth book and in Phemius' account of his own creative powers in *Odyssey* 22. 345ff. Moreover, this is not the first time in Homeric epic that these issues have been raised: the paradoxes of art in its relationship with reality were already implicit in Helen's comments in the sixth book of the *Iliad*: 'these things happen so that we can be made into things of song for the men of the future' (*Iliad* 6. 354ff.) and the *Iliad* employs also other techniques of implied commentary on its own narrative (as, for example, in the *ekphrasis* [interpretive description] of the shield of Achilles in Book 18). By the fifth century, and certainly by the fourth, we can reasonably call these questions traditional.

But what, of course, sets these Homeric incursions into what we might call issues of literary theory apart from Plato's later treatment of some of the same issues is the tone in which they are presented to us. Although the *Odyssey* never suggests that these questions are trivial (indeed, there is a sombre, even tragic, quality to the exchange between Telemachus and Penelope in the first book), nonetheless there is a quality of teasing playfulness about some aspects at least of the *Odyssey*'s treatment of the problematic nature of the work of art. Thus, for example, the paradox presented to us throughout the epic by the stories that Odysseus himself tells within the poem. It is a paradox never made explicit but it teases the poem's audience at every turn: the narrative strategy of the primary narrative of the poem ('Homer's' narrative) offers it as beyond question that Odysseus' own narrative on Phaeacia has the same status as that of the primary narrative itself: it is a true account of real experiences. On the other hand, his various narratives on Ithaca are all, however much they differ from one another, alike in that they are all to be taken as false accounts of experiences that have never occurred. Yet it is equally beyond doubt that the occurrences of the Phaeacian narrative are almost all fantastical, utterly improbable and entirely beyond the experience, both of the internal audience within the fiction of the poem and indeed of any audience external to the poem that may ever have received them, whereas the happenings of Odysseus' Ithacan narratives have a plausibility, a likeness to 'life' and to lived experience, that ought to guarantee their truthfulness.

Again, Odysseus' narratives are in counterpoint with the (imagined) worlds in which they are delivered, in such a way as to disguise these points from us. The part-fantastic, part-magical world of Phaeacia provides the setting for an audience which listens without sense of incongruity to narratives of witches, nymphs and giants, while the intensely 'real' world of Ithaca receives false but 'realistic' tales of raiders and mercenaries, Crete and Egypt, with an equal sense of the appropriateness of the narrated event to the experience of its audience. Clearly Homer is playing games with us, and that is something that Plato, in the *Republic* at least, is equally clearly not doing.

But then, of course, before the *Republic*, there is *Ion*. *Ion* introduces us to some of the problems that face us in getting to grips with Plato's views on art and literature. Is Plato too playing games with us in this highly 'Socratic' dialogue? Clearly Socrates is playing games with Ion but that is not quite the same thing. There is, on the face of it, a problem in reading *Ion* in tandem with the *Republic*, since there is an obvious contradiction between the 'conclusions' reached in *Ion* (that the source of the poet's or the singer's knowledge is not rational but irrational because it comes to him from the gods ['it is the god himself who is speaking': *Ion* 534d 3-4] and that the poet is no more than the mouthpiece, the 'interpreter', of divinity and the singer an 'interpreter of interpreters') and Socrates' ringing assertion in the *Republic* that the entire Greek literary tradition not only systematically misrepresents the truth of human experience and human behaviour but also that it wholly misrepresents divinity itself, which is incapable of resorting to falsity or deceit as it is incapable of inflicting hurt. An obvious way out of the dilemma created by such apparent contradiction is for us to invoke the notion of irony (a strategy to which Iris Murdoch seems drawn in *The Fire and the Sun*) and to assume that the proposition that the poet is merely intermediary for the utterance of divinity is itself 'merely' a kind of joke, a part of the game that Socrates plays on Ion, and not one that we ourselves are meant to take non-ironically as an idea to be entertained seriously.

But it is precisely here that we come up against a characteristic problem facing anyone who tries to assure himself that he has grasped Plato's meaning. For it is hard (I myself would say indeed impossible) to treat the whole of *Ion* as a game in which we, the readers, merely participate as detached observers of the ironical discomfiture of Ion. For when Socrates maneouvres Ion into giving an account of what it is like to perform the great moments of Homeric epic to a vast audience, what we are given (by Plato) is surely one of the classic accounts of the psychology of performance, which only one who was himself in tune with the complexities and contradictions of the performing process could possibly have produced.

Plato makes Ion describe, in answer to Socrates' questions, how at such moments (moments like Odysseus leaping onto the threshhold and pouring out his arrows at his feet in the instant before he begins his revenge on the suitors in the opening lines of *Odyssey* 22, or Achilles setting out on his fatal pursuit of Hector in *Iliad* 22) it is as if he were himself on Ithaca or at Troy; his heart is pounding in excitement or his hair bristling in panic, even though he is at the same time aware of standing in the place of performance in front of twenty thousand persons, all of them 'on his side', to quote Socrates, and aware too, again at the same time, in an apparently wholly detached way, of his audience's response to his performance and of the vital importance to himself as performer that he control that response in an appropriate way. Otherwise, as Plato makes him say, if his audience laughs when his performance requires them to weep, the laughter will be at his expense and the tears will be upon him. There is, surely, no irony in that description: it is not merely games-playing, even if our response to it as readers is, in the context, an ambivalent one. On the contrary, this is an account of one who is able fully to empathize with the performer and his experiences.

For the moment at least *Ion* must remain a problem, one not made easier for us by echoes of the idea that the poet is one possessed by divinity and that his works are produced by 'divine power' ('*theia dunamis*') or 'divine dispensation' ('*theia moira*') in the *Phaedrus*' classi-fication of poetry, like prophecy, as a form of 'divine madness'. But then of course the interpretation of that passage in *Phaedrus* is equally debateable.

However, on almost any reading, the core of Plato's views on art and literature is to be found in the *Republic* and it is to the *Republic* that we must now turn. There are two things, above all, that make that text too problematical for any would-be interpreter. The first is the growing sense of philosophical over-kill that comes over the reader as literature and all its works are done to death repeatedly in Books 2 and 3 and then again revived for a further, yet more comprehensive process of analyti-cal annihilation in Book 10. The second stems not only from the vehe-mence of the onslaught but also from the nature of the target. For Plato is no Mary Whitehouse. His aim is directed not at the marginal, the allegedly outrageous fringe of art-works that offend his moral sensibil-ity, but at the entire Greek literary heritage, including all its master-works, from the *Iliad* onwards to the greatest masterpieces of fifth-century tragedy.

The point is simple but needs to be grasped and moreover given the weight it deserves before we go on to examine what exactly Plato is doing in his none-too-elegant destruction of literary art. For as with Tolstoy's total dismissal of Shakespeare, so with the *Republic* it is difficult not to feel that Plato is at war (and the phrase involves, I think, no exaggeration) with the very best things, the greatest achievements, that his culture had to offer him, or us. We should not, though, be surprised, however dismayed we may feel, since there is an obvious parallel, as well as several links in the tone of the argument and the form that it takes, between Plato's rejection of his own literary culture and Socrates' equally wholesale rejection of the moral culture within which he (and Plato) had been brought up.

We encounter another twist in the paradoxical complexities of Plato's literary persona as soon as we acknowledge that the best state-ment of the shock occasioned by Socrates' gentle but persistent and absolute denial of the validity of the Greek moral tradition is to be found in the words of 'Callicles', the fictional persona of Plato's own dialogue, *Gorgias*. When Callicles asks Chaerephon if Socrates is 'playing games' or being serious in his total rejection of the morality of reciprocity and goes on to describe Socrates' position as one that implies that the whole of human life is an inversion of what is actually demanded of men in their behaviour, we may feel inclined to requisition his language in our own response to the arguments that Plato gives to Socrates in the *Republic*. 'Is he serious?', we may wish to ask, in asserting that what most readers will feel to be among the greatest things in European culture are to be removed from view, taken out of cultural circulation and mockingly dismissed (the standard translations, by the way — suggesting that we should, for example, 'fall down and worship' (Shorey 1930) the Homeric poet and taleteller before ceremoniously expelling him — quite fail to convey the sneering tone of Plato's words *proskynoimen an auton* at 398a 4). Notoriously, though, it is a mark of Plato's greater literary maturity that in the imagined world of the philosophical discussion in the *Republic* there is no 'Callicles' or 'Protagoras' to express dismay and disbelief at the thrust of Socrates' arguments. On the contrary, the response of Adeimantus and Glaukon is almost nowhere more abrasive than 'Absolutely', 'I agree' and 'Yes'. Not for nothing, one feels, did Plato enlist his own brothers as Socrates' respondents in the *Republic*.

I shall look first at some of the arguments that Socrates offers in Books 2 and 3 of the *Republic*, move on to consider briefly what is added to those arguments in Book 10 and then return to consider in more detail the discussion of narrative and dramatic *lexis* in 3. 392-5. Plato's argument starts, persuasively and uncontroversially, as an argument about *paideia*, about bringing up the young. We tell them stories, naturally: are such stories to be true or false? Are they to be 'good stories' ('*kaloi mythoi*') or not? Such are the innocuous but, one feels, disingenuous questions with which Socrates opens the discussion and it is not surprising that Adeimantus has no difficulty in answering them affirmatively. But rapidly we are in very deep water indeed. Socrates' first examples of the 'big stories' told by Hesiod and by Homer which are unacceptable and 'not to be told in our city' (378b1) are perhaps unexceptionable enough, stories such as Hesiod's story of Ouranos' castration by his own son, Kronos. Stories such as these, after all, provide the paradigms for the arguably dubious propositions presented by Theseus in Euripides' *Herakles* 1314ff., by the Nurse in *Hippolytus* 451ff. and, worse still, by Wrong (the 'Unjust Argument') in

Aristophanes' *Clouds* 904ff. These stories cannot be accepted as truth, Socrates argues, since after all 'god is good' (*agathos ho theos*: 379b1).

'God is good' is a proposition not seemingly to be disputed. But for Socrates that proposition turns out to have some far-reaching and disconcerting implications. If god is good, god is incapable of causing harm or hurt. Therefore god cannot be responsible for ill but only for what is good and Homer (that is, Achilles in *Iliad* 24. 522ff.) must therefore be wrong: if god brings hurt upon men, it can only be as punishment, which is by definition beneficial. We may have a passing anxiety here at Plato's inability or refusal to make any allowance for the dramatic mode of representation in casually identifying the fictional character with the poem's author but for the moment it is only a passing anxiety. More shocks are in store.

If god is good ('of course', as Adeimantus says), he is also incapable of change. He is *haplous* (simple) and *alēthēs* (true) and does not depart from his own idea, since whatever is good is unchanging and cannot tolerate *pseudos* ('falsity': an uncomfortably imprecise word). Hence not only are stories of gods deceiving men, even for their own good, by definition false tales but so are all stories which involve the idea of gods appearing in forms other than their own. The premises upon which this phase in the argument of *Republic* 2 depends imply a notion of divinity strangely and perhaps disquietingly similar to a Platonic Form. But the surface of the argument is so placid and undisturbed that we may not notice immediately that we are already being committed to a definition of divinity which is utterly incompatible with that everywhere implicit in the traditions of Greek religion and of Greek storytelling, wherever and by whomever told. There are, strikingly and disturbingly (since no-one in the world of the argument seems to notice), no gods in accepted Greek tradition like the gods offered by Socrates to Adeimantus' unhesitating acceptance in *Republic* 2. Rather they resemble the Apollo of the 'unacceptable' but marvellous lines given by Aeschylus to Thetis (fr. 550; quoted at *Republic* 2. 383b).

If god is good, so too can be men and if they are good, they will not, for example, lament a death, even their own (as Socrates does not in *Phaedo*). The good man is 'sufficient for himself: he does not need another' (387d-e). Thus Homer's description of Priam's lament over Hector or Achilles' over Patroclus are not to be tolerated: we shall ask him not to write such things. It is by now even less clear whether this is because such descriptions misrepresent reality or because they provide a bad example to those who receive them. Furthermore, 'serious men' (men who are *axioi logou*) will not laugh. Still less will gods; nor will they give way to passion or to lust, nor to any desire for food, nor be moved by any wish for gifts or for revenge.

By now almost every recognizable and defining trait of both divinity and humanity as they appear in ancient Greek literature has been excluded from the acceptable picture of reality. In its place we are offered an image of reality as the uniform, the invariable, the homogeneous; the real as completely unchanging and stable, viewed always, by whomsoever it is viewed, as the same; unreceptive of disputed or divided response. This, beyond doubt, is the image of reality that Plato gives us in the language with which, in *Phaedo* as well as in the *Republic*, Socrates describes the Forms. If we should wish to describe works of art as in any sense dealing with 'reality', as enabling us to come to terms with 'the real', we shall clearly be talking about a different kind of reality, one which acknowledges the co-existence of opposites, the presence of irreducible conflict, even of contradiction, within the real; we shall be talking about reality as the arguable. And it is evidently that reality, if we use the word at all, with which we shall want to say that the *Iliad* or the *Oresteia, Bacchae* or *King Oedipus*, deal. The 'quarrel' between poetry and philosophy seems established as beyond question.

When Plato returns to these questions in Book 10, with a sense of doubling back to pick up once more something long since dealt with, we have of course passed through the Cave and a great deal of water has flowed under the philosophical bridges of the *Republic*. The added metaphysical dimension clearly enables him to make further statements about the art-work which are, in an important sense, new. So too does the psychological model of the human personality which, by Book 10, we have also taken on board: that model makes it possible for him to sharpen his point about the damage done to the audience of poetry by what poetry has to offer. Poetry appeals to the non-ratiocinative parts of the mind: it therefore produces contradictory responses by giving free rein to what the 'better' self keeps in check and suppresses. In a memorable phrase, he asserts that poetry 'waters and nourishes' (*trephei ardousa*: 606d) our desires and emotions.

Still later in the book, as he approaches the myth of Er, Plato gives us another image of the soul as it has been altered from its true self by its experiences in the world, so as to be wholly unrecognizable. This is the image of Glaukos as he emerges from his long immersion in the sea: some parts of his body had been broken off, some crushed and smashed by the battering of the waves and his whole person was encrusted with new accretions, of shell-fish, sea-weed and pebbles, so that he looked rather like some kind of monster than his true nature (10. 611c-d). The image, overwhelmingly persuasive, haunting and unforgettable, as so much of Plato's imagery is, is not applied to the personality of the hearer of poetry but we can surely accept it as a telling indication of how far Plato supposed that the human psyche can be distorted by immersion in a medium that perverts its true nature. And for Plato, when he wrote the *Republic*, poetry was undoubtedly such a medium.

Moreover, the attack mounted on poetry, quite specifically, in *Republic* 10 (for poetry, see 595a3), is no longer in the context of *paideia* but within a metaphysical perspective which sees it as providing unreal images of things that are themselves not of the real. The art-bed is image of a bed which itself, because it is a physical object and belongs in the world of physical objects, is ultimately unreal: the art-bed is image of an image of the real. We may be likely to protest that there is no confusion between art-object and the object imaged: we do not try to go to sleep on an art-bed nor sit on Van Gogh's chair, any more than we expect to smell his sunflowers. Moreover on the rules which Plato lays down elsewhere (in *Phaedo* and *Parmenides*, for example) for playing the reality game by invoking the notion of Forms, Plato in *Republic* 10 seems to be indulging in a degree of gamesmanship. Nowhere else do we encounter a Form of a man-made object nor do we anywhere else encounter the notion (597b5-7, 13-14 + c1-d6) that it is god (a god?) who 'made the bed which exists in nature' (*hē en tēi physei ousa*: b5-6); that is to say, created the one bed (the Form) which is of the world of the real.

The corollary, of course, of this proposition is that 'reality' is created by god, and that is not elsewhere a part of Platonic cosmology, even in *Timaeus*; and it will hardly do simply to describe it, as Iris Murdoch does, as a 'picturesque argument'. It is almost as if, here in *Republic* 10, Plato is making up the metaphysical rules by which he conducts the destruction of art and its objects as he goes along and that the new rules exist solely to give a particular bite to the arguments that are to effect that destruction. They have not appeared before and they are not called upon hereafter.

We might ask, then: why? Why does Plato feel the need to create a new set of metaphysical assumptions (an act which is once again not allowed to disturb Adeimantus' equanimity) in order to explain and justify the earlier refusal to accept or even to tolerate the products of poetry? He seems bent on establishing two positions which again appear to stand in an uneasy relationship with each other: first, that art lacks all claim to seriousness, that it offers only the trivial and the unreal; and second, that it is powerfully subversive and has the capacity to disturb and even ultimately to destroy the proper relationship between the parts of the human psyche. Of course, for Plato, there is no inconsistency: unreality does threaten the precarious human grasp on the real and if art is mere 'play', as he sometimes suggests, that is no reason for not taking it seriously. It means perhaps merely that it can be disposed of with the less compunction, the fewer qualms.

But that will not quite do. After all, most of us would agree that Plato is himself beyond doubt an artist and that his writings, his 'works', are beyond question art-works. How could someone capable of creating great works of literary art be so insouciant of denying them any positive value? Our sense of incredulity is likely to be of the same nature as that we feel when we encounter his equally strenuous denial of value to the written, as against the dialectically spoken, word. Can he really be so insensitive to the products of his own creativity? Or is this another form of Platonic (or Socratic) irony, this time masochistic to a degree?

Of course, I have already indicated some reasons for suspecting that he is not so insouciant as he presents Socrates as being. The very fact that he does return to the attack on the work of art in Book 10, when the process of condemnation and execution seemed already to be over, suggests that he is worried that the corpse will not lie down. It is almost as if he feels himself engaged in a life-and-death struggle with something extremely threatening. But why?

Part of the answer, I am sure, lies in the point to which I drew attention some time ago: namely, that the nature of the 'reality' defined by literary art, and already by the masterpieces of Greek literature, is a reality of contradiction and conflict, and that one major function of art is to make it possible to live with contradiction, to accept, in Wallace Stevens' phrase, 'things as they are'. That is not at all the reality defined by Plato's perceptions of the real, which must be simple, pure, stable and which does not tolerate contradiction. There is indeed a war in progress, a deadly serious one, between two entirely incompatible notions of reality and Plato is quite prepared to deploy any weapons that may be to hand in order to win that war. After all, if the fictional worlds of literature, of epic poetry and drama, present a true image of the real, then Plato's image of reality is quite simply false.

But there is another and perhaps equally important aspect to Plato's hostility to the art-work, one which involves the notion of performance. Having dealt with the unacceptable content of the stories told in epic and tragedy, Socrates is made to suggest that the mode of telling is a separate issue which also requires independent discussion. The passage on *lexis* begins at 3. 392e6 and lasts only some five Stephanus pages but it contains some highly significant argument. The focus of Plato's interest is on the mixed mode of story-telling that he illustrates from the first book of the *Iliad*, a mode in which 'narrating' (*diēgēsis* or *apangēliē*, in Plato's terminology) is combined with what Plato calls *mimēsis*, 'imitation', for want of a better English word. Plato's case against this mode of story-telling combines, somewhat idiosyncratically, two points. First, that the narrator (though Plato significantly does not distinguish between 'poet' and 'narrator' and calls both 'Homer'), by using *mimēsis* (that is, by using extended passages of direct speech within his telling of the story) is presenting himself 'as if he were someone else '. (Is he? And if he is, is 'he' 'Homer'?) He is doing his utmost to 'turn' the audience's mind into supposing that 'it is not Homer but the priest, who is an old man, who is speaking'. The second point involves a characteristic piece of Platonic *leger-de-main*: it is that both the narrator and, for Plato far more importantly, the audience of such a mode of story-telling, by involving themselves mimetically (that is, by the kind of empathy so well described in *Ion*) in 'many activities', will become jacks of all trades and masters of none. For the Guardians, who are to have a single skill as 'master craftsmen of the city's freedom', such a risk is unthinkable and *mimēsis*, except of the good and noble (as defined by Plato), is to be at all costs barred from their experience.

But there is clearly yet more to Plato's polemic than this. The whole passage on *lexis* is another example of over-kill. Homeric epic and tragedy have already been dispatched, as we have seen, on the ground of misrepresenting the nature of the real. That, for Plato, is a capital charge. It must surely seem supererogatory now to proceed to a second annihilation based on the way such disallowed story-telling is presented to us. Moreover, there is something distinctly odd about an outright assault on *mimēsis* (as defined in this passage of the *Republic*) which occurs in a context that is itself almost entirely mimetic, and on Plato's own definition. After all, the 'first narrative' (to use Gérard Genette's terminology) of the *Republic* ('I went down to the Peiraeus yesterday ...') only maintains its *diegetic* stance for a few pages and even then is very far from the lifeless 'pure narrative' to which Plato reduces the opening of the *Iliad* (393d- 394a) by stripping it of all *mimēsis*. From the moment when Kephalos leaves, to 'superintend the rituals', the 'story' of the *Republic* is presented to us not as narrative but as almost entirely mimetic discourse. The very fact that we may have some difficulty in thinking of the *Republic* as the 'narrating' of a 'story' is surely evidence enough for the point that I am arguing.

The crucial fact here is that almost all Greek literature down to Plato is what we might call 'performance literature'; that is to say, it is not read by a readership but performed in front of an audience. Homeric epic, in so far as it is mimetic (and Plato's point is an acute one, as Genette's analysis brings home to us), and the whole of Greek drama, by definition, are not story-telling in which the tone, emotional intensity and 'meaning' of the story are controlled by the single commanding voice of the poet. The poet is not there to mould the reader's reception of his story because he has withdrawn from the world of his fiction in favour of other persons who are actors of roles. He gives the floor to his characters, who are in turn presented by autonomous others: the rhapsode, who is his own one-man troupe of role-players, or the troupe of actors. Moreover, drama, by its very nature, is a kind of narrating of story which systematically subverts all that Plato, in this passage of the *Republic*, is clearly committed to establishing; that is, the simple univocality of meaning which is implicit in the perception of reality.

Drama is no more than a passing illustration of Plato's point in the argument of Book 3, an illustration so obvious that Adeimantus is allowed to introduce it, but to consider drama, especially tragic drama, for a moment will help us to see what it is that Plato takes to be so threatening in the nature of the work of literary art. In pure narrative, as Plato would define it, the narrator plays a kind of didactic role; he is in absolute and total control of his audience's 'reading' of the story; it is he who selects not merely the language but also the tone of voice of his narrating; who ensures the univocality as well as the rationality of the narrated events. Contrast with this the 'narration' of tragic drama. By its very mode of presentation, tragedy insists on the 'impurity', the multivalency of experience; it insists upon the interpretability and hence the irreducible plurality of the real. Chorus and characters alike struggle to impose their sense of the meaning of events but always in conflict with others. The aspiration to 'narrate' experience and to control closure and hence meaning is common to all the voices that we hear but is constantly frustrated by the presence of other, competing 'narrators'. There is no privileged voice to interpret experience for us univocally.

Let us briefly take *Antigone* as example. The 'story' of *Antigone* surely achieves meaning, not by enforcing acceptance of one, as against the other, of the conflicting interpretations of events offered us by Antigone and by Creon, nor by privileging the account of Teiresias so as to obliterate those of Antigone and Creon. Any such reading of the play must surely be reductionist. On the contrary, tragic drama seems to require of us, not that we acquiesce in an inevitably reductionist combining of incompatible narratives but that we learn to accept the 'incorrigible plurality' of our experience of the real, the ultimate 'unnarratability', perhaps, of experience itself.

Thus *Ion* turns out to have pointed us in the direction of an aspect of literary art, especially Greek literary art as Plato and his contemporaries experienced it, that goes some way (I think a long way) towards explaining Plato's ferocious hostility ('the ferocity of the attack is startling', as Iris Murdoch rightly says) towards 'mimetic' poetry and drama; namely, its 'performative' nature. And Homer gets special treatment because Plato quite correctly sees in him the same tendency to autonomous but conflicting narratives of 'the story' that tragic drama was later to make its own.

The phrase 'incorrigible plurality' that I have just used is purloined from a poem of Louis MacNeice: 'World is crazier and more of it than we think, / Incorrigibly plural. I ... feel / The drunkenness of things being various' (1964: 'Snow'). That 'drunkenness', celebrated by MacNeice, is one that Plato, at least in the puritanical mood of the *Republic* or the *Phaedo*, would not have wished to feel. On the contrary, the intensity of his commitment to the 'singularity' of the real makes it impossibie for him to observe the paradoxes of plurality with the sophisticated and ironical detachment of his arch-enemy, Homer the performer.

Inspiration and Mimēsis *in Plato*

Penelope Murray

Plato's attitude to poetry is notoriously ambiguous. How can he sing the praises of poets as divine beings inspired by the gods in the *Ion* and the *Phaedrus*, and yet banish them from his ideal state in the *Republic*, declaring at 600e that poets produce nothing but a superficial likeness of the subjects they treat, and have no grasp of truth? On the face of it the notion of the poet as an inspired interpreter of the gods would seem to be incompatible with that of the poet as a feeble imitator of appearances. And indeed many scholars have noted that, with one exception, a passage in the Laws (719c) to which I shall return later, Plato keeps these ideas separate.[1] In this paper I shall first discuss Plato's concept of poetic inspiration, and then go on to consider the relationship between inspiration and *mimēsis*.

I begin with the *Ion*, a dialogue in which Socrates sets out to prove to the rhapsode of the title that his success as a reciter of Homer does not depend on any skill (*technē*) or knowledge (*epistēmē*),[2] a proposition

---

1 On the apparent discrepancy between inspiration and *mimēsis* see e.g. Hackforth 1952: 61; Flashar 1958: 107-12; Rosen 1959: 143; Vicaire 1960: 225-6; Tigerstedt 1969: 66; Pöhlmann 1976: 191-208; Velardi 1989: 115-6.

2 See e.g. 533d1, 536c1, 536d2, 542. The terms *technē* and *epistēmē* are virtually synonymous in this dialogue. See further, Flashar 1958, 27ff., 79ff. The essence of what Plato means by *technē* is summarised at *Grg* 465a, where he says that cookery is not an art (*technē*), but is empiricism (*empeiria*) 'because it has no rational understanding of the nature of the patient or the prescription, and is thus unable to give a reason for its procedure in every case. And I cannot call anything which is irrational an art'. Despite problems of detail in the text and interpretation of this passage, on which see Dodds 1959 *ad loc.*, the general point, that a *technē* is based on a rational principle and can therefore always explain its procedure, is clear. See further e.g. Rosen 1959, 136ff. and below, n.19.

which is first put forward at 532c6 and then repeated with monotonous regularity throughout the dialogue. After some preliminary questioning Ion is quickly reduced to *aporia* and asks Socrates why it is that he excels in speaking about Homer (ironically using the verb *euporō* at 533c6 just at the point where he has reached *aporia*), but is at a loss as far as any other poets are concerned. Socrates replies at 533d that Ion's ability does not depend on *technē*, but on a divine force (*theia ... dunamis*). Just as a magnet attracts iron rings and induces in those rings the power to attract other rings so that a long chain can be suspended from the magnet, so the Muse inspires a chain of people possessed by divine enthusiasm.

With this image of the magnet Socrates shifts the focus of the dialogue away from the specific question of Ion's skill (or lack of skill) as a rhapsode and moves on to the larger subject of poetic inspiration in general. For, as he explains later on (533e), the rhapsode is the middle link in a chain inspired by the Muses: first there is the poet, then the rhapsode, then the audience. The implication of this image is that what is said about rhapsodes also applies to poets (and vice versa). There has been much debate about the 'real subject' of the *Ion*. Is it an attack on Ion in particular or on rhapsodes in general? Is it an attack on poetry or on its interpreters? Or is the dialogue really about poets and poetic inspiration? But perhaps these are the wrong questions to ask. For, as Velardi has pointed out (1989: 113), Plato is concerned with the whole process of poetic communication, which involves the poet as author, the rhapsode as communicator and the audience as recipients. The image of the magnet at the beginning of Socrates' speech strongly emphasises the interconnexion between the different elements in this chain of poetic communication.

The Muse inspires a whole chain of people who are *entheoi* or *enthousiazontes*, for as Socrates goes on to say (533e5) all epic poets, or rather all good epic poets, recite (*legousi*) all their fine poems not through skill (*ouk ek technēs*), but in a state of enthusiasm and possession. This is a startling statement. We all know that poets traditionally claimed to be divinely inspired, but no-one had ever said that poets lack skill. Furthermore, lack of *technē* is not the sign of a bad poet; it is specifically good poets who are devoid of skill. Ion himself is, of course, a good rhapsode, as we see from the beginning of the dialogue where Socrates congratulates him on winning first prize at the festival of Asclepius at Epidaurus. The fact that Socrates uses the term *legein* both of poetic composition and of poetic recitation suggests that he is not interested in distinguishing between the poet as composer and the rhapsode as reciter; so far as he is concerned in this dialogue, their activities are parallel.[3]

Just as good epic poets recite their fine poems when inspired, so too good lyric poets compose their fine songs (*ta kala melē*) when they are not in their right minds. This is another startling statement: had anyone ever said that poets were actually out of their minds when composing? Indeed the words *ouk emphrones.. .poiousin* at 534a2 are almost a contradiction in terms, since *poiein* and its cognates when used of poetry generally refer to the craft aspects of poetic composition. Two images underline the irrationality of lyric inspiration, the repetition of the words 'lyric poets' at the beginning and end of this section (533e8, 534a1 and 534a6) strongly suggesting that these images apply specifically to them. First they are compared with Corybants who dance when they are out of their minds; the initial point of comparison here would seem to be music. Socrates goes out of his way to distinguish betweeen epic and lyric poets and to stress the musical element in lyrical composition — melody, dance and rhythm — perhaps in order to make the comparison between poets and Corybantic dancers seem plausible. Once he has established that comparison he can then conveniently forget that it was introduced specifically in relation to lyric poetry. When these lyric poets embark on melody and rhythm, they are filled with Bacchic frenzy, *bakcheuousi*, a word which picks up the dancing of the Corybants (*orchountai* at 534a10), but also broadens the picture of frenzied ecstasy. Not only are they dancing, they are possessed like Bacchic women who draw milk and honey from rivers when they are out of their minds, an image which suggests supernatural strength and fluency as well as divine possession.

Socrates claims that the poets tell us this themselves (534a6-7), but in fact they do no such thing. Bacchic and Corybantic ritual had never had anything to do with poetic inspiration, but Socrates manages to make the analogy look plausible by producing a kind of collage of traditional material. Of course wine had been associated with poetry and song from Homer onwards, but as Tigerstedt has pointed out (1970: 175-6), drunkenness and divine possession are not the same thing, even

---

3 This point is stressed by Velardi 1989: 50. On the use of the term *legein* see further, M.L. West, 'The singing of Homer and the modes of early Greek music', *J.H.S.* CI (1981) 113-15; J. Herington, *Poetry into Drama: Early Tragedy and the Greek Poetic Tradition* (Berkeley and Los Angeles 1985), 13, 224-5.

amongst the followers of Dionysus. Some have adduced Archilochus fr. 120 as evidence for a connexion between poetic and Bacchic frenzy: 'I know how to lead off the dithyramb, the lovely song of the lord Dionysus, when my wits are thunderstruck with wine'. But the source of inspiration in this fragment is not Bacchic ritual as such, but wine, which Plato significantly does not mention in this passage of the *Ion*. It is the portrayal of Bacchic ecstasy such as we find in Euripides' *Bacchae* which lies behind Plato's image of the poet as Bacchant rather than the *topos* of the drunken poet. Plato no doubt exploits the age old connexion between wine, poetry and song, symbolised by Dionysus himself as god of the vine and as patron of Greek drama, in building up his picture of the frenzied poet;[4] but we should not underestimate his originality in assimilating poetic inspiration to Bacchic ecstasy.[5]

The streams of milk and honey at 534a5 of course recall Euripides' *Bacchae* (142-3, 708-11) where the ground flows with milk and honey for Dionysus' frenzied worshippers. But they also recall Pindar's words at *Nemean* 3.76-9: 'I send you this honey mixed with white milk ... a draught of song on the breath of Aeolian pipes'. Milk and honey are associated not only with Bacchic ecstasy, but also with poetry, and Plato exploits these associations in order to bring together two different kinds of experience: Bacchic ecstasy and poetic inspiration. The poets tell us, says Socrates, that they bring us their songs from gardens and glades of the Muses, culling them from honey-flowing streams like bees. Honey was indeed associated with words from Homer onwards, and in the lyric poets in particular honey is often used as a symbol for poetry. It is also associated with prophecy, and specifically with pro-

---

4   On wine and song see F. Lissarrague, *The Aesthetics of the Greek Banquet*, trans. A. Szegedy-Massak (Princeton 1990), 123-39; on Dionysus and Greek drama see C. Segal, *Dionysiac Poetics and Euripides' Bacchae* (Princeton 1982); and on Dionysus and poetic inspiration see the judicious remarks in R.G.M. Nisbet and M. Hubbard, *A Commentary on Horace Odes: Book II* (Oxford 1978), 316-7.

5   Dr. Andrew Barker points out that Pindar *Dithyramb* 2 (= fr. 70b, ed. B. Snell, rev. H. Maehler, Leipzig 1975) provides positive evidence of the distance between the poet and Bacchic *mania* in more traditional accounts. Here Pindar's description of his new-style dithyramb vividly emphasises frenzy, wildness and Bacchic fervour, as against the dreary artificiality of earlier compositions. But he goes on: 'the Muse has set me up as a chosen herald of wise words (*sophon epeon*) for Greece'. The poet who produces 'wild' poetry representing ecstasy and frenzy is himself very far from being out of his mind. See further Barker 1984: 59-60.

phetic inspiration in the *Homeric Hymn to Hermes* (11.552ff.) where the poet describes the Bee Maidens of Mount Parnassus (three virgin sisters who teach divination), who speak the truth when they are inspired by feeding on honey. The connotations of honey imagery have been fully discussed in several studies, notably by Scheinberg (1979), who shows how widespread the association was between honey, bees, poetry and prophecy. The mere mention of honey in a poetic context is enough to bring to mind the whole range of these associations; honey, we should remember, recalls not only the sweetness of poetry, but also the truth of its content.

The poet as bee is therefore a traditional image, as is the idea of the poet culling his songs from the garden of the Muses. One thinks, for example, of Pindar, *Olympian* 9.26: 'I dwell in the choice garden of the Graces', or of Aristophanes, *Frogs* 1299-1300 where Aeschylus speaks of 'culling the sacred meadow of the Muses'. The verbal parallels with the passage in the *Ion* are obvious, and it is through precise verbal echoes such as these that Plato succeeds in making his overall picture of the frenzied poet look plausible.[6] Socrates adds an additional point at the end of the sentence: 'poets too [i.e. like bees] fly through the air' (534b3). Just when we are on the point of grasping the metaphor it flies off again, for poets are birds now as well as bees, an image which reminds us, for example, of Aristophanes *Peace* (827ff.) where the slave asks Trygaeus:

> When you were up there in the clouds, did you see anyone else flying around there?
> No, except for two or three dithyrambic poets flitting about collecting preludes.

Similarly in the *Birds* (1373ff.) Cinesias comes in quoting Anacreon: 'I fly up to Olympus on light wings; I fly from one path of song to another'. He wants wings in order to go up to the clouds and collect preludes. But significantly he adds that his whole art, his whole *technē*, derives from the clouds. This is parody, of course, but the example shows that however light-weight and airy dithyrambic poetry may be, Cinesias can still claim that it is a *technē*.

Socrates' speech resonates with familiar images, but when he goes on to interpret that imagery he does so in a way which subverts many

---

6 For further details see my commentary on the *Ion*, Cambridge forthcoming.

of the traditional claims which poets made. 'A poet is a light, winged and sacred thing', as we have seen already, but when Socrates endorses that picture by explaining that the poet cannot compose until he is out of his mind (*ekphrōn*) and his reason has left him we seem to be moving into the realms of Socratic/Platonic fantasy. I claimed earlier that no-one before Plato had ever said that poets were literally out of their minds when composing, but perhaps I have over-stated the case. Perhaps there is a reference to this idea in Aristophanes *Acharnians* (395ff.) where Dicaeopolis calls on Euripides and asks the slave:

> Is Euripides in?
> He's in but not in, if you see what I mean.
> How can he be in and not in?
> Easily. His mind is out, collecting scraps of poetry, and so not
> in. But he's in upstairs, composing a tragedy.[7]

Again there is possibly a parody of the notion of poetic *enthousiasmos* in Aristophanes *Thesmophoriazusae* (40ff.), where Agathon's slave emerges from the house and says: 'A band of Muses composing lyric poems dwells inside my master's halls'.[8] But it is difficult to find any trace of the idea of poetic inspiration as a form of possesion in literature earlier than the fifth century. Indeed it seems very likely that the idea was first formulated during this period, and that it was Plato above all who developed the image of the frenzied poet which became a commonplace for centuries to come.[9]

Dodds (1951: 82) guesses that the idea may have been a 'by-product of the Dionysiac movement' which sounds plausible enough, but again it looks as if Plato was the originator of the image of the poet as Bacchant. Another possible source for the idea of inspiration as a kind of frenzy, *furor poeticus*, is the old analogy between poetry and proph-

---

7   See M.S. Silk, *Interaction in Poetic Imagery* (Cambridge 1974): 121; Verdenius 1983: 44 n.134.

8   As implied by the comments of K.J. Dover in *J.H.S.* 1970, 231.

9   See Tigerstedt 1970; Woodruff 1982a; Verdenius 1983: 27-8. The term *enthousiasmos* first occurs in Democritus, fr. 18, and both Cicero (*de Orat.* 2.46.194 and *de Div..* 1.38.80) and Horace (*A.P.* 295-7) name him in connection with the notion of *furor poeticus*. For an attempt to reconstruct Democritus' views see Delatte 1934. On the relationship between Democritus and Plato see Tigerstedt 1969: 72-6.

ecy, which Plato certainly exploits in this passage in the *Ion* as elsewhere. Having said that no poet can compose until his mind has left him (and there is still the implication that he is talking about lyric poetry), he goes on to make a statement about all composition: no man so long as he keeps his mind can compose or prophesy (*chrēsmōdein*). Characteristically Plato introduces a new point here (534b7) at the end of a sentence; a new point but one that is not entirely unexpected since the picture of inspiration which he has built up is one that belongs to the sphere of prophecy.

We know, of course, that the association between prophecy and ecstatic inspiration is ancient and widespread. The word *mantis* (seer) is etymologically connected with *mainesthai* (to be mad), and the Pythia at Delphi provides a classic example of prophetic enthusiasm in the literal sense: the priestess, so it was believed, became *entheos*, filled with the god, who spoke through her, using her merely as a passive medium for his message. Cassandra, as portrayed in Aeschylus' *Agamemnon*, provides another obvious example of this phenomenon. We also know that in many primitive societies poet and prophet are not differentiated; a single figure, the seer, combines the functions of both.[10] There are several indications that this was once the case in ancient Greece: for example, the overlapping of the domains of Apollo and the Muses points to an original unity of poetry and prophecy. In Homer the functions of *mantis* (seer) and *aoidos* (bard) are clearly separate; but Hesiod recalls an earlier stage when he describes how the Muses singled him out to be a poet and inspired him to sing of the future as well as the past (*Theogony* 32). He represents himself here as a *mantis* rather than as a Homeric *aoidos*. The analogy between poet and prophet is a commonplace in early Greek poetry, and it is often therefore assumed that Plato is doing nothing new in characterising poetic inspiration as a form of *enthousiasmos, ekstasis* or *mania*, as if it were exactly analogous with the ecstasy of the Pythia. But I would argue that whatever conditions may have pertained in the pre-literate, pre-historical period, whatever the etymological evidence may suggest about an original unity between poetry, prophecy and an altered state of mind (on which see Nagy 1989: 26-7), the picture of poetic inspiration that we

---

10 See H.M. and N.K. Chadwick, *The Growth of Literature*, 3 vols. (Cambridge 1932-40); James L. Kugel (ed.), *Poetry and Prophecy* (Ithaca and London 1990).

find in early Greek literature does not correspond with the frenzied portrayal of a Cassandra or a sibyl. Plato claims that his notion of *furor poeticus* is entirely traditional: in the *Laws* (719c) he says that there is an 'old story (*palaios mūthos*) that the poet, whenever he sits on the Muse's tripod, is not in his senses, but like a spring lets whatever comes into his head flow freely'. But in reality the figure of the mad poet is a Platonic myth.

It would seem that despite the appearance of continuity, Plato's doctrine of poetic inspiration in fact represents a radical break with the past. He takes over the traditional view that poets are divinely inspired, but transforms it by emphasising the passivity of the poet and the irrational nature of the poetic process. He differs most significantly from his predecessors in maintaining that inspiration is incompatible with *technē*. The craft elements in poetry had always been important, and by the time Plato was writing, the word *poiētēs* (maker) had come to designate the poet par excellence. The implications of the term *poiētēs* are discussed by Nagy (1989: 23-4):

> Whereas the *aoidos* had remained in the sacral realm of prophecy, as evidenced by the institutional dependence of the *aoidos* on the divine inspiration of the muse, the *poiētēs* entered the desacralised realm of poetry as we are used to it, where the very notion of inspiration is but a literary convention. The *poiētēs* was a professional; he was a master of *technē*, the work of an artisan. In the *Frogs* of Aristophanes, the very art of tragedy is consistently called *technē*.

It is curious that Plato should revitalise the notion of inspiration in such a vivid way precisely at the point when inspiration had become nothing more than a literary convention. He does this partly by breathing new life into a cluster of metaphors about poets and poetry which were not exactly dead, but which had become conventional. If a poet describes himself as a prophet, a bird or a bee what are the implications of such images, asks Plato, and he comes up with some very striking answers. He also invents some extraordinarily powerful images of his own, notably the poet as Corybant or Bacchant. The total effect of his highly skilful collage[11] is to provide an overwhelming image of irrationality, at least so far as the poetic process is concerned. He has not yet tackled

---

11 I borrow this term from Velardi 1989: 57.

the content of poetry in the *Ion*, and in so far as he touches on that subject at all, he is perfectly complimentary: poems are consistently described as *kala* (fine or beautiful) throughout the dialogue.

In fact Plato constructs his account of poetic inspiration in the *Ion* so that it is deliberately ambiguous. By using the language of divine possession Plato maintains a link with the traditional concept of poetic inspiration, but turns this concept upside down. In the early Greek poets, the divine origin of poetry is used to guarantee its truth and quality,[12] and there is still an implication of that sort in Socrates' words here, especially at 534d. Despite its eulogistic tone, however, this speech undermines the authority traditionally accorded to poets by depriving them of *technē*. And we cannot ignore its context: as I said earlier, the image of the magnet at the beginning of the speech emphasizes the interconnexion between the various elements in the chain of poetic communication, and it is difficult, therefore, to separate our judgement on the activity of the rhapsode (which must surely be negative) from our judgement on the activity of the poet. Like *Ion* we are left in a state of *aporia*, unable to decide how to read Socrates' apparent eulogy of poets. It is ironic, certainly, but how ironic?

The negative implications of Plato's theory of inspiration are apparent in several other dialogues. In the *Apology* (22b-c) Socrates professes to be dismayed to find that the poets whom he questioned were quite incapable of explaining the meaning of their poetry, and concludes that they compose not through wisdom (*sophia*) but by a kind of instinct and inspiration (*phusei tini kai enthousiazontes*) like seers. Again, as with the *Ion*, the value of the poetry itself is not necessarily diminished by the fact that poets cannot understand their own productions; but the 'wisdom' traditionally accorded to poets is certainly called into question. In the *Meno* (99c-d) Socrates asserts that statesmen like Themistocles owed their success not to the possession of wisdom or knowledge, but to inspiration:

> So far as knowledge is concerned, they do not differ from seers and soothsayers who, when inspired, say many true things, but they know nothing of what they say.
> - So it seems.

---

12 See Murray 1981: 90-2; Verdenius 1983: 27-8.

- Isn't it right, Meno, to call men divine who, without thinking, are often highly successful in what they do and say?
- Indeed.
- We should be right then to call divine those seers and soothsayers whom I just mentioned, and poets of every description. And we should say that men who take part in public affairs no less than these are divine and inspired, being possessed and held by god, when they are successful in speaking on many important subjects, although they know nothing about what they are saying.

The irony of this passage is all too apparent:[13] Plato uses the language of divine posession in this context (exactly the same language as he uses of poets in the *Ion*) in order to stress that politicians have no knowledge of what they do. If anyone is successful without the aid of reason — be he poet, seer or politician — he must be divinely inspired, a proposition which, though leaving open the possibility of valuable products (seers and poets say many fine things; politicians can speak well on important subjects) nevertheless undercuts the authority of the practitioners.

More ambiguous and less obviously ironic is the celebrated passage on poetic *mania* in the *Phaedrus*. In his speech of recantation at 244a Socrates suggests that madness is not simply an evil; on the contrary, our greatest blessings come to us through madness, provided that it is divinely given. Four types of divine *mania* are discussed: prophetic madness bestowed by Apollo, telestic or ritual madness, whose patron is Dionysus, poetic madness inspired by the Muses, and erotic madness, caused by Aphrodite and Eros. Socrates describes poetic *mania* thus (245a):

> The third type of possession and madness (*katokochē te kai mania*) comes from the Muses: taking a tender and virgin soul it rouses and

---

13   Those scholars who regard this description as a compliment to politicians (e.g. Flashar 1958: 112; Vicaire 1960: 31 and 353) fail to deal adequately with the following objections: in view of Socrates' negative verdict on politicians in the *Gorgias* (517) it is difficult to take his praise of them here seriously; the emphasis on their lack of knowledge can hardly be complimentary; the treatment of Anytus, Socrates' accuser, is clearly ironic; Socrates concludes by stating that the hypothesis that virtue (*aretē*) comes by divine dispensation can only be verified by an enquiry into the nature of virtue itself. The dialogue thus ends in *aporia*, and its conclusions cannot be regarded as certain. See further Tigerstedt 1969: 41-5; Sharples 1985: 187.

excites it to Bacchic frenzy in lyric and other sorts of poetry, and by glorifying the countless deeds of the past it educates the coming generations. Whoever comes to the doors of poetry without the madness of the Muses, persuaded that he will be a good enough poet through skill (*ek technēs*), is himself unfulfilled, and the sane man's poetry is eclipsed by that of the insane.

The contrast between poetic inspiration (described only here as *mania*[14]) and technique recalls the case of Tynnichus in the *Ion* (534d-e), a poet who composed nothing worth mentioning except a paean which is one of the finest of all lyrics, and which he himself described as 'an invention of the Muses'. But the passage in itself contains no hint of the irony with which Socrates treats the subject of poetic inspiration elsewhere.

So far I have stressed the novelty of Plato's emphasis on the irrationality of the poetic process; but it should not be forgotten that the powerful emotional, and therefore irrational, *effects* of poetry had always been recognised by the Greeks. The myth of Orpheus, the supreme example of the inspired musician exercising magical powers over nature itself, embodies an essential aspect of Greek thinking about poetry. From earliest times poetry was thought of as an enchantment, as is reflected in the use of the term *thelgein* and its cognates to describe the magical, and potentially dangerous, effects of song.[15] Specific emotional responses to poetry are described, for example, in the *Odyssey* when Penelope weeps as she listens to Phemius' song (1. 336), and

---

14 In early Greek literature the words *mania* and *mainesthai* are used to describe many kinds of behaviour which deviate from the normal, ranging from pathological insanity to mild unreasonableness or perversity. They are also commonly used in connection with various temporarily heightened or irrational states such as battle-frenzy, Dionysiac ecstasy and sexual desire. So when Plato speaks of the *mania* of the worshippers of Dionysus or of lovers he is using the word in contexts which are already familiar. Similarly his description of prophecy as madness is not new: Heraclitus (fr. 92) had already referred to the Sibyl as speaking 'with maddened mouth', and, as I have said, the association between prophecy and ecstatic inspiration was ancient and well established. But it seems very likely that the connexion between poetry and the *mania* word group was first made by Plato, which is in itself an indication of the originality of his views. See further, Verdenius 1962; Tigerstedt 1969: 64. On the significance of *mania* in general in Plato's work see Nussbaum 1982: 92-106.

15 See e.g. S. Goldhill, *The Poet's Voice* (Cambridge 1991), 60-66 with bibliography there given.

Odysseus is reduced to tears by the songs of Demodocus (8. 83-95, 521-34). According to Herodotus (6.21), the tragic poet Phrynichus dramatised the capture of Miletus so graphically that the whole audience was moved to tears, and fined him for reminding them of their misfortunes. Gorgias' *Helen* can be seen as an attempt to rationalise and analyse the emotive power of poetry.[16] His description of the effects of poetry on an audience who feel 'the shudders of fear, the tears of pity, the longings of grief' (*phrikē periphobos kai eleos poludakrus kai pothos philopenthēs; Hel* 9) is particularly interesting in view of Ion's claim at 535c that when he recites something pitiful his eyes fill with tears; when it is something fearful or terrible, his hair stands on end in terror and his heart leaps. What is different in Plato is that it is not just the audience who are carried away as they listen to the poetry, but the performer too. And there is the basic assumption running through the dialogue that the *poet's* mental state when composing is exactly analogous to that of the rhapsode when reciting.

Indeed Plato makes no distinction between composition and performance, a fact which, as Havelock demonstrated, clearly reflects the oral nature of Greek culture. Poet, rhapsode and audience all experience the same frenzied enthusiasm: Ion's soul dances (*orcheitai* 536b8) whenever he hears the poetry of Homer just as poets themselves are likened to dancing Corybants (*orchountai* 534a1) when they are filled with the Muses' inspiration. The audience, like Ion, weep and are amazed as he enacts Homer's words (535e). There is, of course, irony in the fact that Ion has to keep his eye on the audience's responses in order to make sure of his financial reward; but his enthusiasm is perhaps not quite as spurious as, for example, Tigerstedt (1969: 21) supposes. Plato is well aware of the paradox of acting whereby the actor can appear to be completely transported and yet conscious of his effect on an audience. As Ferrari points out (1989: 96) 'Ion is not actually lost in a world of his own; but his mind is lost to its proper function of understanding'. Indeed Ferrari has interestingly suggested (1989: 92-99) that it is precisely the theatricality of poetry which lies at the heart of Plato's critique. A skilful performance, such as Ion's, can transport us into an imaginary world, but it does not engage our understanding;

---

16   See Segal 1962; Havelock 1963: 161 n.25 and 145-60; De Romilly 1973. On the question of Gorgias' influence on Plato see Flashar 1958: 68ff.

and Plato infers from the emotional state of both rhapsode and audience that the poet when composing similarly projects himself into the imaginary world of his narrative, without understanding anything of what he does.

The idea that the poet's state of mind can be inferred from the actor's is in fact a persistent one in antiquity, as Cicero testifies in the *de Oratore* (2. 193-4). Remarking on the ability of an actor to arouse emotions in an audience by appearing to experience those emotions himself, he says:

> If that actor cannot act without grief, although he plays the part daily, do you think Pacuvius [the tragedian] could have written it in a calm and relaxed state of mind? Of course not. Indeed I have often heard that no-one can be a good poet whose mind is not fired with a kind of inspiration akin to madness — a view which is said to be found in the writings of Democritus and Plato.

Cicero here equates the notion of *furor poeticus* with the ability to feel emotions, and, like Plato, assumes that the emotional transport of the actor is analogous to the frenzied enthusiasm of the poet.

It is striking that in the *Ion* and other dialogues in which poetic inspiration is discussed there is no mention of *mimēsis*. In the *Republic*, however, the opposite is the case: we have *mimēsis*, but no inspiration. The subject of poetry is introduced in the context of how the Guardians of Plato's putative state should be educated. I wonder what weight we should give to the prefatory words at 376d9-10: 'Let us educate our imaginary citizens as if we were traditional story-tellers (*hosper en mūthoi muthologountes*)', especially since *mūthoi* (stories) are defined at 377a5 as being 'in general fiction (*pseudos*), though they contain some truth'. The whole discussion is prefaced with words that draw attention to its own status as a kind of *mūthos*, warning us, perhaps that what follows should not be taken entirely literally in all its details.

The first point established (377b) is that *mūthoi* have a profound effect on the young, and it is therefore of paramount importance that the stories they are told should be *kalon* (morally appropriate). Stories are traditionally the province of poets — Homer, Hesiod and the rest — but most existing poetry will have to be rejected because it misrepresents the nature of the gods (377e), and encourages moral weakness, such as cowardice and fear of death, by giving a false impresssion of the after life. It is the content of such poetry to which Plato objects, a point which is made very forcibly at 387b:

> We shall ask Homer and the other poets not to be angry with us if we delete all passages of this kind. It is not that they are unpoetical or unpleasant for the general public to hear; indeed the more poetical they are the less should they be heard by children and men who should be free, fearing slavery more than death.

Plato here sets up an important distinction between form and content: what makes poetry poetical is apparently the way in which the content is dressed up in order to make it seductive, the implication being that poetry is nothing other than a form of rhetoric.[17] If the content is false then the poetry is all the more dangerous, a point which Plato picks up and expands in Book 10 (see especially 601, quoted below).

The discussion in Book 3 moves from the question of content to form at 392c6. Poetry tells stories in three ways: by means of simple narrative, by *mimēsis*, and by a mixture of the two. *Mimēsis* is defined at 393c:

> When he [Homer] makes a speech as if he were someone else, shall we not say that he assimilates his speech as far as possible to that of the supposed speaker? ... Is not to assimilate oneself to another, either in voice or in gesture, to represent (*mimeisthai*) that person?

This is what happens in tragedy and comedy (394b6). It is also what happens in rhapsodic recitals such as Ion's, as described at *Ion* 535b. Socrates asks the rhapsode about his state of mind when he sings of Odysseus revealing himself to the suitors, or of Achilles rushing at Hector, or one of the piteous episodes about Andromache, or Hecuba or Priam:

> Are you at that moment in your right mind? Or does your soul, taken out of itself and inspired, imagine itself present at the events you describe? ...
>
> - How vividly you have proved your point, Socrates; and I shall speak frankly. Whenever I recite something sad, my eyes fill with tears; when it is something fearful or dreadful, my hair stands on end in terror and my heart leaps.

---

17   Cf. *Grg* 502 with Dodds 1959 ad loc; Halliwell 1988: 127-8. For the distinction between form and content see also *Rep* 378e4-9a4.

Plato does not use the term *mimēsis* in the *Ion*, preferring instead to speak of enthusiasm, possession and inspiration, but the experience here described bears a marked resemblance to the notion of *mimēsis* in Book 3 of the *Republic*. In both dialogues the activity of reciting and the process of composing poetry are treated analogously, indeed no clear distinction is made between them. Homer impersonates his characters no less than Ion does, so that in this sense at least *mimēsis* and *enthousiasmos*, so far from being incompatible, are actually one and the same thing.

When Socrates returns to the subject of poetry in Book 10, he says that they were right to have excluded all mimetic poetry (595a5) from their state. In fact they did not. At 396d, for example, Socrates suggested that it would be in order for a decent man to imitate a good man behaving steadfastly and reasonably; and at 398b he concluded his discussion of the role of poetry in the ideal state with the words: 'We ourselves for our own good should employ the more austere and less pleasing kind of poet and story teller, who would imitate (*mimoito*) the style of the good man'. But it now transpires that *mimēsis* in Book 10 means something different from what it meant in the earlier discussion. In Book 3 *mimēsis* means something like mimicry or impersonation and is to be understood primarily in terms of performance: to imitate a character, whether you are a schoolboy, a rhapsode or a poet, is in a sense to become that character. But in Book 10 painting is taken as the prime example of an imitative art, which leads to quite different consequences.[18] For one thing the analogy with visual representation enables Plato to introduce a metaphysical dimension into the discusion. Whereas the performer assimilates himself to, and therefore becomes like, the characters he represents, all the painter does is to produce a superficial copy of the appearance of things; *mimēsis* is now the equivalent of holding up a mirror to reflect the external world, a worthless activity which merely reflects the insubstantial world of particulars. This argument, which Plato applies wholesale to poetry as well of course, has to be understood against the background of the theory of Forms, as Socrates explicitly points out at 597a5. The poet, like the painter, is nothing but a specious imitator of appearances, whose representation stands, in Plato's famous words, at third remove from

---

18 See Annas 1981: 336-44; Nehamas 1982; Halliwell 1988: 7-11, 117-22.

reality (597e). Consequently all poetry is now *mimēsis* and condemned as worthless, whereas in Book 3 only certain types of poetry were classified as mimetic and therefore potentially dangerous.

Poets are not even given the status of skilled craftsmen, as is apparent from the way in which Plato plays around with the words *poiein* (to make) and *poiētēs* (maker), a word which by Plato's time had come to be used predominantly of the poet. In the passage from 596c-d, for example, the specious making of the poet is unfavourably compared with the genuine making of the craftsman who makes furniture. Although words like *demiourgos* and *cheirotechnēs* (both meaning craftsman) are used of the poet and the painter, it is pretty clear that they are used ironically: a craftsman who could make everything [i.e. like the poet or painter] would be 'a wonderfully clever man' (596c2), 'an amazing sophist' (596d). Plato is particularly anxious to discredit poets precisely because they have the reputation of being masters of all forms of skill (*pasas ... technas epistantai*, 598e). But for Plato the practitioner of a craft is always a better judge of poetic descriptions of his craft than the poet is, for the latter has no knowledge of his subject matter. If Homer really possessed the skills which are represented in his poetry he would have practised those skills rather than producing poetic imitations of them. The same argument is used against rhapsodes in the *Ion*, where Socrates says that if Ion really understood the art of generalship and the other skills to which he lays claim, he would be a general rather than earning his living as a rhapsode (541b-c).

In the *Ion* the rhapsode's obvious lack of skill is 'proof' that he is divinely inspired: since he is successful, yet does not seem to have any *technē*, he must be inspired. Although Ion himself lacks *technē*, there is apparently such a thing as rhapsodic *technē* (538b4, 539e3, 540a-b), but we are never told what that might be. In the *Republic* Homer's lack of knowledge does not carry with it the corollary that he is divinely inspired. Nor is the poet credited with having any skill whatsoever: the only thing he can do is to imitate (*mimeisthai*):

> Similarly [like the painter] the poet uses words and phrases to lay on the colours of every art, though he knows nothing except how to imitate, so that other people like himself, judging by the words, think that he really has something to say if he speaks about shoemaking or generalship or anything else in metre and rhythm and harmony. These have such great enchantment by their very nature. I think you know what the content of poetry amounts to when stripped of its musical colouring and left on its own. (601a-b)

At this point we want to say that at the very least the poet must have some skill because he knows how to use the formal features of poetry in such a way as to make his representations persuasive, but Plato does not even allow that possibility. His extreme reluctance to grant poets any *technē* whatever, both here and elsewhere in his work,[19] must surely be seen against the background of the increasing emphasis on the professionalism of the poet's vocation in contemporary society.

The final and most damning charge against poetry (605c6), and indeed the reason for its banishment, picks up and expands on views which have already been put forward in Book 3. Poetry appeals to the lowest element in our souls, stirring up our emotions, making us slaves to pleasures and desires which ought to be kept firmly in check if we are to live the good life. Annas (1981: 342 and 1982b: *passim*) points out that one of the deep seated problems about Plato's treatment of poetry in the *Republic* is that he seems to hold two inconsistent views. On the one hand poetry is important and dangerous, and so has to be severely censored as in Book 3 or expelled altogether as in Book 10 — although even here he does leave open the possibility that a defence of poetry could be constructed by men who are lovers of poetry without being poets themselves (607d-e). On the other hand poetry is a trivial and fatuous thing as he tries to prove (unsuccessfully, as Annas argues) by the inappropriate analogy with painting. But how incompatible are these views? Plato never underestimates the powerful *effects* of poetry: the direct content of poetry may be trivial, but its ethical implications and psychological effects are significant, and often thoroughly corrupting. Poetry is deceptive, as Plato makes clear at 601a-b, because ordinary people do not realise how trivial it is; they, we, are seduced into believing what poets say precisely because of its appeal to our emotions. It is dangerous because we are taken in by its 'natural magic' and

---

19 See Schaper 1968, 21-48. Plato does occasionally imply that the poet is a craftsman of sorts. Thus at *Rep* 601d it is said that there are three kinds of *techne* relating to any one subject, concerning the user, the maker and the imitator respectively. But it is clear that the imitator is inferior to other craftsmen in that his expertise, such as it is, is not based on knowledge of his subject matter (602). Cf. *Laws* 670e (with 669a-b) where it is said that although musical composers should understand *harmonia* and rhythm, they need not have knowledge of whether any given representation (*mimēma*) is good or bad. Perhaps the implication is that poets and musicians are incapable of having such knowledge.

deceived by its emotive power, so that we are incapable of judging its content.

Annas suggests (1981: 342-4; 1982b: 20-1) that to find Plato's views on poetry we should do better to look at other dialogues such as the *Ion* and *Phaedrus* in which the poet's gifts are taken more seriously. But the degree of irony which surrounds the topic of poetic inspiration in both these dialogues makes it very difficult to arrive at any settled conclusion as to the seriousness or otherwise of Plato's views; whilst I would not go so far as those critics who regard the *Ion* as merely ironic, it does seem to me to be more playful than serious. Similarly I agree with Rowe (1986: 10) that the tone of the *Phaedrus* is predominantly 'light, ironic and playful'. The setting outside the city walls in the country (230d) is significant,[20] as is the fact that Plato repeatedly alludes to Socrates' inspired state (235d, 238c-d, 241e, 257a, 262d, 263d). Plato makes Socrates behave uncharacteristically, putting set speeches into his mouth and pointing out that he is not responsible for what he is saying; as usual the notion of inspiration involves a lack of knowledge on the inspired person's part.

I do not intend at this point to add anything to the continuing debate amongst professional philosophers as to the interpretation of the *Phaedrus* as a whole; and it is obviously dangerous to extract passages from a dialogue as complex as this and discuss them out of context. But anyone interested in the subject of poetic inspiration must of necessity single out the words on poetic *mania* at 245a (quoted above, pp.36-7) for special comment, if only because of the centrality of this particular passage in the later classical tradition.[21] Here at last, it is often claimed, we have Plato's true views on poetry. But despite what is said in this passage, there is the extraordinary fact that later on in the dialogue at 248d-e Socrates rates the life of the poet sixth in order of merit after the philosopher, the king, the politician or businessman, the athlete and the seer. The language he uses is significant: the highest form of life is that of 'the lover of wisdom or beauty, a follower of the Muses or of love',

---

20   See e.g. Rowe 1986: 135 and Ferrari 1987: 1-36.

21   This passage, together with the *Ion*, provided the basis for the development of the Renaissance doctrine of *furor poeticus*. See B. Weinberg, *A History of Literary Criticism in the Italian Renaissance* (Chicago, 1961) vol. 1, 250-51. See also M.J.B. Allen, *The Platonism of Marsilio Ficino* (Berkeley and Los Angeles, 1984) 41-67.

whereas the sixth form of life is that of 'a poet or a practitioner of some other imitative art'. Some scholars attempt to eradicate this contradiction by referring to the distinction Plato makes between inspired poets and mere technicians at 245a.[22] But there is nothing in the text at 248d to suggest that the poet here is any different from the poet who is described in such fulsome terms at 245a. The contradiction between Plato's low rating of the poet's life and his earlier exaltation of the poet as divinely inspired must rather be accepted as an indication that Plato's attitude to poets and poetry in this dialogue is just as equivocal as it is in the *Ion*. Poetry remains a mimetic art, and the *Phaedrus* does not, after all rehabilitate poets, for the true devotee of the Muses proves to be the philosopher, who devotes himself to the highest form of *mousikē*, which is, of course, philosophy.[23] The ending of the dialogue (278c-d) where Plato asserts the superiority of the spoken over the written word also suggests very little change in his attitude to poets: if Homer and the poets along with speech writers and law givers had knowledge of the truth when they wrote and could defend their words in conversation they would deserve to be called lovers of wisdom. But a man who has nothing more valuable than what he has written, who has spent time twisting words, sticking them together and pulling them apart is rightly called a poet or a speech writer or a maker of laws. The one thing poets are consistently unable to do throughout Plato's work is to give an account of what they have composed. The conclusion of the *Phaedrus*, therefore, like the *Republic*, suggests that the poet is merely a manipulator of words, with no more grasp on the truth than anyone else.

I began by saying that the notion of the poet as inspired appears to be incompatible with that of the poet as imitator. But there is one passsage in the *Laws* (719c) where the two views are brought together:

> There is an old story ... that when the poet sits on the tripod of the Muses, he is not in his right mind, but like a spring lets whatever is at hand flow forth. Since his skill is that of imitation (*tēs technēs ousēs*

---

22 See e.g. Hackforth 1952: 84; Vicaire 1960: 53-4; Nussbaum 1982: 89. For criticism of this view see e.g. Ferrari 1987: 118-9 and 257-8.

23 See Nussbaum 1982: 88-91; Rowe 1986: 181; Ferrari 1987: 40.

mimēseōs), he is often forced to contradict himself, when he represents contrasting characters, and he does not know whose words are true.

Mimēsis is used here in the same sense as in *Republic* 3; in fact *mimēsis* and inspiration are identical.[24] *Mimēsis* in the sense of impersonation is just as irrational as inspiration in that in both cases the poet does not know what he is doing, and is therefore incapable of judging his productions. It is the poet's lack of knowledge which Plato consistently attacks, whether that attack is veiled in the ambiguous language of praise, as in the *Phaedrus* and *Ion*, or is more explicitly hostile as in the *Republic*. Even the concept of the poet as imitator of insubstantial appearances, explored in Book 10, is consistent with the idea of inspiration to the extent that it denies the poet knowledge. For Plato poets are masters of truth in no sense, for they have no skill and no means of understanding what they say. And they are particularly dangerous because they infect everyone with whom they come into contact with the same irrational frenzy as they themselves experience. This seems to me to be a far cry indeed from the images of the poet that we find in pre-Platonic literature.

---

24 As emphasised by e.g. Velardi 1989: 115-7.

Myth, Allegory and Argument in Plato
Mary Margaret McCabe

I Myth and allegory

If the job of a philosopher is analysis, maybe he has no business telling stories; if philosophy is about argument and truth, it should shun myth and allegory. Now when Aristotle writes philosophy, he writes arguments. When Plato writes philosophy, he writes stories, myths, allegories. Inside Plato's stories, if we are lucky, skulk some arguments, aimed at some unfortunate interlocutor and only indirectly pertinent to our philosophical concerns. Aristotle's arguments, by contrast, are directed straight at his audience; they are immediate and accessible. So Aristotle is easier on the philosophical eye. Why didn't Plato write like Aristotle?

What is wrong with philosophers telling stories?

a) Truth?

First of all, whatever a myth is, what it *isn't* is straightforwardly true — nor is it directly false. If I tell you that I caught a bus last week, then I might be telling you the truth — and if I said I met the man in the moon, you might say I was just lying (or mad). But if I tell you the story of Odysseus and Polyphemus you may think I'm telling a myth. Whatever that means to you, perhaps you won't be worried about its truth value; the important question about Odysseus and Polyphemus is not whether it really happened or not, but (perhaps) how the Greeks thought of barbarians, or why they found Odysseus' joke about 'Nobody' funny. So however outrageous, myths still matter — perhaps they explain how we understand ourselves, often against an alien background; their oddity may help the explanation along, rather than getting in its way.

b) Poetry

So myths and allegories are not literally true. But if myths are stories which hide the truth (or just miss the point altogether) has the philosopher any business using them? Plato's attacks on the poets suggest not. The only stories we should hear, he suggests in the *Republic* (376e ff.), are those which are true (and uplifting). The trouble with the poets is that they offer us mere imitations, at the second remove from truth (597e). So the poet either knows what he imitates or not (599a ff). If he knows, why not tell us; if he doesn't know, why bother to talk at all? (Cf. Osborne 1988) The trouble with poetry is that it has no devices for distinguishing the true from the false, and it has no justification for the false at all. Poetry contains the trap of the soap-opera, where we become so absorbed in the doings at Ambridge or Albert Square that we cannot tell where fiction ends and reality begins. We are prisoners in the televisual Cave, staring at the screen and never discriminating between the truth and the lies.

c) Imagery

Perhaps, then, myths are neither true nor false, but distanced from reality by being images of what is real and what is true. They are, that is, fashioned to suit the inadequacies of belief, the state of mind of people enmeshed in the sensible world, susceptible to the persuasive words of the poets and orators, who observe what is likely at the expense of what is true. Allegory (one might think) behaves in rather the same way. Look how Plato offers an allegory — the Sun — for the intelligible world dominated by the Form of the good:

> But, my lucky friends, let us leave for now the question of what the good itself is, for it seems to me to be beyond the scope of our present attempt to arrive at what I think about that now; instead I should like to describe something that seems to be an offspring of the good, and very like it, if that is pleasing to you; if not, I am happy to leave it.
>
> No, describe it, he said; you will pay your due to the parent another time.
>
> I wish I could pay my dues, I said, and you could collect them, and not just the interest [the offspring]. So collect this interest and offspring of the good itself. But take care lest against my will I deceive you, giving you a false-coined account instead of the interest.
>
> We will take care as best we can, he said; but just tell us.
>
> (*Republic* 506d-7a)

Here the point is that the sun is *not* the Form of the good. The allegory works because there is not a direct assimilation of the allegory to what it represents; instead, there is a distancing effect between the image (the sun) and its reality (the Form of the good), a distancing effect which is, we might think, somehow fundamental to the impact of the allegory.[1] That is all very well — but images (Plato is often thought to have said) are a bad thing, the mere appearances of the sensible world, which obscure the reality behind and get in the way of the philosophical soul. How on earth are we to understand them?

d) Cash-value

We might want to treat myths as crude versions (or subversions) of reality. Perhaps, then, we can cash the myth in for its corresponding truth? But Socrates argues against being too clever. At *Phdr* 229b ff. Phaedrus asks whether this is the spot where Boreas raped Oreithuia; no, not here, but a mile away, responds Socrates (is this myth a fact?). How should we interpret the myth, asks Phaedrus; *is* the story true? We could, of course, rewrite the myth as the history of a girl being swept away by the wind. But who cares about that, says Socrates, when he still does not know himself — he has no time for this alien story:

> If someone disbelieves in these [mythic monsters] and wants to re-duce each thing to what is likely in each case, using as it were some rustic wisdom, he will need a lot of spare time. But I have no spare time for things like that; and this, Phaedrus, is the reason. I am not yet able, as the Delphic saying has it, to know myself — it would seem absurd to me if while I was ignorant about that, I investigated things that belonged to other people. So I let these matters [monster-stories] alone and just believe the common view about them; and, as I just said, I investigate not them, but myself, to see whether I am some kind of beast more complex than Typhon and more bad-tempered, or a gentler and more simple creature, sharing by nature in some divine lot, not like Typhon at all.
>
> (*Phaedrus* 229e-30a)

---

1 Compare the effect of the 'chinese whispers' introductions of the *Symposium* and the *Parmenides*: a told b; b told c; c told d ... about this meeting between Socrates and his interlocutors. Cf. McCabe 1993b: ch. 4.

So Plato has good reason to reject the images and stories of the poets, which offer reality at several removes. Instead perhaps he should have written like Aristotle, eschewing myth and imagery; maybe he should have got on with the Delphic business of knowing himself.

But he doesn't — he writes myths, myths, what is more, of his own (no room for the anthropologist here), and allegories and stories as well as arguments. And he presents his stories in the terms I have described.

The myths are *alien*, they do not belong — hence, for example, the *Phaedo's* myth is second-hand (107d); the cosmology of the *Timaeus* does not belong to Socrates, but to Timaeus; and in the *Phaedrus* Socrates describes the soul under the influence of magic, and his story belongs, not to Socrates, but to Stesichorus (242c ff.).[2]

And the myths are *images*, not reality. The sun is a child of the good, a likeness of reality (*Rep* 509a), similar to the good but not identical with it (509c). A charioteer with two horses is an image of the soul (*Phdr* 246a), accessible to human ignorance. And the cosmologies of both the *Phaedo* and the *Timaeus* are 'likely stories' (*Phd* 108c, *Ti* 29c-d). Why should we take any of them seriously?

Perhaps we shouldn't. Perhaps we should attend to the health warnings on myth and allegory — 'beware of what follows'. Remember the equivocal introduction to the Sun allegory: 'take care lest against my will I deceive you, giving you a false-coined account instead of the interest'. It is as if Plato said, 'now I shall tell you a lie'. Are we to believe him? Or are we to believe the lie? Can we now believe the lie? What is the point of this sleight of hand?

One (obvious and rather dull) answer might be that Plato wanted to blandish us into reading his arguments — so he dresses them up in literary finery to seduce us into philosophical attentions. Or perhaps his myths and allegories do what he says they do — they illustrate the points in his arguments that he cannot demonstrate or argue for fully — literature supplies what philosophy lacks. The Platonic texts, on that view, are complex vehicles for philosophical dogma, instruments of persuasion, not weapons of argument. They are put together to persuade, not to demonstrate; and the remarks the texts make about rhetoric or poetry or deceitful propaganda are *ad hominem* attacks on Plato's opponents, not taken to apply to his own procedures.

---

2 Cf. Mackenzie 1988 on the requirement that explanations belong to their explananda.

II Argument

Where does that leave argument?

a) Truths with reasons
An argument may be thought of in Aristotelian mood, as a connected series of propositions, where the earlier — the premisses — give reasons for (they cause) the later — the conclusion. Thus, for example,

> All creatures with trunks are pachyderms
> All elephants are creatures with trunks
> All elephants are pachyderms.

Arguments like this (as Aristotle was the first to observe, e.g. at *Prior Analytics* 26b26 ff.) have two important characteristics: firstly they are valid in a perfectly obvious way (they *look* valid); and secondly their validity can thus be formalized (All B are A; All C are B; So all C are A). If the premisses are true, the conclusion will be true; the conclusion is true because the premisses are true. So the argument is explanatory. But what that means is that when we have the argument, we understand the conclusion — that is what understanding is — seeing why something is so, understanding the reasons why it is true. Now suppose that arguments like this, with true premisses and conclusion, represent facts in the world; that is why the premisses are true. Understanding, we may say, is a state of mind (not a state of affairs in the world out there). But if an argument directly generates understanding, understanding is itself caused by the argument's presenting 'truth with reasons'. So the cognitive state is directly consequent upon the argument itself — the argument is, we may say, transitive; and understanding requires no further cognitive or psychological content. Understanding is, as it were, a feature of the world, and nothing particularly to do with *me* the understander, except in so far as I provide the head for the understanding to be in.... Is that right? Does understanding *just happen* when we come face to face with an argument?

b) Explanation
That makes it all look rather too easy. Think again about explanation, the reasons that lie behind the truths. How does explanation work? Plato (characteristically) approaches this issue by posing some puzzles (in the *Phaedo*, 96 ff.).

Puzzle i) Imagine that Socrates is smaller than Simmias by a head. How can the head's difference between Socrates and Simmias explain *both* Socrates' smallness *and* Simmias' tallness?

Puzzle ii) Think about 'two'. How is it that instances of two may be explained *either* by the division of some whole into two parts, *or* by the addition of one unit to another, so that 'two' seems to have two opposite explanations?

The problem here seems to be this: neither the 'head' nor 'addition or division' explain properly, because in the first case we have the same explanation for different phenomena; in the second case different explanations for the same phenomenon. Can such accounts really be thought to explain? Surely, instead, we need some strict rules for explaining, so that we end up with the same explanations for the same phenomena, different explanations only for different phenomena. We need to be direct, to cite what exactly fits the explananda. When we explain, then we should say, for example, that 'the beautiful things are beautiful by virtue of the beautiful', 'the large things by virtue of largeness', 'two things by virtue of two'. Now the explanation of things' being beautiful or large will be the *form* of beauty or the *form* of large. This gives the proper account each time, and avoids contradictory-seeming muddles. This Socrates calls his simple-minded answer.

This account of explanation works piecemeal or one by one — each item is explained by citing its own explanation, by citing what belongs to it (it gives the *oikeios logos*, the 'explanation that belongs'). Does that sort of explanation work? You can see that if an explanation does *not* belong to the explananda, it cannot explain *them*. But then if the explanation does 'belong' does it do any explaining? The trouble with the simple-minded explanation is that it may turn out to be so close to what is explained that it never explains at all — simple-minded explanations are too thin to give us understanding.

c) Understanding

So far I have posed two questions about explaining and argument:

i) (about explanation) Is the simple-minded answer too thin, so that it doesn't provide any real understanding at all?

ii) (about understanding) Is there no positive psychological content in understanding, so that argument is just passively received?

Plato's account of full understanding tries to answer both questions by explaining both the systematic nature of explanation and the active role played in understanding by the mind.

1. Systematic understanding. Both Aristotle and Plato think that it is an important part of the philosophical method to connect things together. In the *Prior Analytics* it is the combination of the two premises which generates the conclusion. In the *Republic* the philosopher understands the symbiosis of the forms, analogous to the natural connection of the phenomenal world (hence the allegory of the Sun, 506 ff.). In the *Theaetetus* (184 ff.) reason contrasts opposites, compares similiarities and thus comes up with the common terms such as sameness and difference. In the *Phaedrus* and later, the best way to do philosophy is to find systems and structures — 'collection and division'.[3]

Why is connectedness, system, so important for Plato? If we can contextualise our simple-minded explanation among other explanations, we come to understand how it is that they explain. If we see that the beautiful and the good are connected; or that being and unity are related; or that sameness is different from difference, then we come to understand what sameness and difference, being and unity, beauty and goodness are. (They are, if you like, mutually explicatory). The first condition that Plato offers for understanding, then, is *connectedness*, the interrelation of one Form (or one idea or whatever) to another.

But just connecting one explanatory item to some other is still pretty thin as an explanation. Instead, Plato offers a most stringent condition for proper explanation, that the connections should be *exhaustive*. Thus proper explanations turn up when we grasp the whole system, the entire structure — and thus can explain anything by contextualizing it among all the others. Thus, for example, the philosopher of the *Republic* sees a whole intellectual world; and is infallible in his prescriptions for the phenomenal state.

The notion of cognitive context offered by this sort of explanation can further be understood by explaining how it is for the best. This is a *teleological* account of explanation. Plato appears to hold that if something is ordered, its order is good order. So understanding order is understanding good order; and ordered explanations thus show how everything is ordered for the best. So full understanding is grasping the order of things, for the best.

---

3 Cf. McCabe 1993b: ch. 9 on the importance of collection and division in Plato's account of personal identity.

There are, then, three conditions for understanding, increasingly stringent: i) connectedness; ii) within a complete system; iii) where the system is organised for the best. This gives a 'fat' notion of understanding by contrast with the thinness of the simple-minded answer.

The trouble is that fat understanding seems wellnigh impossible to acquire. Think here about 'Socrates' autobiography' in the *Phaedo*. Socrates complains about the inadequate theories of his predecessors, in particular their failure to show how everything was tied together and ordered for the best (their failure to offer a teleological explanation). He was never more disappointed than when he read the work of Anaxagoras, who postulated a divine or cosmic Mind — and then left it nothing to do. What Socrates hoped for is an entirely systematic and exhaustive account of the universe; instead what he gets are some mechanisms — with a spare part, Mind, which ends up doing nothing at all.

> ... But I was dashed, my friend, from this optimism, when I read further and discovered that the man made no use at all of Mind, nor did he connect any reasons together with the ordering of things, but cited airs and aithers and waters and many other silly things like that.... I should then gladly have become anyone's pupil to discover such an explanation [how things are tied together by the best and by necessity], however it might be; but I was deprived of that, and I could neither find it myself nor learn it from anyone else....
>
> (*Phaedo* 98b-c, 99c)

Now Socrates' irritation with Anaxagoras is not just disappointment; after all, if that were the case, there is nothing to stop this (fictional) Socrates from simply revising Anaxagoras' account. But that he does not do — instead he embarks on a different investigation which culminates in the simple-minded answer itself.

Why is Anaxagoras such bad news, and the simple-minded answer so good? What is at issue here, I think, is the nature of scientific theorising. Anaxagoras' theory failed where Socrates' answer succeeds — in its simplicity, its economy. The great advantage of the simple-minded answer is that it is thoroughly economical; whereas Anaxagoras' account is not only expensive, but even profligate in postulating explanatory bits and pieces that do no work at all. William of Ockham[4]

---

4   As tradition has it — but see the Kneales (1962) for a more sceptical view.

later forged this complaint into a razor — 'entities are not to be multiplied beyond necessity' — which shaves off those entities that seem otiose, redundant, extra to the theory under scrutiny; and the razor is still plied by modern theoretical physicists. Think — from the ancient world — about an example from Aristophanes' *Clouds* (365 ff.). Socrates says that the clouds are divinities. Does he not think that Zeus, Poseidon and the rest are gods too? Why should they be? Socrates responds — we have enough gods with the clouds, they explain the rain and everything else — there is no need for any more gods than those. Socrates' autobiography in the *Phaedo* makes a similar point (as indeed Plato does elsewhere, compare *Parmenides* 130e). Extra entities should do some work in a theory; if they don't, there is no point in having them at all. Here are Ockham's classical origins.

Proper understanding, therefore, needs to be systematic, teleological — and mean with its entities. How mean should it be? That is a matter of how you define 'necessity'; Ockham's razor does not produce bald reductionism, but forces us, instead, to justify the entities we want — and that is a tricky business.

2. *Active mind.* Moreover, fat understanding is a cognitive state, an active character of the mind, not just something that happens to the philosopher from the outside. When we think about systematic understanding, we may be thinking about what is understood; Plato, like Aristotle after him, supposes that explanation gives understanding because explanation is systematic. Aristotle, when he talks about demonstration and understanding, seems to suppose that explanations (structured arguments) are not only isomorphic with understanding (which is structured in the same way) but that they are transitive — if an explanation is complete and I 'have' it, then I understand. Here, the active psychological element in understanding is minimal. (I have reservations about whether this is true for all of Aristotle's works — for example, the *Rhetoric* makes great play of the active participation of the audience of a speech — but it is true, I think, for the more strictly logical or epistemological works.)[5]

But for Plato there is a central psychological condition on both his logic and his epistemology. At *Theaetetus* 184b ff., for example, Socrates offers

---

5 But see here Burnyeat 1984.

a refutation of the thesis that knowledge is perception. He argues that although the senses can perceive their special objects, they are unable to grasp 'what is common'. It is not by means of the senses, that is, that we say that something 'is' or 'is not', or that we make judgements about sameness and difference, likeness and unlikeness, one and many. Instead, those judgements are the province of the soul, *working by itself*. What the soul does is to calculate and to judge; the soul is active in reasoning, understanding is done by souls, not just suffered by them.

But how? How does the soul come to understand? What is it that makes the soul think for itself—or harder still, understand itself? Return now to argument. The English expression 'argument' may mean 'giving truths with reasons', as we saw. It can also mean a dispute, a debate, a controversy between two (or sometimes more) sides. Controversies progress, typically, by the vigorous giving of reasons by either side—so Kinnock may have an argument with Major about dirty water by giving an argument about the relation between water privatisation and inefficient purification plants. We may give arguments to win arguments — at any rate, the giving of an argument is generally good tactics in controversy, since the argument given persuades us to believe the conclusion. Moreover, no good controversy is without argument—the 'did','didn't' brigade can hardly be said to argue at all. In practical terms, then, the two senses of 'argument' are connected by reasons and reasoning.

This sort of argument has a counterpart in the ancient world —*dialectic*.

> First of all we should approach the search for understanding by considering the puzzles that should first be posed; these consist in the opposing views that people have taken on some issue, even including some theses that have been left unconsidered. For asking a good puzzle is useful for getting a good answer; for the later answer is a solution of the earlier difficulties, and it is not possible to solve them without understanding what ties them together — as perplexity makes clear for inquiry. For when we are puzzled, we suffer just as those who are tied up suffer — neither of us can move forward. So it is necessary to examine all the difficulties first, for their own sakes, and because someone inquiring without asking questions first is like someone walking without knowing the destination, or being able to recognize it when it is reached. Such a person has no clear objective; the person who has looked at puzzles first has. Moreover, exactly as happens in court, the person who has heard all sides of the case must be better able to judge.
>
> (Aristotle *Metaphysics* 995a24-b4)

Formally, a dialectical argument represents two lines of (deductive) argument, where either the premisses of both lines are compelling, but the conclusions inconsistent, or where the premisses are exhaustive but the conclusions of either line untenable. The use of such arguments in the ancient world was widespread — from Zeno through the sophists and Plato's *Parmenides* to Aristotle and beyond into the Hellenistic period. Now dialectical arguments (pairs of dialectical arguments) could be destructive or constructive. They destroy when, like the arguments of the sophist Gorgias, they promote nihilism or despair. They build when they establish a thesis by refutation (as Aristotle and possibly Zeno do), or where they force us to grapple with serious philosophical problems. Plato's *Parmenides*, for example, presents a series of paired and apparently exhaustive arguments which lead to the conclusion that everything and nothing is true. The effect of such a conclusion is to force the reader to re-examine the arguments, and to think hard about a connected set of metaphysical questions (What is it to be the same as oneself? What is it to be here or now?). In cases such as this, the arguments come in pairs; the dialectical effect is achieved by each of the pair acting as a critique of the other — simply because they represent radically different ways of thinking about identity, or space, or time. From the logical or argumentative point of view, then, the pairing of the arguments is fundamental.

But still why present arguments in that irritating way? Plato's use of dialectic runs parallel to his understanding of understanding — since it emphasizes the critical assessment of the arguments, and demands a state of consistency in the soul — and that corresponds to the demand that explanation should be systematic.

Aristotle suggests that a crucial feature of the process of dialectic is learning to *judge* between two lines of argument. The activity of dialectic is not necessarily to change our basic assumptions (by making us believe, for example, that monism is true), but to make us understand the assumptions we have, by judging between the alternative arguments, and coming to a full explanation of why we think the way we do. The crucial thing here, surely, is judging — that is when *we* understand (cf. McCabe 1993a). This view runs through Plato's account of philosophical activity. The Socratic elenchus, for example, by the dialectic of question and answer forces the interlocutor to be critical of his beliefs. The intellectual gymnastics of the *Parmenides* posit an unbearable choice between pairs of untenable hypotheses. And the *Sophist* claims that thinking is silent speaking, a dialogue within the soul. So opinions are stages in that dialogue; and their truth value is explained by the activity of the soul. It is the soul, not the world, who makes mistakes, by making a bad fit, a bad connection — perhaps by the wrong association of a predicate term with a subject or by a failure in consistency. Mistakes, if you like, are a matter of imagination, not fact; and the explanation of falsehood must bring with it some account of what goes on in the mind. The dialogue in the soul is a matter of making the right connections between the stages in the arguments that go on *in our minds*.

Why is it so important that dialectic goes on in the soul? When Socrates confronts his unfortunate interlocutors, he demands that they 'say what they believe'; but in the end they discover that what they believe is inconsistent. Why does that matter? It matters because consistency in the soul (consistency of our beliefs) is a primary condition of *who we are*, and a necessary condition for the health of the soul. When Socrates is defending his emphasis on consistency against the sophists' denial that consistency matters (e.g. at *Euthydemus* 287) he presses the importance of the unity of consciousness, as opposed to the cognitive discontinuity urged upon us by Protagoras' account of truth. Socrates insists that we can usefully ask the question 'Who am I?' and receive an answer in terms of the consistency of my beliefs (if we ever arrive at such a state). Here once again the central notion is one of fit, of systematic connections and the unity that this then brings with it. But psychological unity matters because that is a state of psychological health and good order — so consistency is something we are driven towards for ethical reasons — because of 'what's in it for us'.

The drive towards consistency is something the philosopher may exploit. Socrates was an irritating man to meet, because he forced you to face the inconsistency in your soul. Likewise any dialectical argument insists that we untie the knot of the puzzles because we cannot bear to stay puzzled; and we certainly can't move that way — or even get away from Socrates. In the same way, Plato later suggests, the sensible world pushes us towards understanding, because it confronts us with manifest puzzles. Think about three of your fingers. Your index finger seems both large (compared to your little finger) and small (compared to your middle finger) — how can such a case explain what large and small are? Or hard and soft?

> The sense which is about hardness must also be about softness, so that it reports to the soul that it feels both hard and soft.... So in cases like that the soul is bound to be at a loss what the sense means by hard, if it calls the same thing soft.... So it is plausible to suppose that in cases like these the soul, summoned to calculation and reason, tries to consider

whether there are two reported items or one. But if there are two, they must each be one, different from each other ... and if each is one, the soul will think the two separately — otherwise, it would think them to be one.

(*Republic* 524a-c)

The challenge posed by such apparent contradictions is resolved by the soul *in* the soul; and the challenge is dynamic just because inconsistency is unbearable, a logical, metaphysical and ethical black hole which we must and do resist.

I say blithely 'we'. But of course the drama of a Platonic dialogue does not seem to be about us at all — but rather about Socrates, Theaetetus, Glaucon, Simmias and company. Surely it is they who search for consistency — we just watch from the sidelines.

Think about that claim again. The characters in Plato's philosophical stories are fictional; they have no souls, and no deep desires to arrive at consistency. The only real live souls involved in the Platonic dialogues are the souls of his readers, us. How does he involve us in dialectical argument (passive as we may be)? How, if our state of soul matters so much, can we be brought to get our souls in order? How does the passive reader become the active dialectician?

III Myth and allegory again

Now return to myth and allegory, and consider three examples:

a) The allegory of the Sun in *Republic* 6. The sun is the source of light and growth; in the same way the form of the good is the cohesive force in the intelligible world.

b) The myths of judgement in the *Gorgias*, *Phaedo* and *Republic*. Virtue is its own reward because it is the best state of soul. And into the bargain, virtue receives the rewards in the afterlife of eternal happiness and the release from the cycles of incarnation.

c) The creation myth of the *Timaeus*. The world is structured as it is because it is the product of a benevolent heavenly craftsman who reconciled the good sense of reason with the pig-headed workings of necessity and produced the world as we see it to be.

There is something fishy about each of these stories. They are, remember, *images*; and they *belong to someone else* (to Timaeus or to the old tellers of tales in contrast with, for example, the simple-minded answer which just belongs to what it explains). What is more, these stories discourage our immediate assent: the myths are discordant with the arguments of the body of the dialogues. First, the allegory of the Sun, as we have seen, declares its own doubts in its introduction — is Plato going to tell us a lie? Second, the myths of judgement sit uneasily in their contexts: the *Gorgias* myth is a long speech presented within a dialogue that attacks the rhetoric of speechifying; the *Phaedo* myth turns up at the end of a dialogue designed to show that the care of the soul is worthwhile even though we don't know what will happen after death — and yet the myth tells us what will happen after death; and the *Republic* myth details the way in which justice receives its rewards in an uneasy coda to the arguments of the dialogue to show that justice is its own reward.[6] In each case, the straight arguments of the dialogue argue for the importance of knowledge and the exculpation of the vicious; and yet the myths insist both on the moral responsibility of the soul and on its receiving its just deserts. And, third, the myth of the *Timaeus* is hedged about with doubt, since it describes a world that is only accessible to the inferior cognitive activities of belief — and claims just to offer an *eikōs mūthos*, a likely story.

So do the myths matter? Do they have any philosophical function? We might expect them to do some explaining, to give us some under-standing. But what principles of explanation do they obey? Scientific reasoning, I suggested, is cut short by Ockham's razor. But myths are not. There are no principles of economy that govern mythologizing — you can have as many chimaeras and hydras as you like, so long as it's a good story. And so it is with Plato's myths — the Sun, the eschatologies and Timaeus' cosmology are all profligate of both entities and explanations — they are at the opposite extreme from simplicity and the simple-minded answer. How, then, can they be integrated at all into the arguments?

Dialectic, I suggested, provided us with two opposed lines of argument. This dialectical relation holds, I suggest, between the myths and the formal arguments in the dialogues. Myths and straight arguments

---

6 For more detailed argument cf. Annas 1982a, Mackenzie 1981: ch. 13, Sedley 1991.

are counterposed because they obey radically different principles of explanation; and thus, just as with the dialectic of the *Parmenides*, each is a critique of the other. Thus Plato's myths, so far from being confirmations of what he says in the body of the dialogues, are challenges to what is said there; and it is by the straight arguments that they are themselves challenged. So the combination of myth and argument is itself an argument — of the dialectical sort. It is left to the reader to untie the knot.

Hence, I suggest, Plato's 'image' imagery. Earlier I canvassed the view that myths were inferior entities because they are images and so mere appearances. But let us consider again Plato's approach to the philosophical dividend from an appearance. The trouble with particulars is that they offer conflicting appearances (cf. *Phd* 74 ff.; *Rep* 523 ff.). This does not entail that they are not really there (that kind of scepticism is resisted, e.g. at *Phaedo* 100a, 'Perhaps my image is not altogether right; for I should not agree that someone who investigates what is in words (*logoi* — theories) is dealing with images any more than someone considering what is in deeds...'), nor does it imply that they are only partially what they are said to be. Instead, Plato's problem is that they are *cognitively incomplete*. My index finger is not an illusion, like the Cheshire Cat, but a puzzle; and it is for that reason that it is held to be an image of what is real (the form of large, for example). 'Images' in this sense are not unreal, not illusions, but worrying. So then if a myth is an image, that may be because it offers simultaneously the true and the false; it is not thus liable to disappear, but instead to threaten our understanding. Images are not self-explanatory; and they are cognitively confusing; they conflate messages; they render the person who thinks about them unable to distinguish between what is true and what is false. Images on their own, on such a view, have the same effect as eristic arguments — they contradict each other and fail to provide a proper and consistent view. Provide them, however, with the proper explanation, and the contradictions fade; the philosopher can be a king in the sensible world because the philosopher can determine and disentangle the puzzles presented by the conflicting evidence there. Myths, then, may be arguments — dialectical arguments, incomplete without their other arm. And they are dialectical arguments directed at the reader, challenges to the consistency in his soul.

IV   Timaeus' teleology

Let us consider one example of how this might work: the likely story of the *Timaeus*.[7] Now in this dialogue the mythical context is rather more tricky than usual. The conversation purports to take place the day after the conversation of the *Republic*; and the figures of Socrates and Timaeus are set carefully against the mythology of earlier sages like Solon — whose own claim to know what he is doing is debunked in comparison to the older and wiser Egyptians. But Timaeus is still an expert (is he?), and it is he (not Socrates) who offers a cosmology.

The cosmology itself is a myth, a likely story, told instead of the truth. This contrast between what is true and what is merely likely is set up in the epistemological premiss of Timaeus' account, where he separates completely the two worlds — the world of being and the world of becoming — and their respective cognitive modes — knowledge and belief.

> First of all, in my opinion, we should make the following distinctions: What always is, and has no generation? What always becomes, but never is? The former is graspable by thought with argument (*logos* — word? theory?), since it is always the same; the latter is opinable by opinion with irrational (*alogos* — without argument? etc.) sense-perception, since it is subject to generation and corruption, but never really is.
>
> (*Timaeus* 27d)

What Timaeus himself has to offer is strictly belief, about the world of becoming; although he persistently tries both to bridge the gap between the two areas (e.g. at 30b7-8) by a harsh juxtaposition of truth and likelihood; and to widen it (as for example in his despairing comments about reasoning at 52b). Here, as in the allegory of the Sun, the story begins with a challenge:

> So if, Socrates, in so diverse an account about gods and the generation of the whole cosmos, we become unable to produce arguments (*logoi*) which are altogether consistent with each other, nor precise, do not be amazed. But if we produce nothing less than what is likely, bearing

---

7   Compare Osborne 1988 & forthcoming, McCabe 1993b: ch. 6.

in mind that I the speaker and you the judges have a human nature,
it would be reasonable to look no further once we have found a likely
story....

(*Timaeus* 29c-d)

How are we to make the arguments agree with themselves (be consistent)? How are we to *judge* the likely story? The context may be mythical — but the instructions are dialectical, opening with a fierce tension between truth and likelihood (30a-b), knowledge and belief — and argument and myth.

Timaeus offers a cosmology; and (echoing the *Phaedo*) the cosmos is described in the terms used by the early Presocratics — earth, air, fire and water; flux; and atomic particles. But Timaeus also promises a *teleology* — to show how god (the demiurge) made the world to reconcile the opposed principles of reason and necessity; and thus how the world is for the best. How far does Timaeus' cosmology answer the complaints of the *Phaedo*? Is this teleology useful and economical? Or extravagant and otiose?

If we are looking for an explanation for how everything is for the best, we might think first about practical reasoning. Suppose that I want some chocolate cake, and there is some chocolate cake over there. I can explain my walking over there and stuffing my face by pointing to the *telos*, the chocolate cake, and explaining that I did as I did out of desire (or greed or whatever) for that end. This is an *intentionalist* model of teleology where 'the best' is explained in terms of *somebody finding it best*.

Alternatively, 'the best' might be explained in terms of things *actually being best*. Aristotle, for example, explains living organisms in terms of their proper (natural) function (e.g. at *Parts of Animals* I. 1). As in a plant the leaves are for photosynthesis, the roots for gathering water, so the whole plant is 'for being a plant' in the right way. Or more generally, we could say that things which are ordered are intrinsically better than things which are chaotic — ecological balance, for example, is a good thing because it is nature in order. Order, on such a view, is good in itself; a structure is teleologically explained if it is understood in terms of its order. Let us call this the *natural* model.

Either the intentionalist model or the natural model of teleological explanation could be used to explain both individual and universal teleology: to use both seems like carelessness. On the one hand, an individual outcome can he explained as its agent aiming for the best; or the universe can be explained as the product of divine intention. Or on the other hand, an organism can be ordered for the best — and so can a whole universe. The intentionalist model then generates the notion of a creator, a god who determines the goodness of the whole universe by having the universe reflect his intentions. The natural model, on the other hand, may represent the universe as a living organism (the Gaia hypothesis, for example) or as a working mechanism (like a clock, perhaps).

But on either view the teleological explanation asks us to believe more than we are given by the data of sense-perception. An organism's being well-ordered is a feature of it over and above its just being an organism; a divine creator would be an entity extra to the physical entities of the physical world. Against such a view of the universe someone (an extreme Ockhamist) might argue that we should invent no extra entities, that our explanations should be as thin as they can be (let us call this character a reductionist). So the teleologist and the reductionist are at loggerheads: the former asks us to believe in an expensive account of the world in order to understand it; the latter goes for stringent economy and wields the razor with enthusiasm.

The trouble about this confrontation is that it seems irreconcilable. If entities are not to be multiplied beyond necessity, the teleologist and the reductionist disagree about *what counts as necessity*, about what grounds are enough to justify an ontological overload. And now we find just that sort of conflict turning up in Plato. Socrates (I argued) rejected Anaxagoras for reductionist reasons; but Plato's myths offer an abundance of teleological theories. The eschatologies of the *Gorgias*, the *Phaedo* and the *Republic* give us a view of the world organized for the best by means of final (or not so final) judgements — a political motif. The Sun allegory illustrates a good natural order, on the analogy of an ecological account dominated by an overriding goodness. And the *Timaeus* offers us teleology under several different descriptions.

Timaeus' cosmos is order brought out of chaos by the divine craftsman, the demiurge. So the cosmos is for the best both because it is the object of the demiurge's intentions and because it is ordered. It is also beautiful because it is a copy of a beautiful original — the intelligible universe. But because it is the only copy of the intelligible universe, it is exhaustive and complete, and so a perfect copy. What is more, because this world is made of reason imposed on necessity, it is rational (and so good); and because rational, alive — and so good.

This, if you like, is a case of teleological overkill. The thesis that teleology is a product of the divine aesthetic sense is overlaid with the claim that the universe is ordered; and the claim that the universe is a perfect copy (of a perfect original) is further supplemented by the proposal that the universe is alive (and so itself possessed of intentions towards the best). The reductionist might argue that none of these claims is needed; the moderate teleologist might suppose that one is enough; but this teleological myth gives us a series of different stories about the excellence of the universe. The myth offers us two counter-poised accounts. i) The universe may be good because god made it. Or ii), (supposing god to be a creature of myth) the universe is good because it is ordered as if a god made it. The question is which of these accounts, if either, is true?

If we put the myth of the *Timaeus* against the background of Socrates' complaints about Anaxagoras, we may see how the mythical context allows us to challenge its extravagance and its consistency. We may see at the same time that the drive towards teleology represented by the myth is a counter-challenge to the thinness of the reductionist account (of Socratic simple-mindedness). The same sort of contrast — between the rich extravagance of the myths and the austerity to be found in plain arguments elsewhere — appears in the details of Timaeus' story. Consider an example.

> The third type is the permanent space which does not admit decay but presents a place for whatever has generation itself, grasped by the lack of perception, by some bastard reasoning, scarcely credible. We look to it as if in dreams, and we say that everything that is must be in some place and to have some space — for that which is neither on earth nor in the sky is nothing. Since we are at the mercy of this dream, we are unable to discriminate and speak the truth, either about these things and what is akin to them, or about the sleepless and true nature. On the one hand, since not even that on condition of which the image exists belongs to the image, but the image is always carried around as a phantasm of something else, the image must therefore come to be in something else. But on the other hand the truth comes to the rescue of what really is, so that so long as one is one and the other the other, neither will come to be the other, nor will they become thus one and two at the same time.
>
> (*Timaeus* 52a-c)

Timaeus suggests that the phenomenal world (a copy of the ideal world) is made from three components: the stuff from which the model is made; the shape of the original; and the copy itself, the composite of the two. But the stuff from which the cosmos is made is itself a monster from a myth — the 'receptacle of becoming', the indefinite formless 'something' which has no shape, no description, is not graspable at all except as in a dream — something we cannot even mention as the substrate of all becoming.

The Presocratics, of course, loom large here; but the early mythmakers perhaps loom larger. Timaeus' explanation cites something which is itself the product of necessity, not reason, which is unmentionable and indescribable, mere stuff, inaccessible to reason. What sort of nightmare mythical monster has Timaeus produced? How can we reason about it? How can we even be persuaded that it is there?

In the *Theaetetus* Socrates has a dream.

> The things of which there is no account are unknowable ... while the things that have an account are knowable.... It is only possible to name each one itself by itself, and no other predicate can be attached to the name, neither that it is, nor that it is not: for that would already be to attribute being or not being to it, which we must not do, since someone could only mention it itself. So we must not say 'it' or 'that' or 'each' or 'only' or 'this' or anything else in addition; for all those things run around and are attributed to everything, although they are different from the things to which they are attributed, but this, if it were possible to mention it and it had its own account (*oikeios logos*), should be said without all these attributes.
>
> (*Theaetetus* 201c-2a)

How, Socrates asks, can I understand things which are ungraspable, inexplicable and unknowable? What sort of a dream is that? The arguments of the *Theaetetus* suggest that these monsters fail to contribute to our knowledge; the mythical context of Timaeus' presentation suggests that their mythical status may threaten their necessity as entities. And yet Timaeus describes it as a safe and simple-minded answer (49d ff.).

The same sort of extravagance turns up all over the *Timaeus*. For example, the demiurge, like a divine pastrycook, makes world-soul out of slices of sameness and difference. But, ask the *Parmenides* (e.g. 139b ff.) and the *Sophist* (compare the ontologies of 244 ff. with the discussion of Sameness and Difference at 255 ff.), can sameness and difference really be understood as slices of things? If I am different from you, is that because I have a piece of difference in me, which makes me so? Do you have one too? What is the difference (challenges

Euthydemus 301a ff.) between having a piece of difference and owning a cow? Is difference really a thing?

Or think about the forms, the models which the demiurge uses to stamp character on the unmentionable stuff. They seem to be separate entities; but do we need them? If Timaeus wants to argue that there are forms for every natural kind, every relation and every value, is his account plausible? The *Parmenides* argues for parsimony in postulating forms; and the contrast between the Eleatic view represented in the *Parmenides* and the extravagant teleological view offered in the *Timaeus* could not be more extreme. Timaeus suggests that we can give a teleological argument if we go for the expense of a myth. Parmenides argues that we cannot escape the reductionist objection (if the intelligible world is just extra, is it worth having?). We should be at least sceptical about any claim which supposes that a giraffe is made of a Form (giraffe) stamped on some stuff. *Is* that a likely story?

What did Plato think? That is (by now, I hope) the wrong question. Myth is a difficult medium for Plato, because myths seem not to represent direct truths. Arguments, on the other hand, are presented in the dialogue as incomplete without myths. What then is the relation between myth and argument? The connection is, I have suggested, itself argumentative. The myths and the arguments are set up as dialectically opposed to each other, offering opposed accounts of central metaphysical questions. In particular, the mythological enterprise offers ontological (and teleological) extravagance, while the argumentative enterprise tends to a reductionist view. Therefore the myths and the arguments are fundamentally inconsistent with each other; the challenge is *to the reader* — to arrive at a consistent position. The point of the dialectical contrast is that *we must judge* between the rival claims — in the case I have discussed, of the reductionist to be economical; of the teleologist to offer a fuller and more comprehensive explanation. We do that by the process of 'compare and contrast' vital to proper understanding; and we aim at a theory fully consistent and complete — such a theory, and not some closing myth, must have the last word. What Plato gives us, then, is arguments, and the criteria on which they are to be judged. The judgement is up to us; we are to blame, the god is blameless.

Speaking about the Unspeakable: Plato's Use of Imagery

Manuela Tecuşan

It is well known that the length and frequency of poetic passages in Plato appear to conflict both with his verdict against the poets and with his request for sober arguments, based on reasoning alone. This conflict has prompted scholars to seek a hidden metaphysical value in imagery. The other option seems to be to conclude that Plato either was not serious in his dialogues or systematically contradicted himself.

But it is possible to think that Plato neither assigned a high function to images in philosophy nor contradicted himself by using them. I wish to develop three aspects of this idea:

> I Images have a didactic function which increases in importance as we advance towards Plato's last works. I shall start from a passage in the *Politicus* which illuminates this function.

> II I shall examine next what is said about particular images: Ship, Beast, Charioteer, Sun, Cave, Statue, Letters. The comments suggest that images are designed, broadly, either (A) to persuade (eg. by recapitulating an argument or recalling a position) or (B) to make clear what the speakers mean (e.g. in controversy or correction). They never provide proofs or have a genuine heuristic value. (A) and (B) tend to impose different requirements: images must be relevant either as wholes or in virtue of their details. But I have little space to analyse here how the image itself works.

> III Finally, I shall consider the value of imagery in the light of Plato's position on the truth of images.

I

Robinson considers that examples and images form in Plato a continuum:

> There is no brief description that successfully conveys a general idea
> of this feature; but it is something like 'the use of cases' or 'analogy'.
> It ranges without break from the clear use of cases in what we should
> naturally call epagoge to something that we should say is not a use of
> cases but a use of images or icons. At one end it is epagoge and at the
> other imagery. (Robinson 1953: 41-2).

This situation is made more difficult by Plato's terminology (to the
extent that we can attribute one to him). Aristotle understands by
paradeigmata particular cases, as used in the inductive syllogism to
reach the universal (*Prior Analytics* 2. 24, *Rhetoric* 1356b12ff.). Plato
uses this term in different and sometimes obscure senses,[1] but a
considerable number of what speakers call *paradeigmata* are examples
in discussion. Socrates says for instance 'let us take a *paradeigma* of
each, so as to grasp the *tupos*' (*Republic* 559a). The *tupos* in question is
a category of desires, the necessary; he chooses as *paradeigma* the desire
to eat bread in order to keep alive. In the *Meno*, Socrates asks the
young man to define virtue using the *paradeigmata* of definitions
offered previously (77a). *Paradeigmata* at *Philebus* 13c refers back to
cases adduced at 12c-d to show that pleasures are of many different
sorts. At 53c Socrates takes the white to serve as *paradeigma* for
pleasure. The *Laws* lays down the examination of courage as *paradeigma* for examining higher virtues. The *Sophist* posits several
paradeigmata (221d, 226c).

For our 'image' Plato uses the terms *eikōn, eidōlon, mimēma, phantasma,
homoion, homoiotēs*. These terms have wider applications, but *eikōn* is
frequently used by the speakers to refer to a procedure adopted in their
conversation or in philosophical debate in general. *Eikōn* is in most cases
distinct from *paradeigma*.[2] It is a legitimate designator for 'image', be-

---

1   Applied to Forms (*Euthphr* 6e), world (*Ti* 27e-9d), contents in soul (*Rep* 540a-b, 561e),
    constitutions (*Rep* 557e, *Laws* 739b-e), lives (*Rep* 617d-8b). *Rep* 592a-b does not mean
    that Callipolis *is* a *paradeigma en ourano* (Moline 1981) but *has* one.

2   Most often they are opposites, e.g. *Ti* 37c-d: time (*eikōn*) - eternity (*paradeigma*).

cause this is what the word normally means in Greek.[3] The portions of text where speakers officially recognise *eikones* are among the best-known exemplars of Plato's sense of metaphor and poetical style.

Yet sometimes Plato applies the term *eikōn* to examples. At *Gorgias* 517d Socrates runs through a list and points to Callicles: 'I use the same *eikones* on purpose, so that you may more quickly understand'. *Eikones* refers to a typical element of the Socratic *epagōgē*: the trivial example which speakers accuse him of using all the time (*Gorgias* 490c-1a), familiar from the refutations of the early dialogues: clothes and shoes, smiths and tanners, doctors and cooks. This is a minor occurrence, maybe a joke; a few other places are difficult to judge;[4] if asked, Plato may give us the favourite reply, 'Let us not quibble about words'. But the use of these words is puzzling in the *Politicus*. The Stranger gives an account, unique in Plato, of the *phusis tou paradeigmatos* (277d-e), and then refers to his several *paradeigmata* by the term *eikōn*: 'Let us return to the *eikones* with which it is necessary to compare the royal ruler all the time' (297e). This includes the main *paradeigma* of Weaving: the Stranger completes the definition of the King *kata tēn eikona* (309a-b). But in the diaeretic dialogues *paradeigmata* are integrated in the method of division. It seems that Plato normally uses *eikōn* and *paradeigma* for distinct procedures, and yet from time to time the terms are interchangeable.

Plato does not give us conclusive accounts of what an *eikōn* is for him, but his evaluation of poetic procedures in philosophical inquiry is notoriously low. Given that *paradeigmata* are important in the diaeretic dialogues, an equation *eikōn* = *paradeigma* would embody the highest function that he ever allowed *eikones* to have in philosophy. Let us assume that *kata tēn eikona* (Weaving, 309b) means the same to Plato as *kata to paradeigma* (Shepherd, 275b), and see briefly what this highest function is.

The Stranger makes his points through the example of Letters (277d-8e). Three items are relevant to my purpose: the role and nature of *paradeigmata* and why we need them.

---

3 *Eikōn* is primarily associated with painting and sculpture. The meaning 'statue' occurs in Plato (*Phdr* 235d9, *Criti* 116e, *Laws* 930e-1a). The *zōgraphos* or his activity are frequently evoked in passages about imagery, some of which do not mention *eikones*.

4 Eg *Rep* 538c, 375d, *Men* 72a8; cf. *Prt* 330a-b.

1. With the help of *paradeigmata* the pupil does not learn new letters, but consolidates his capacity to recognise known letters in more difficult syllables (278a-c). This indicates that *paradeigmata* must be used by someone who knows already, to orient and guide someone else, and not to get proofs.[5] Ideally, a teacher does not err with his examples. It would be interesting to see how the Stranger's failures and corrections in dividing according to the kinds (277) fit into the picture, but this is beyond my scope. We find illustrated in the dialogue an interesting extension of the principle of 'recognizing': the Shepherd grows into a myth (268e ff.) which points out mistakes in the division (274e). It is a form of *paidiá* subordinated to the *paradeigma* and made to serve serious purposes, as a sort of counter-example. A related use of *paradeigmata - eikones* occurs at 298a-300a.

2. *Paradeigmata* are 'smaller' than the object studied (277d1-2); examples must be simpler and easier. This is a very familiar requirement in both diaeretic dialogues. The *Sophist* posits the Angler as a *'paradeigma* for the bigger thing'*, the Sophist, in order to 'practise the method of tracking him down on some easier quarry first'; for 'it is a good idea to take something comparatively small and easy before attempting the big subject itself' (218c-e). The *paradeigmata* of Angler (*Sophist* 218e) and Weaving (*Politicus* 279a-b) are introduced by *ti dēta* questions in search for smaller objects of study. The Letters themselves are a study of *paradeigmata* done 'on a small particular case of *paradeigma*' (278e).

3. *Paradeigmata* are indispensable (277d1-2) because the mind cannot recognise familiar or known items when they are present in unfamiliar or unknown compounds (278c-d). If we did not have this congenital defect we should not need them; for we do not pursue the divisions of Weaving for its own sake, but in order to become better philosophers (285d). *Paradeigmata* have no value in themselves.

The items described at 277d-8e help us to find the same element in different compounds. This idea is important in Plato's late epistemology. *Paradeigmata* operate 'when something *on tauton* is rightly believed to exist *en heterōi'*, so that this common part, *sunachthen peri hekateron,*

---

5   The method of inferring from cases corresponds to what Aristotle calls *epagōgē* in the *Topics* (I. 12) and attributes mainly to Socrates in the *Metaphysics* (M. 4). But a large part of Plato's cases are not inferential; they illustrate or recapitulate something already demonstrated, or emphasise a point which does not need demonstration. The diaeretic dialogues do not aim to give proofs, but definitions.

makes it possible to reach 'one single true judgement about both things' (278c3-6). We see the principle at work in the comment at 275b: the Shepherd stretched in contrary directions, wanting to show a feature which the king has in common with others (*agelaiotrophia*), and his specific feature as king (*epimeleia tēs anthrōpinēs trophēs*, 275b). The *Sophist* recommends us 'to be able to follow our statements step by step and, in criticizing the assertion that a different thing is the same or the same is different in a certain sense, to take heed of the exact sense and respect in which they are said to be one or the other' (259c-d). The presentation of the method of dialectic at *Politicus* 285a-c indicates that Sameness and Difference are connected with the two steps of division and collection.

Thus use of *paradeigmata* must be a part of the dialectical exercise. But the Stranger says at 286a that we should train in dialectic in order to be able to reach the greatest subjects, *ta megista kai timiōtata*, because these subjects have no *eidōla* or *homoiotētes*; they can be apprehended by reason alone. If *paradeigmata* are a part of the dialectical training, we expect them to take us away from images as far as possible. Yet *paradeigmata* are, in an undefinable sense, images. Thus it seems that we use images in an exercise which enables us to reach subjects or modes of thought which have no images (cf. a similar transition in *Posterior Analytics* 2. 19). They are small units at the bottom of a process which ends up very high. In helping us to 'recognize' they create a bridge between trivial and important matters. But the need for this bridge springs from a defect, and the procedure requires a competent guide.

Bearing this in mind, let us take a few *eikones* from Plato's text and see what situation they reflect.

II

The Ship (*Republic* 487e-9a) is a part of Socrates' attempt to justify the claim introduced at 473c-d, that philosophers should be political rulers.

This claim was made under interesting circumstances. At 472c Socrates starts to explain that the whole inquiry we witnessed was a quest for exemplary items on which to 'fix our eyes', but 'our purpose was not to demonstrate the possibility of realizing such ideals'. He is nonetheless willing to make the concession desired by Adeimantus: 'if we can discover how a state might be constituted most nearly answering to our description, you must say that we have discovered the possibility you demanded. Would you be happy with that?' (473a-b). Adeimantus of course is, and Socrates stipulates a method to turn the city real: 'we must try to discover ... what exactly goes wrong in our cities ... and what is the smallest change, preferably in one thing, that would bring the good constitution in them' (b). Next he introduces the philosophic rulers. This idea appears as an immediate application of the practical method; having such rulers would be the 'smallest change in one thing'. But we have not discovered yet what goes wrong in actual cities.

This must be a turning point in the history of Callipolis. The passage suggests that the utopia is only to begin, although we may have considered ourselves well into it. Socrates started with the First City (370-1), then had it rapidly expanded into the Feverish (372). These were not normative projects but *paradeigmata*, samples purer than reality can offer, destined to satisfy better than historical examples some condition in the argument about justice, so that inquiry may advance. At least this is what Socrates declared at 369c: 'let us build then a city from scratch, *en logōi*; its author, it seems, will be our needs [*chreia*]'. But the account turned normative by stages: after the first purification, completed at 399e, the city incorporated more and more of Plato's standards and beliefs. The philosopher-king is the strongest expression of the change, and this character provokes the most fascinating part of the story, down to the end of Book 7 where Callipolis is completed.[6]

The *eikōn* must answer the following question: 'How can it be right to say that our cities will never be freed from their evils until philosophers become rulers, when we agreed that philosophers are *achrēstoi* to cities?' (487e). *Achrēstoi* [without use, but see below] refers to an objection just formulated by Adeimantus (c-d). According to the objection, only the best philosophers are *achrēstoi*; the rest are worse.[7]

Plato was fully aware that the idea of philosophers ruling in cities was very hard to accept. He presents it as a 'supreme paradox', difficult to formulate (473c), submits it to heavy attack (473e-4a), and gives it a long defence with epistemological ramifications; yet he omits something essential. At 474c Socrates promised to show that 'the study of

---

6 Socrates considered it established when he proceeded to the soul (427c-d) and intended to discuss next the inferior constitutions (445c-d), but the others were intrigued about the community of women and asked him to hold on. The problem of feasibility arose from such matters.

7 *allokotoi* ('aloof, estranged') and *pamponeroi* (which can mean 'ill', cf. Luc. *Abd* 14, as in 'altered food', Epich. 14).

philosophy and political leadership belong by nature' to philosophers, but he convinces us only that what belongs properly to philosophers is the study of philosophy. After 484e he draws a portrait of the philosophical character to establish that he has qualifications of two sorts, *kakeina kai tauta*, but the second sort contain no proof of political capacity. Plato left undefended what appears to us to be the crucial side of a matter which he considered extremely difficult to render acceptable to people. The short dialogue at 484b-d suggests that he may have remembered again that guardians are 'hounds'. At 375d this *eikōn* helped us to see how it is possible to have two opposite features in a single individual — one related to philosophy, the other to action. But the possibility of this combination does not justify Socrates' lack of concern with the issue of political ability here. If the objection picks up this element, as it seems to, then it is strong.

Socrates does not proceed with another argument; he agrees with Adeimantus (487d10). Thus the *eikōn* must answer the question at 487e from a position of agreement with the opponent's premiss, 'philosophers are *achrēstoi*'. But this is not exactly what happens. The subject of the Ship is 'the *pathos* incurred by the best people at the hands of the state' (488a), or 'the *diathesis* of states towards true philosophers' (489a), and its lesson is that 'philosophers are not honoured in our cities' (489a9). In fact Socrates has an answer for Adeimantus' question and will give it soon: philosophers become *achrēstoi* because the philosophical nature is easily corrupted. What is the Ship doing?

The case is interesting because Plato tells us a few things about the *eikōn*. Most importantly, it is not intended for proof: 'I hope that you will not ask to find out that the condition I described corresponds to the relation of state to true philosophers by putting the *eikōn* to the test, but that you will see my point' (489a). Its function is this: 'teach [*didaske*] this *eikōn* to the man who is surprised that philosophers are not honoured in our cities, and try to convince him [*peithein*] that it would be far more surprising if they were' (a-b).

The Ship depicts a world defined by: a shipowner, identified by Aristotle with the Demos (*Rhetoric* 1406b3), who is noble and strong but dull and naïve about business on his ship, and a crew of sailors whose standard of value and achievement is to obtain from him command of the ship, while contemptuous of the profession which teaches you what to do when in command. This is an abbreviated description of the present world. It conveys under symbolic form the results of an absent inquiry for the first step of the method propounded at 473b, to find out 'what goes wrong in our cities'.

Socrates says that the matter cannot be described in imagery because the *pathos* of the best is unique (488a), so the *eikōn* must be a non-existing animal:[8] a fairy-tale, something which cannot happen. But the matter has a non-iconic account, as we know from the *Gorgias*. Apparently it is Adeimantus' question which compels Socrates to make an *eikōn* (487e). The next few lines present a situation familiar from other dialogues: the opponent insinuates that Socrates is at home with such procedures, and Socrates complies. This play should not hide from us the fact that Socrates is 'forced': Socrates uses an *eikōn* because Adeimantus is in the state of the stranger at 489a, who needs to be 'taught and persuaded' in this fashion. He questions basic truths for which Plato has no time at the moment. We may feel deprived of the inquiry promised at 473a, but the thought is familiar enough for Plato to expect his interlocutors to share it. Adeimantus offers a view which compels Socrates to compress a grave matter into a childish tale because he has other things to say. The situation on the Ship acts as a premiss which did not even need to be formulated.

The method seems useful because it calls to mind old positions in a vivid and brief form, and indicates the new direction which they will take. The specific element of the Ship in relation to our argument is the occurrence of the true pilot in the last sentence. It is typical of Plato to introduce different angles to the same thing. The true pilot turns the *eikōn* into a description of how it may happen that the competent and good appear as useless idlers; that a role is already decided by others in a manner which contradicts reality but is neverthless accepted by all. If you are a true pilot and happen to be invited on that ship, what else is there for you to do than look foolish?

The *eikōn* puts an end to all objections and complaints to the philosophic rulers. How does it do this? Let us look at the unusual order of the statements. Instead of opposing Adeimantus directly, Socrates first agrees with him. There is some truth in what Adeimantus said, and Socrates respects it: he sets off next to explain the *ponēria* and *phthora* of actual philosophers (489d-90e), and it will result that the philosophical nature is corrupted precisely in circumstances such as on the Ship. But

---

8 *tragelaphos* ('goat-stag') was popular in Greek decoration; the name is sometimes given to drinking-coups (Diph. 80, Antiph. 224.4). On all this see Blaydes on Ar. *Ba* 937.

the proposition that philosophers are *achrēstoi* is true in a narrow sense. Between the two points of assent (487e and 489d) Socrates inserts a picture which renders phenomena on a larger scale. On this scale, the opponent's proposition appears as a possible result of prejudice, and Socrates' assent is ironical. When he says at 489d that he has 'explained the cause of the *achrēstia* of the good people', he reveals that *achrēstoi* in his assenting proposition at 487e meant 'unused', and not, as Adeimantus intended it, 'useless'. The *eikōn* corrects the mistake with a vivid illustration of this difference, followed by comments which fix the point didactically (489b-d).

We may for our part find that Adeimantus' objection is well founded and his question apposite. If we do this it is because we think that Plato's argument lacks something. But the point is that Plato does not see this; his conception of politics in relation to knowledge makes him consider the basic demonstration already finished.

Nobody wants to be a member in the crew of the Ship. We may think that, by introducing his relativistic angles, Socrates intimidates Adeimantus, using the insidious effect which Plato was so aware that images have. This is true. Plato uses the image in order to bring home to a speaker what was to him an obvious truth, because this truth reduced the speaker's objection to a prejudice. But this is not to impose a new dogma, as a dubious proof that philosophers are naturally designed for politics certainly would; it only makes it possible to conceive that, in a world 'most nearly answering to our description' (473a), true philosophers can rule unhandicapped by the current prejudice, so that it makes sense to carry the discussion further. In the uncertain realm of politics in the *Republic*, this is an invitation to freedom of thought and revision of received ideas and authority.

*

The Beast (*Republic* 588b-9b) is, like the Ship, an animal which does not exist, in the family of Chimaera, Scylla, or Cerberus (588c).[9] It is an '*eikōn* of the soul made in words', dedicated to the proponent of the thesis that injustice is profitable: the man must 'see what he means' when he

---

9 The dialogue at 588b-e sounds as if it accompanied the making of the *eikōn*, or came from a play which showed it being made. This seems a joke about the forthcoming controversy, which is not a real one.

claims this, and then be 'gently persuaded' to reason. The *eikōn* is very
clear when you know what has happened in the nine Books so far. It
weaves together the main lines, and occurs at a point where everything
has been demonstrated; Socrates has just crowned the contrary proposition with the three arguments on pleasure. But we can doubt that the
imaginary opponent, or any speaker in Book 1, would make much of
the *eikōn* if they had not stuck to Socrates up to this point. The Beast
recapitulates the whole story; taken out of it, it loses its meaning. The
case of the Ship is similar in that it asks us to be familiar with Plato's
position in other dialogues.

*

The Ship is a short-cut; the proper explanation would be much longer.
Plato sometimes presents his *eikones* as second-best options which offer
an advantage in a certain situation. Such is the famous comparison
which governs the myth of the soul in the *Phaedrus*, 'let the soul be
likened to the union of powers in a team of winged steeds and their
winged charioteer' (246a). Socrates introduces the image thus: 'The
nature of the soul (*hoion men esti*) would be the object of a divine and
long account, but that with which it resembles can make the the object
of a human and shorter account'.

In what sense is the long account 'divine'? In the *Republic* Socrates
embarks on the topic of the soul's tripartition with the warning that

> we shall never apprehend this matter accurately from such *methodoi*
> as we are using now in our arguments; for there is another *hodos,*
> *makrotera kai pleiōn,* leading to these results. Yet the present methods
> may be suficient for the purpose of our previous statements and
> inquiries' (435c-d).

At 503e-4b the 'longer road' turns out to be that of the science which
pursues *ta megista mathēmata*, dialectic. These passages assure us that
tripartition can be established dialectically;[10] but it must be difficult to
give a proper scientific account of soul, with the hypotheses of immor-

---

10 The reference to virtues at 504a4-6 has raised doubts whether the road, which is
obviously the same in the both passages, does not lead to different studies in each
case. I think that *auta* at b1 refers primarily to soul and tripartition. Plato recapitulates;
he mentions the analysis of virtues as it emerged from the account of the soul.

tality and tripartition not leading to contradictory conclusions. The Charioteer occurs in the *Phaedrus* after the argument that soul is immortal (245c-6a). It seems intended to present tripartition in a way that avoids difficulties; for it helps Plato to describe non-dialectically, in a fairy-tale, 'how it is that living beings are called mortal and immortal' (246b). The tale is beautiful, and also true: the Charioteer would not exist if Plato did not hold tripartition. But it renders this truth very loosely. The *epithūmētikon* and *thūmoeides* which we know from the *Republic* are not opposites in the same genus — as would be a good and a bad horse.

I interpret the introductory words as a warning that the form of presentation through images and myths sets aside difficulties when it is not necessary to solve them on the spot, and allows us to abbreviate matters considerably, but one should not expect from it real explanations about the nature of things. The other account is 'divine', I think, not in the sense of being inaccessible to mortals, but of belonging to dialectic. It is probably 'longer' because the method requires much preparation and training. Plato's myths of the soul are certainly longer than the half-line definition of soul as 'self-mover' in the *Laws* (896a); but the diaeretic dialogues show how much systematic exercise on small and easy subjects is required in order to reach the definition of a difficult subject through the method described in the second part of the *Phaedrus*.

The function of images such as the Charioteer and their relation to truth is best formulated by Plato himself in the *Phaedo*, at the end of the myth: 'No sensible person should take at face-value the details of my presentation. But it seems plausible to me, since we have evidence that the soul is immortal, that either this or another account about our souls and their future inhabitations is true. It is worth risking to have this belief; for the risk is noble. We should use such accounts to charm ourselves [*epaidein*], and this is why I made it so long' (114d). They are, like the Ship or Beast, imaginary animals created to bring before the eyes, for correction and persuasion, states of things for which Plato himself had an argument.

*

But are we sure that Plato always had an argument behind his *eikones*? Socrates seems to deny this at the summit of the *Republic*. He refuses to speak about the most important thing and the object of dialectic, the Good, although the dialectical method forces you always to say what you think on a subject. Pressed hard by the others, he offers to speak about 'what seems to me to be the offspring of the Good and the thing most similar to it' (506e). This is the Sun, whose account is an *eikōn* (509a9) or *homoiotēs* (c6) for the account of the Good. The Sun is followed at the beginning of Book 7 by an *eikōn* which the speakers find 'strange' (515a4): the Cave. This situation seems to furnish the main evidence for the view that images in Plato render metaphysical truths.

Socrates' attitude is paradoxical; we must see the paradox in a clear light. What is it that he refuses to say? Adeimantus wants to find out Socrates' position in the 'many and violent disputes', which Socrates has just dismissed (505b-d), between parties who hold that the Good is pleasure or knowledge. Adeimantus' reply at 509a, 'for you certainly don't mean that it is pleasure', shows that he has not abandoned the original track; and Socrates shuts him up with a strong word, *euphēmei*. The discussion at 505b-d gives the feeling that there is something wrong with the definitions as such. Maybe they are ill-formed because they identify the genus, concept, property, or predicate 'good' with particular species, objects, substances, or nouns under it. What Plato thinks at this stage is impossible to know, but the direction taken by his method shows a growing need for correct categorisation. Maybe the present objection takes further Socrates' objection to enumerative definition, familiar from the *Meno*. In any event, when he bids us to leave aside the question of what the Good itself is (506d-e), he refers to a specific question, which confines the answerer to a choice between two sides in the dispute of the *Philebus*.

Socrates gives oblique answers to Adeimantus, but on careful reading we discover that the problem whether he himself has knowledge about the Good does not even arise. Adeimantus' question is not appropriate because it asks for an opinion, and mere opinion is of no value in this case (506c1-5). Then Adeimantus asks for an account of the Good of the same kind as the previous accounts of the virtues (506d). But Socrates insists that the method used for soul and virtues, although sufficient for limited purposes, was not the right one; his words at 506e1-2 strengthen this. He replies to Adeimantus that his present capacity (*parousan hormēn*) may not be up to the task of talking about the Good in the same fashion.

Speaking through *eikones* may appear as a good procedure because Socrates offers to do this after declining to employ an inferior method. But at the end of the Sun he tells us that what he said is only what *seems* to him (509c). He warns that his account might be *kibdēlos* and deceive us without intention (507a), and he throws doubt on the whole story right after interpreting the Cave: 'God knows if this is true' (517). He makes himself ridiculous at 509c1-4, just as he anticipates at 506d6-8 that he would if he followed the deficient method. All these details suggest that Socrates has decided to give what Adeimantus asked, an opinion, from the moment of offering to draw the *eikōn*; he adopts deliberately a procedure which he considers to be inappropriate, without telling us whether he might have done otherwise. Trying not to fall in the abyss of the Unwritten Doctrine, I shall venture two guesses:

1. In our passage Socrates, with skill and irony, avoids committing himself on the question of his own knowledge. But when Glaucon asks what are the *tropos*, *eidē*, and *hodoi* of dialectic, wishing to learn more about this wonderful science whose *dunamis* he just glimpsed, Socrates replies:

> For my part I would not lack the good will, but you, Glaucon, will not be able to accompany me; you would no longer see an *eikōn* of the subject of my speech but the true thing itself, as it appears to me — it's not worth considering whether rightly or wrongly. (533a)

This indicates that Socrates has in mind more than he says. It is more plausible to think that he speaks through *eikones* to make the company follow, than because he cannot do otherwise. This sort of language requires good acquaintance with your subject. Ironically or not, Socrates appears unconfident that he can construct fabulous animals about the Good; he will manage pretty well with the Cave; but this is as far as he can go in making *eikones*. He gives an idea of what dialectic is, but would not describe it in this language; we have to read that in other dialogues. Sun and Cave may be adjustments to the interlocutors, like the Ship.

2. Socrates refuses to say that the Good is knowledge or pleasure but says that it is *like* the sun. Both answers state opinions, but the second is better than the first. Perhaps the *eikōn* contains primarily advice to find out *how* the Good is instead of *what* it is?

This line suggests that there is a good seed in the bad procedure. As we see in the *Politicus*, we must have a correct description of the thing in order to define it. The *Politicus* compares the definition with a 'portrait' (277b). Is the Sun a very young brother of the Shepherd: an attempt to draw a 'portrait' of the Good? The *eikōn* is not a picture of the Good as much as an example of how the Good works; the offspring does not look like his father but rather behaves like him. We can make sense of Sun and analyse it because we take it as an illustrative example, giving up other questions about the Good. Socrates does not prove anything here, but at least we can follow his meaning up to a certain point.

The Cave is different. It is notoriously difficult to interpret because we cannot say to what exactly it refers. Robinson (1953: ch. 11) has shown in detail that it does not illustrate the Line; we do not find any segment correctly represented in it. At 517a-b Socrates asks us to apply 'this *eikōn* as a whole [*hapasan*]': not to analyse it. He says that it refers to 'what has been said before'; but he will also relate it to what comes next (532b-c).

*

The good seed in the bad method seems to be a slight change which makes the *eikōn* more of an example than a picture. We cannot put a finger on the difference; but let us return for a moment to the diaeretic dialogues. In the *Sophist paradeigma* seems to be, not the Angler, the 'small thing' itself, but what we do with it: the procedure in reaching definition. The common thing between Angler and Sophist (at least according to 218e and 221c) is that both have a *logos*. But in the *Politicus* the Stranger does not seem to refer to a procedure so much as to the referendum of the example: the *paradeigma* at 279a-b is Weaving, and what makes it a *paradeigma* is the fact that it has *tēn autēn politikēi pragmateian*. The state of things in the two dialogues is complex, but in principle the Angler aims to be an example of correct division, whereas Weaving integrates the example itself. Plato's examples and metaphors tend towards these two poles, but the movement around each pole seems chaotic because he does not keep 'metaphor' as a separate category. The first pole offers an abstract model; the second pole suggests a physical relation between two things. But this leads to what *we* regard as metaphors. Take Weaving. Each individual has a natural disposition towards *to andreion* or *to sōphron*; the King weaves the state from these two opposite fabrics, and his *huphasma* is the best. 309a-b shows us how this is done: the King must treat those disposed to bravery as the warp, *stēmonophues*, and those disposed to wisdom as the woof, *krokodes*. To us, the notions of *krokē* and *stēmōn* of state are metaphors which make the Stranger's point more vividly; he seems to regard them as indispensable aids in the division. Weaving yields a final description of the King and his art (311a-c), greeted by Socrates as an equivalent of what was done in the case of the Sophist (311c).

Something similar happens at *Republic* 429d, where Socrates offers to explain an element in the definition of courage by comparing it 'with something which seems to me similar to it'. He stops in order to make plain a point which his interlocutor failed to understand. The definition claimed that courage is a 'preservation' (*sōtēria*), in danger, of one's beliefs about what is dangerous and what is not. Glaucon did not grasp the notion of 'preserving' beliefs; Socrates makes it physical. He takes a case to illustrate a claim already made; this is one role of examples. But, whereas at *Sophist* 226c several *paradeigmata* bring out a single feature, here a single case is analysed into several features, and the analysis ends up in metaphors which arise from linking terms in pairs which do not make sense out of context: *doxa* is *deusopoios*, *phoboi* are called *rhummata*. Unlike the fabulous image whose details do not matter, this kind of image is good because its details display characteristic features.

The procedure of the *Republic* is to construct a city 'in words', keeping it faithful to some basic premisses. At the beginning of Book 4 Socrates compares this procedure with the making, not of goat-stags or other fabulous creatures, but of statues faithful to the original, in which eyes are not implausibly beautiful compared with the whole body (420d). The passage is interesting. It suggests that Socrates' imaginary city acts as a mental picture; gives us three examples of drawing such pictures; and applies to the method rules of verisimitude from the figurative arts. It is clear that this kind of picture must, almost like examples, make some point. Their value depends on how adequately they incorporate or conform to conditions set by the argument. But they do have a feature opposite to examples: we must pick up the points for ourselves, for nobody states them explicitly.

Images such as these come closest to examples, without being examples in the proper sense. What would Plato call them? Simmias calls *eikones* the wrong counter-examples of Lyre and Coat, through which the Thebans attempt to demolish Socrates' proposition that soul is immortal (*Phaedo* 87b3, d3). The representation of mind as Wax and Aviary in the *Theaetetus* expands the example into a picture where hypotheses or mistakes can be 'seen' and discussed in better light. The picture itself does not 'test' or 'discover' anything; it only illustrates an idea which already exists.

*

But the celebrated tablet from which Socrates reads justice in the *Republic* seems to show that Plato used such procedures in investigation and proof.

> The *zētēma* [inquiry] we are undertaking is not at all easy; it calls for good sight, I think. Since we are not *deinoi* [highly skilled], I advise that we employ the *zētēsis* which we should use if someone bade us to read small letters from a distance when we did not have a good sight, and then someone else observed that the same letters might exist elsewhere, in bigger shapes, on a bigger surface. It would be a godsend, I think, to read those first and only then to examine the smaller, [to see?] if they are indeed the same. (368c-d)

After reading the big letters which tell what justice is in the state (432b-3c), Socrates recapitulates the method, saying that 'we must apply back to the individual what revealed itself in the state', and if something different reveals itself in the individual 'we will return to the state and test it there' (434d-5a).

To derive truths about the soul from truths about the state seems to be the 'bad method' of which Socrates complains, for this is what he presents before the complaint at 435d. 'The city was found to be just because it had in it three kinds .... Then we shall judge that the individual has the same forms in his soul too, and that, in virtue of *pathē* identical with those in the city, they deserve the same appellations'. But does Plato really apply this method?

1. Socrates never explicitly checks the hypothesis 'if the letters are indeed the same'. 368e and 435b disclose that man and state have in common precisely the unknown factor which we are trying to calculate, justice: 'a just man will not differ at all from a just city in respect of Justice'. It cannot be right to infer that all the letters are the same. The bigger tablet allows us to see the unknown letters more clearly, but this does not mean that both have the same text. We are very far from the Letters of the *Politicus*, which teach you to recognize the same thing in different combinations. But Socrates' knowledge of the soul derives indeed from better methods: he will establish tripartition through the law of noncontradiction (437a). Is this the 'check' of the hypothesis?

2. Socrates never applies the cautious test recommended at 434d-5a: man and state are isomorphic. But this points to an important premiss in Plato's political thought. The state differs from the individual only in quantity or size; Callipolis is a Socrates drawn very large. We often feel in the *Republic* that, in spite of being smaller, the soul has logical priority. Civic *sōphrosunē* emerges from individual *sōphrosunē* at 430e, when we are not permitted yet to look at the small tablet. At 435e Socrates says that the forms and qualities present in the state are brought there by individuals who possess them; but this annuls the bad

inference at 435b-c. The five constitutions enact, as Nettleship said, an ideal 'history of evil', whose principle is in the structure of the soul (1901: 295).

The method of reading from bigger letters seems to give us an explanation constructed upside down. The Stranger would not agree to look at the bigger tablet first, unless he believed that the city is a smaller subject — something like an angler. In interpreting this difficult case, we must pay more attention to Socrates' warning that the reason why we need larger letters is that our sight is not very good.

III

Plato's few accounts of *eikōn* connect it with language and thought. In the famous picture-theory of the *Cratylus*, according to which words imitate, represent, or portray things, *eikones* are qualitative entities which do not contain all the features of the representandum (432a-c; that would be as absurd as a statue which resembles the man inside), yet have an *orthotēs* of their own, which makes it possible to apply the distinction true / false to statements and words (431c-d). How to conceive this correctness Socrates does not say, except for the eliminatory statement that it is not like correctness expressed quantitatively in numbers. The *Philebus* tells us that *eikones* can be true or false (39a-e); but these 'paintings' reproduce our *doxai*, not the world, and do not take linguistic form.

The *Sophist* states that an *eikōn* is something between being and not-being (240c) which results from the blending of the Different with belief (*dianoia*) and speech (*lexis*, 264c). This process explains the possibility of *apatē* in general. Unlike in the *Cratylus* and *Philebus*, all images are false; true statements do not seem to be iconic. But:

1. The original division of *eidōlopoiikē*, image-making, contains *technai eikastikai* which make faithful reproductions of the original, and *technai phantastikai* which make deceitful appearances (236a). This start encourages us to think that there is a difference between *eikones* and *phantasmata* with respect to truth or reality. The Stranger returns to the division at the end (264c), which means that he held it throughout. Unfortunately he is not interested in the icastic branch because he follows the sophist on the other side; so he tells us nothing more about it.

2. In the announcement that one cannot talk seriously about the possibility of false statements (*logoi pseudoi*) without destroying the

Parmenidean position, the Stranger exemplifies *logoi pseudoi* by *eidōla*, *eikones*, *mimēmata*, and *phantasmata* (241d-e). We hear again of *eidōla*, *eikones*, and *phantasiai* when the demonstration is completed (260c). These passages give the impression that, in spite of the division above, there is no (or no important) difference between *eikones* and *phantasmata*.

Eikones in these sentences and *eikones* in the division are slightly different items which Plato does not put together. We may think that, when he defines *eikōn* at 240c, he does not mean 'image' of the kind produced in the first branch of *eidōlopoiia*, but 'image' produced by the whole art, *eidōlon*. But the notion of image, whatever we call it in Greek, remains unclear. The sophist is a bad character and so is his art, *phantastikē*; his good brother is the philosopher.[11] Is the twin art, *eikastikē*, any good in philosophy? If an image cannot be entirely real, to what extent can a faithful image contain truth for Plato?

Eikones, originally owned by *zōgraphoi* (*Protagoras* 312d), are readily at home in poetry, literature, music, dance — all *technai* working 'through the production of *homoia*'.[12] Plato's position with respect to these arts is very drastic in the *Republic*. But in the *Laws* we witness a spectacular change. Magnesians must spend their lives in what looks like an only briefly interrupted festival. They are expected to sing and dance in prescribed manners which the Athenian thinks out in amazing detail. They are supervised by top specialists who rank high in the state; expertise in music occupies almost a whole book. All this is the task of *paideia*, understood as training of the sense of pleasure and lower instincts. Why so much effort on this? Because the road of *paideia* is as strict as the road of dialectic. If the highest subjects can only be attained through reason, persuasion alone reaches the child's soul: other faculties than pleasure are absent in him. Education in Magnesia, far from forbidding the arts as it does in Callipolis, operates mostly through artistic imitations of the good, which progressively fashion and refine our sense of pleasure. But Plato's argument against persuasive procedures survives: they cannot guarantee their truth.

---

11   Sophistry appears as the opposite of dialectic in many dialogues. Robinson (1953: 84-6) comments interestingly on this antinomy.

12   In the *Laws* all arts are *eikastikai* (667c-d), and *eikōn* is 'artistic image' (668c). Cf. *Rep* 401b-c, *Laws* 655b, 667-9.

Eikones, too, remain inferior; we take one at 897d-8b because human eyes cannot perceive the motions of Wisdom directly. But Plato's use is more obviously didactic. The Puppet serves to emphasize the importance of *paideia* (644c) and thus prepares us to listen to the odd argument about wine; it acts like a 'charm'. But it also lends itself to analysis, helping us to notice possible changes in Plato's conception of the soul. The Athenian's manner assures us that he knows well where he is going even when we should doubt it. The Puppet is an authoritative expression of experience and knowledge.

The diaeretic dialogues do not abandon imagery so much as integrate it in the disciplined form of examples in the exercise of division. At this stage Plato is more explicit about the role of images in the operations of the mind. The *Laws* gives us a measure for appreciating Plato's evolution. This evolution does not betray inconsistency; it reveals another side of what Robinson termed 'Plato's constructive personality'.

Reflections of the Sun: Explanation in the Phaedo[1]

Christopher Rowe

The theme of the seminars which provided the foundation for this volume, as originally described to me, was 'Plato's views about the capacities of language to describe/represent perceptibles, with some focus (not exclusive) on the *Timaeus*'. I shall in fact touch on the *Timaeus* only at the very end of this paper, in a couple of sentences. But there are good reasons for my choice of the *Phaedo*: not just because I happen recently to have completed a commentary on the dialogue (Rowe 1993a), but because the parts of the dialogue I shall be discussing constitute one of the most important discussions in the whole of Plato about how to talk about perceptibles, or 'particulars'. The method of inquiry they propose is actually represented as a substitute for the grand ambitions of the sort of account we find in the *Timaeus*; but this is partly disingenuous, since the *Timaeus* actually presupposes the same sort of method. I also have some things to say about the relationship between the *Phaedo* and that part of the *Republic* referred to in the overall title of the seminars: 'The Language of the Cave'.

*****

At *Phaedo* 99c-d, Socrates proposes to describe a 'second voyage' (*deuteros plous*) which he has been undertaking towards the search for

1 This paper is a version of a longer and more detailed one (Rowe 1993b), adapted to a seminar context, and is printed in virtually the form in which it was originally read at Warwick in February 1992. I should like to express my thanks to the audience on that occasion for a stimulating discussion, which served to weaken my belief in parts of the interpretation proposed, without however destroying it.

the *aitia* of ('the reason for'?)[2] things. The first voyage seems to have consisted of his reading of Anaxagoras, which ended in failure: he had hoped to find in Anaxagoras the kind of teleological explanation which appealed to him, but was disappointed. Since then, he has set out again, but with rather lower expectations: the phrase 'second voyage', as *Politicus* 300c seems to confirm, has connotations of 'second-best'. The goal of this new voyage is still the *aitia*, or an explanation of *ta onta*, by which he means perhaps everything that there is in the ordinary world, but whatever he discovers will not be what he had originally hoped for, and presumably still hopes for. At best, we may suppose, it will be consistent with that; but it will not be the real thing.

(I am aware of having already dipped my toe, or perhaps even a whole leg, into a controversy here: some people — for example, Wiggins — think that Socrates undertakes his second voyage precisely with the hope of finding the sort of explanation he had previously been deprived of. '[W]hat he now envisages is a way of achieving it that bears the same relation to the hope he had entertained of Anaxagoras' book as rowing to one's destination against wind and tide bears to the hope of simply sailing thither with a fair wind'.[3] But this interpretation seems largely to depend on a reading of a later passage in the *Phaedo* which I shall contest, so for the moment I may set it to one side.)

Socrates begins his promised account of his *deuteros plous* with a new image, which is the source of my title. He compares the kind of procedure involved in his first voyage to looking directly at the sun in eclipse; if people do that, rather than looking at its image in water or something like that, they get blinded. In just the same way, he had thought that he might suffer a kind of 'blinding of the soul' if he went on looking at things themselves directly with his eyes, and trying to grasp them with each of his senses. Instead, he decided to take refuge in *logoi*, which I shall take to mean 'propositions' (see below), and to examine the truth of things in them.

---

2   The case for abandoning the more traditional rendering of *aitia* as 'cause' is convincingly argued in Vlastos 1973b, 78-102. Frede 1980, 222-3, 227 alleges a difference between *aitia* ('reason' or 'explanation') and *aition* ('cause') in the relevant context in *Phd*; later in the dialogue, however, the terms appear to be used in identical fashion ('the reason for this is that ...': 110e2, 112a7-b2).

3   Wiggins 1986, 2. (This explanation of the phrase *deuteros plous* is itself ancient: see Burnet 1911, *ad loc.*)

This might give the impression that the new method is a second-best to looking at things directly, as well as to sailing breezily towards his preferred, teleological, type of explanation. But Socrates moves immediately to correct this impression: 'But perhaps', he says, 'it's in a way not like what I was comparing it with: for I don't agree at all[4] that the person who examines the things that are in propositions is studying them more "in images" than the person who examines them in direct experiences' (99e6-100a2).[5] The latter person is someone like Anaxagoras, or the scientists in general: it is they who try, unsuccessfully, to understand things by looking at them directly. The reason why this is just as much, or more, a matter of 'examining the things that are "in images"' than examining them 'in propositions' is presumably that the objects of perception are themselves images (or can be described as images), i.e. of the forms. (This is, or relates to, a common way of describing the relationship between particulars and forms elsewhere in Plato — particulars are 'likenesses', 'shadows', or 'imitations' of forms: it does not figure in the *Phaedo*, except rather obliquely here, perhaps for reasons connected with the earlier argument from recollection, which needed to stress the difference of particulars from forms.)[6] 'Propositions', or 'things said', are also images, or analogous to images, in so far as they reflect the truth about 'the things that are'. Since these 'things that are' are, in the present context, things in the ordinary world, i.e. particulars, we might think that *logoi* would then turn out to be images of images — and so actually worse off than unmediated (?) perceptions of things. But the crucial point is that the specific type of *logoi* or propositions that Socrates has in mind will turn out to *include reference to forms*, because they will explain particulars in terms of their relationship to forms (of which more anon). To this extent, they will be images directly of reality, given that forms represent the originals of which particulars are images.

But in fact this ought to be clear already, when Socrates talks of being *blinded* by the direct use of the senses. He was talking in exactly the same way a few pages before: he was 'so blinded by this sort of inquiry

---

4 Or 'I don't wholly agree'?

5 'Direct experiences' here translates *erga*: cf. Dixsaut 1991 ('expériences directes').

6 Whether particulars are like or unlike forms is consequently left open: contrast 74a2-7 with c11-d2.

[i.e. by looking at things in the way that the scientists do] that I unlearned even the things that I thought I knew before' (96c5-6): that is, the sorts of answers that 'wise people' gave when asked for explanations raised puzzles in other cases too, in which he'd previously thought he was secure — e.g. that we get larger through eating and drinking, and so adding to our bulk. The puzzle is just how anything can come about through the rearrangement of *other* things; which is the kind of idea that he found when he read Anaxagoras, and which is the cause of his (potential) 'blinding' in 99d. So the contrast is not, except ironically, between being blinded by the brilliance of the real thing (the sun, or ordinary things in general) and managing to see it successfully, but at one remove; the real contrast is between not seeing anything at all, and seeing things with at least some degree of success, which Socrates thinks and hopes he can do, and has done, 'in propositions'.

To sum up so far. There are three kinds of routes which are talked about in the present context: 1. the direct route to a preferred type of explanation, which Socrates hasn't been able to find; 2. a second-best route, which will take him, and us, at least somewhere; and 3. the route chosen by Anaxagoras and his 'wise' scientific or materialist colleagues, which leads to a dead end. The second route, which is the one Socrates has embarked on (the 'second sailing'), and the only one presently available and useful, is somehow 'in propositions'. It is his description of his voyage on this route that I want to try to follow out in the main part of this paper.

He started out, he tells us, by 'hypothesizing on each occasion whichever *logos* I judge to be strongest, and positing as true whatever seems to be in accord with this, in connection both with *aitia* [i.e. explaining anything] and with everything else, and as not true whatever (seems) not (to be in accord with it)' (100a3-7). Such *logoi* (because more than one seems to be envisaged) are, presumably, the *logoi* from which the new method 'in *logoi*' begins; and if they are 'hypothesized', they presumably take the form of propositions (*logos* is minimally 'thing said', but I take it that any 'thing said' which could be usefully hypothesized would have the form of a complete sentence, or could readily be translated into one). What then are these hypothesized propositions?

I have already indicated that they crucially *refer to forms*. This emerges explicitly in what follows, when Socrates explains what is involved in this new method of hypothesizing: he hypothesizes 'that there is something beautiful by itself [a form of beauty] and good and large and everything else' (i.e. something beautiful by itself, something good by itself, something large by itself, and so on: a single form in each case: 100b5-7). His next move is to say that anything else that is beautiful, or whatever it may be, is so just because it 'participates in' the corresponding form (100c4-6). We might try treating this as something which is 'in accord with' the hypothesis of the existence of the forms; on the other hand, a version of the idea turns out to be combined with the form-hypothesis to provide the starting-point for the last argument for immortality (102b1-2), which gives the *raison d'être* of the whole of the present context, so that it seems better to treat it as itself part of what is hypothesized.

In that case, however, Socrates seems to end up by explaining his method in terms of a *single* hypothesis; whereas he said that he began from '*whichever logos* seems to me to be strongest' — and that, again, seems to imply more than one. The answer to this puzzle may, I think, lie in 100d3-8: 'in my plain, artless and perhaps simple-minded way I hold this close to myself, that nothing else makes (the particular thing) beautiful except the presence of (the form), or its being associated (?) with it, or in whatever way and manner (it makes it beautiful) by having come to be added to it;[7] for I no longer affirm this with confidence, but (only) that it is by the beautiful that all (particular) beautiful things come to be beautiful', i.e. I do not want to commit myself on this as I do on the main hypothesis. What if we supposed that the apparent reference to hypothesized *logoi* in the plural in 100a is in fact a reference to the various different possible ways of describing the form-particular relationship? The basic term for this relationship is 'participation'; but Socrates seems to see the need — as well he might — for saying what, more precisely, this 'participation' might amount to, and suggests a couple of possibilities, with an indication that there may be others, without committing himself to any particular one. My suggestion is that when he talks about hypothesizing 'whichever *logos* I judge to be strongest', he means that he puts his form-participation hypothesis in whatever seems to him at the time ('on each occasion') the most defensible version. After all, 100a does seem to suggest uncertainty, and the only area in which he actually goes on to admit any real uncertainty is

---

7 Or 'in whatever way and manner we describe (the relationship)'. There is a textual problem here, but it does not fundamentally affect the main point. (A third way of describing the relationship would be in terms of original and likeness: see above.)

over this matter of the precise specification of the form-particular relationship.[8]

Armed with this suggestion, I now go on to the next crucial passage. Socrates indicates how Cebes should use the recommended kind of account to deal with the puzzles that caused so much trouble. This is in 100e5-102a1; my interest is in the last part of the passage, from 101c8. What Cebes should do is to say goodbye to the subtleties proposed by 'wiser' people, and cling to 'that safety of the hypothesis'; i.e. he should cling to the hypothesis (that F things are F 'by the F', or through participation in the F) in virtue of its safety, which has just been demonstrated: with it, at least we don't get into the difficulties that the other or 'wiser' type of 'explanation' gets us into. Now someone might propose firmly accepting the hypothesis for just that reason. But Cebes would not commit himself until he had first considered whether its consequences harmonized with each other or not — which is what Anaxagoras and company failed to do.[9] Supposing that he had found nothing to disturb the hypothesis there, he would then accept it. But there would come a time when he had to 'give an account' of it. Here, he would follow the same procedure as before, i.e. by using the method of hypothesis: he would propose whichever of those (hypotheses) 'above' seemed best, until he reached 'something adequate' (101e1).

I shall not comment on the rest of the passage, because it is not directly relevant to my immediate concerns, although it is itself full of difficulty. The part that I have paraphrased is one of the most disputed passages in the whole of Plato. My paraphrase does, I think, make fairly good sense of it down to 101d5, and I have not found anything better in the literature. But the last stage of the recommended method is particularly puzzling. What precisely does 'giving an account' of the hypothesis entail? What are the hypotheses 'above' that are talked about? And what does it mean to arrive at 'something adequate'?

---

8   The existence of forms, and the 'participation' of particulars in them, are of course still officially hypotheses; they are nonetheless things that Socrates is evidently prepared to 'affirm with conviction' (*diischūrizesthai*). See further 107b4-9.

9   The 'consequences' of the hypothesis are its applications to particular cases. The basic question is whether it can always be applied with the same success (since it is supposed to give us *the* explanation of things).

A common way of approaching these problems is to call in the sixth book of the *Republic*, which describes what seems on the face of it to be a similar process: the use of hypotheses, connected with forms, as a means of access to something higher, allowing reason to travel 'as far as the unhypothetical, to the first principle of the whole' (*Rep* 511b6-7), i.e., apparently, the form of the good. What exactly all *this* means is itself far from clear, but in its language, and in the general shape of the ideas involved, it seems to echo the *Phaedo* passage pretty closely. In which case, it looks reasonable enough, given no better alternative, to suggest that the *Phaedo* is adumbrating the more complete account of the higher processes of dialectic which we find in the *Republic*; or in other words that the *Phaedo* too envisages a possible release for us from the darkness of the Cave into the light of the Sun, where all will become clear.

There are, however, a number of difficulties with this reading. In the first place, the *Phaedo* does not accord any special place to the form of the good; where it is mentioned, it is simply listed along with others (100b5-7, 75c9-d3, 76d8-9; cf. 78d3-4). Then again, there is no mention of anything 'unhypothetical' in the *Phaedo*. This might be thought a small matter, but I think it is not. If we look at what Socrates says at the end of the final argument for immortality, we find him suggesting that we may in the end have to make do with hypotheses, at least in this life (107b4-9); and in the myth, the final revelation of truth seems to be said to be reserved for those fortunate souls which go after death to join the company of the gods[10] — if indeed there are any who achieve this end.[11] The hollow in which we live is a prison which holds us until we die: after death, if we have not succeeded in freeing ourselves from the influences of the body as far as is possible during our lives, we will descend into still deeper prisons. The whole picture of human life and

---

10   114c2-6. Only these souls evidently achieve that complete release from the body which Socrates has earlier treated as a necessary condition of achieving wisdom (64a-68b).

11   The careful eschatology of the myth identifies an intermediate category of souls who are adjudged to have lived with exceptional piety, but who have nevertheless not achieved full purification from the body (114b6-c2). This category, which is translated after death to the surface of the 'real' earth, seems to include Socrates himself, who expects only to 'meet' (different) gods (69e1-2, 63b-c; cf. 111b-c), rather than to become divine himself (82b10-c1). Yet it is he who is the paradigm of the philosopher (see especially 76b8-12).

its possibilities (and limitations) is, I think, different. In the language of the Cave, we can get to the entrance, perhaps, but no further.

Another more general issue needs to be raised: to what extent is it legitimate to read one dialogue in the light of another? It is in principle possible that Plato could have inserted passages which needed to be read with others in other dialogues in order to make them fully intelligible (although even this presupposes a more systematic organization in his writing than is immediately obvious); or passages which could only be properly understood by those with some sort of inside knowledge — and I have already mentioned one likely small example of this, at 99e6-100a3. However, there is a considerable problem about supposing that he could be doing this in the particular passage in question. This is that what Socrates has said is 'wonderfully transparent' (*enargēs*) — 'even to someone of small intelligence' (Echecrates), 'to all those present' (Phaedo), and 'to those who were not there, but are hearing it now' (Echecrates again). Maybe all those present were insiders (and indeed all of them do seem to be represented as belonging to a group which has regularly been involved in conversation with Socrates: 59a, with 75c-d, 78d), and Echecrates and the others in Phlius too. And maybe Echecrates, or Plato, overestimates either or both the clarity of what was said and what might be intelligible to an outsider, or 'someone of even small intelligence'. All the same, the emphasis on the *enargeia* of Socrates' account is striking (and can hardly be written off as ironical), and seems to me to suggest that it ought somehow to be intelligible, at least at some level, in itself.

That would mean looking for some way of interpreting the passage from within the resources offered by the *Phaedo* itself. The first requirement will be some set of hypotheses, somewhere in the surrounding context, which could be described as 'above' the original hypothesis about forms and participation. Is there any such set available? I believe that there is: namely, the set represented by the various different ways of describing the form-particular relationship which were referred to in 100d. Socrates' claim there was that 'nothing else makes the particular thing beautiful except the presence of the form, or its being associated with it', etc. These alternatives are alternative *possible* ways of describing the relationship, and can therefore plausibly be taken as 'hypotheses' — and if they are, as I suggested, the sorts of *logoi* in question in 100a ('I began by hypothesizing whichever *logos* seemed to me strongest'), then they will actually have been referred to as such. Can they be said to be 'above' the form-participation hypothesis? The question is, of course, what it means for one proposition to be 'above' another. To judge by the purpose for which 'hypotheses above' are to be called in, i.e. to enable the 'giving of an account' of the original one, a proposition will be said to be above another if it provides a defence, justification or explanation of it; and that is just what the propositions of 100d will do in relation to the basic form-particular hypothesis, since they are different ways of spelling out what it *means* to say that particulars 'participate' in forms, or that particulars are what they are 'by' the forms. We may compare the first part of the *Parmenides*, where Parmenides tries in a similar way to force Socrates to cash out the term 'participation': 'do you mean ...?', or 'do you mean ...?' As it turns out, no satisfactory solution is found, and yet Parmenides himself seems to imply that one can and must be discovered, in order to preserve the possibility of talking about anything (*dialegesthai*, 135c2). Just so, Socrates has suggested in the *Phaedo* that he will bring in the forms in relation to any and every subject ('in relation to explanation *and everything else*', 100a6). But even if we restrict ourselves to the matter of explanation, we shall clearly need a satisfactory account of how forms relate to particulars; it will be no use resting everything on a hypothesis one of whose central terms is essentially a place-filler — which is how Socrates seems to treat the idea of 'participation'. According to the interpretation I am suggesting, he anticipates someone saying to Cebes 'but just what does this alleged relation of "participation" amount to?' His next move will be to sort through the available substitutes, and 'hypothesize' the one that seems to him best (recall Socrates' reference to himself as 'hypothesizing whichever proposition I judge to be strongest'); and he will evidently continue this process, until he comes to 'something adequate', which I take to mean some version (whether it be 'presence', 'association', or anything else) which is capable of meeting all available objections. Again, there is no indication that the method will ever rise beyond the level of hypothesis. What we will end up with will perhaps be just a 'hypothesis worthy of acceptance', which is how Simmias described the hypothesis of forms itself at 92d6-7.

On this interpretation, the 'hypotheses above' are only 'above' the original one;[12] they do not form a series of ever-ascending hypotheses,

---

12 Or rather, of part of it (that particulars are what they are by participation in the forms); but it is to this part of the original compound hypothesis that our attention has been directed since 100d.

of the sort that is usually discovered in the passage at the end of *Republic* 6.[13] Socrates' sole concern is with the conditions of talking intelligibly and fruitfully about particulars, things in the ordinary world. (He seems to assume, in the *Phaedo* at least, that we can do so.) The essential condition, he suggests, is that we begin with the hypothesis that forms exist, and that particulars derive whatever character they have (and their names, 102b2) from some as yet incompletely specified relationship with them. All of this is perfectly compatible with some more ambitious inquiry into the *aitia* of things, of the sort which is adumbrated in the *Republic*, and on which Socrates hopefully set out in his aborted first voyage in the *Phaedo* itself. But his second voyage has a much more limited objective. The sun, as we might say, is for the moment beyond the horizon.

I want now to turn to the immediate use that Socrates makes of his basic hypothesis, in the final argument for immortality. The version in which it appears in this context is 'that each of the forms is something, and that the other things [i.e. particulars], by coming to share in these, have the names of these very things' (102b1-2). It would take too long to give (and defend) a complete analysis of the argument; instead I shall try simply to single out the relevant aspects of Socrates' strategy. Here too I shall have to cut corners, since this new section of the dialogue is only slightly less problematic than the one we have just been considering. But in a seminar context, it may be acceptable, and even appropriate, just to suggest a *possible* reading of a difficult passage.[14]

What I propose is as follows. Socrates brings three categories of entity into play: first, forms; second, particular things like cabbages or kings; and third, what he calls *ideai* or *morphai* (or 'the F in us'), which (after Vlastos among others) I shall translate as 'characters' — a set of things which things in the second category have by virtue of sharing or participating in things in the first. (Things in the second category might, I suppose, reduce to the third: since the same analysis ought to be applicable to any feature of them, they would apparently turn out just to be bundles of 'characters'. But that takes us into deep waters, which

---

13 Whether correctly or not is another question, but in any case one beyond the brief of the present paper.

14 For a detailed defence of the reading suggested, see Rowe 1993a.

I shall skirt round. I shall also not try to say where soul fits in — though perhaps it is *sui generis*.) To put it crudely (though there may be no other way of putting it), the strategy is to treat these 'characters' as if they were miniature versions of the corresponding forms. They are of course unlike forms in that they pass in and out of existence, but in other respects they behave just like them: in particular, they exclude their opposites, if they have them, and if they don't, but are essentially linked with one of a pair of opposites, they will exclude the opposite of that. Thus Simmias, for example, is tall (by comparison with Socrates); but he is also short (by comparison with Phaedo). In this case, he has both the 'character' of tallness 'in' him and that of shortness — but, Socrates insists, it's only Simmias who's both tall and short, not the tallness (or shortness). Threeness doesn't have an opposite, but nevertheless always brings one with it, i.e. oddness, and will never come to be even. Take any group of three things (say Simmias, Socrates and Phaedo): it will be three in virtue of having the character of 'threeness' in it. If the group then becomes even in number (because Socrates dies), threeness itself won't have become even, because of course it is no longer there.

The shape of this peculiar stuff is determined by the needs of the argument for immortality (Socrates will next introduce *soul* as something else which lacks an opposite, but always brings an opposite — life — to whatever it comes to occupy, i.e. body ...). What interests me in the present context is the sort of thinking about forms and particulars which underpins it. The first and obvious point is that it is implied that for any x to be F (where x is a particular, and F any property which it has) is for x to 'share in' the F (the relevant form); and further, that to say of any x that it is F is to assert that x participates in the F. Next, this relationship can also be described by saying that a 'character', F-ness, inheres in, or 'occupies', x. Now in the course of the argument from recollection, Socrates suggested that some particulars necessarily fall short of the forms, apparently because, unlike the forms, they are capable of being both F and not-F (74bff.): thus any two sensible things that are equal to one another are capable also of being unequal, i.e. to other things — just as Simmias is capable of being both tall and short. But the same consideration does not apply to the 'characters' of equality, tallness and shortness, which will remain exactly what they are, i.e. equality, tallness and shortness, so long as they subsist. All the other considerations which are brought in elsewhere to impugn the reality of particulars seem equally to relate to the bearers of attributes, not to the attributes ('characters') themselves: if a particular beautiful thing, say, may only be beautiful now, not tomorrow, or only in this respect, not in that, or only to some people, not to others,[15] still, if it is beautiful now, in this respect, and to those qualified to judge such things, there is beauty there, and it will be true to say that there is. It may only be an evanescent and qualified beauty (compared e.g. with the beauty of things on the true surface of the earth, as described in the myth), but it is nonetheless beauty.[16] In this sense, and provided that we are aware of all the relevant qualifications, our statements about the world may be not only true but unproblematical.

The point at which problems *do* arise is when we leave out these qualifications: when we behave like the prisoners in the Cave in the *Republic*, and think these temporary, partial exemplars of beauty (or whatever) are all there is to it. There is no incompatibility here either between the *Phaedo* and the *Republic*. The *Republic* is centrally concerned with the question about how we acquire knowledge about the most important things: not only about beauty, but about justice, and about the good itself. The Socrates of the *Phaedo* agrees that it is no use looking to acquire this sort of knowledge from ordinary experience; he treats the senses simply as an obstacle to the acquisition of knowledge (64aff.), except in so far as they may put us in mind of its proper objects (74aff.). The only major point of difference between the *Phaedo* and the *Republic* is the one that I have already pointed out, that the *Phaedo* does not envisage the possibility of acquiring complete wisdom in this life; and it is perhaps only the *Republic* which does suggest such a possibility (though maybe Diotima's revelations in the *Symposium* also imply it). Elsewhere, it seems to me, the emphasis is on the limitations of human understanding which receive such stress in the *Phaedo*.[17] This might raise some interesting questions about the status of the *Republic*, and also about the theses of the so-called 'Tübingen school' of interpreta-

---

15 See especially *Rep* 474-80, with *Smp* 210e-212a.

16 Or, to take a different example: a pair of objects in one corner of the room will still be precisely equal in number to another pair in the opposite corner. It may only be equal to it in number, and there will be many other groups of things to which it is not equal (in number); but there is nothing in Plato's argument which should make him want to deny that it is equal, in the specified respects.

17 See especially *Phdr* 278d, which makes explicit what is already implied in the myth at 248aff.

tion.[18] But these I must pass over. The immediate point is that these limitations to our understanding seem ultimately likely to prevent our giving a *complete* account of the physical world, however successful we may be in describing parts of it. That brings us to where the *Timaeus* begins. We must be satisfied, Timaeus says, because we are merely human, with a 'likely' (? *eikōs*) account of an 'image' (*eikōn*) — an idea which recalls Socrates' implied characterization at *Phaedo* 99-100 of scientists like Anaxagoras as dealing with images, in so far as they spend their time looking directly at things. Is Plato admitting, in the *Timaeus*, that any account of the world given from a human standpoint must, inevitably, depend on the observed relationship between its parts, and that only a god could describe it, as it were, from the top down?

---

18   See e.g. Krämer 1990, Pesce 1990.

Plato and the Sightlovers of the Republic[1]

Michael C. Stokes

Though its relevance to the Cave will become apparent, this paper's conclusions are, like those of Gail Fine (1978), limited in scope almost entirely to the final argument of *Republic* 5. It is perhaps best introduced here in relation to Fine's article: agreeing that Plato does not endorse in Book 5 a two-world theory, and that the context of his argument is significant, I disagree with her grounds for these views and prefer an account of 'being' in the argument mainly in terms of existence to her veridical terms. My reason for the importance of the context and for doubting Plato's endorsement in this Book of a two-world view of Forms and particulars is, broadly, that the argument is dialectical. Its conclusions are reached by steps some of which are due to the predicament the 'sightlovers' of the dialogue are contextually landed in. Thus we should not saddle Plato himself with any other than the *literary* responsibility for either the course or the conclusions of the argument. This paper will make a piece of dialectic out of a set of arguments which readers may have cherished as interesting if erratic Platonic philosophy.

The lovers of sights and sounds, *philotheāmones* and *philēkooi*, appear at 475d in a discussion of the philosopher. The philosopher, in parallel with the *philoinos* or oenophile and others, is tentatively described as

1 This paper was read in various drafts to the Durham University Philosophy Seminar, the Centre for Research in Philosophy and Literature of the University of Warwick and the Seminar in Ancient Philosophy at the London Institute of Classical Studies. I am deeply indebted to friendly critics on each occasion who have saved me from numerous errors of omission or commission; mistakes that are left are my fault alone.

desirous (475b8-9) not just of some *sophia* (wisdom) but of all wisdom. Socrates suggests that one hard to please (*duskherainonta*) in subjects to be learnt is not a lover of learning or wisdom; the philosopher is willing to taste any and every subject, and goes gladly and insatiably to work at learning. The reader's experience of philosophers may bear this out; but Glaucon objects. He wishes to distinguish the lovers of sights and sounds from the philosophers; the lovers of sounds fanatically pursue choral performances, and presumably the sightlovers behave analogously; it would be absurd to place them among the philosophers. Socrates agrees: they spuriously resemble philosophers, he says.[2] It is against the dialectical background of these spurious lovers of wisdom that Socrates introduces to the *Republic* the Forms and the accompanying epistemology. This paper argues that this background explains much in the argument that would otherwise need to be explained away.

The true philosophers, Socrates suggests, love seeing the *truth*. Glaucon seeks an explanation of this. It would not be at all easy, Socrates says at 475e6, to put across to someone else, but Glaucon, he thinks, will give him the point he needs next. Socrates' reason for singling out Glaucon is unclear: Glaucon is not specially docile in discussion (witness his objection mentioned above); he is not elsewhere characterized as significantly expert on the Theory of Forms; though he readily accepts the identity of an individual's and a city's justice at 435a, being thus disposed to accept the singleness of abstracts such as 'justice', he is surely not unique in this, even though what Adeimantus accepts at 368d-e is somewhat less explicit. Socrates' language at 475e6 is strong; but perhaps it just makes a fine compliment to Glaucon's quickness of uptake. I have said more below (pp. 118-19).

The points Glaucon accepts are not simple; but we may skate rapidly (with Plato's Socrates) over some thin ice. 'Honourable' and 'dishonourable' or 'beautiful' and 'ugly' (*kalon, aischron*) are opposites, and are therefore two [distinct things]. Since they are two, each must be one. This offers Glaucon an *argument* of sorts for the unity of 'beautiful' and

---

2 *Pace* Gosling (1977: 309 and elsewhere), there is nothing here to make one suppose that the sightlovers are confusable with philosophers proper: what the sightlovers go out and learn is not in Socrates' eyes properly learnable; it is Glaucon, not Socrates, who speaks at 475a of the 'learning' the philosophers love as possibly including sights and sounds. See also n.10 below.

of 'ugly', and does not simply assume it. Without stopping to ask of 'beautiful' 'one *what?*', we continue skating. What is true of 'beautiful' and 'ugly' is true also of 'just'/'unjust', 'good'/'bad', and all kinds. Each is 'one' itself, but seems many, appearing everywhere, by sharing in actions, bodies and (according to the MSS) each other. On this basis Socrates distinguishes the only true philosophers from sightlovers, lovers of skills and doers (476a-b). The distinction has sight- and sound-lovers enjoying beautiful voices, colours, shapes and things crafted from them, whereas their mind cannot see or enjoy the nature of the beautiful itself.

Much has been written on expressions like 'the beautiful itself'. But it is simplest to think of 'itself' in this passage as meaning 'by itself'. That such expressions are at this stage of the dialogue already technical terms seems an unnecessary assumption based on a very uncertain view of what Socrates says to Glaucon at 475e6 (see above). One can then discern in this passage a fair antithesis between beautiful thises or thats, whether they be sensible objects or sensible properties or both indiscriminately, and on the other hand 'the beautiful' *simpliciter* or, less technically, 'the beautiful [considered] by itself'. Plato's Socrates' suggestion is then true, that those capable of going to and seeing 'the beautiful by itself' are few.

One cannot, indeed, *see* 'the beautiful by itself'. One has to use one's intellectual powers of abstraction to conceive it. Such intellectual effort — for effort is needed — is not to everyone's taste or within everyone's capacity. Few would have thought it worthwhile, or been able, to accomplish the task of abstraction apparently envisaged. Those who did no doubt deserved to be called 'lovers of wisdom'. But it is another question whether they earn their description as 'sightlovers of the truth' (475e4); is any kind of truth — truth-value truth, genuineness, realness — to be gained by such abstraction? It is open to doubt, of course. But Plato gives us a Socrates who is prepared to fight dialectically for his views, and not merely an intellectual bully imposing them.

Before we come to the fight, let us set up the contestants: in the red corner, the sight-and-sound-lover. (S)he acknowledges beautiful things, whether objects or properties or both; but does (s)he accept 'beauty by itself'? Never. (S)he doesn't acknowledge such a thing now, and even if led to the *gnōsis*, recognition, of it (s)he is unable to follow. 'Beauty' here (476c2), for some obscure reason, replaces 'the beautiful'. But the sightlover, Socrates asks, does (s)he live in a dream or awake? Explaining this, isn't the dreaming state one in which, awake or asleep,

one thinks X which resembles Y is in fact Y? Given that that *is* what
it means to be dreaming, Glaucon agrees that the sightlover is dreaming. In this context, then, the sightlover thinks that the beautiful things
are the beautiful itself. It is not possible to claim more than plausibility
here, but one way to envisage this as a live possibility is to suppose
the sightlover to take 'the beautiful' in a collective sense meaning 'the
set of beautiful things [or properties, or both]'.

If you were like this and I asked 'Show me the beautiful,' you
might take me to see a Cathedral and a castle, take me to a
symphony concert, introduce me to your lover, and show me your
exquisitely bound copy of McGonagall. You might also, or alternatively, point out the beautiful colour of the Cathedral's stone, the
imposing thickness of the castle walls, the sheen of the book's
binding, and so forth. If I said next, 'Show me the beautiful, or
beauty, by itself', you would not instruct me in intellectual abstraction; you would say 'But I've shown you all those beauties', or 'all
those beautiful things'; 'What more do you want?' (or, 'What more
can I do?'). If I said, obdurately, 'The beautiful, please, by itself',
you would reply 'There's no such thing. I can't show it you. If you
want to see what I think you must mean by that gibberish, come
and see more sights.' Now if you say that, and if you yourself seek
out the sights, you are very like the sightlover in the *Republic*. You
take 'beauty' or 'the beautiful by itself' to be another way of saying
'the set comprising beautiful things'; you think there are beautiful
concrete things, and/or even beautiful perceptible properties such
as beautiful colours, but not 'the beautiful' in the abstract. The
Hippias Major (compared by Turnbull 1988: 33f.) presents perhaps
an extreme version of the syndrome. Now Plato in the *Phaedo* and
Symposium had already talked about abstractions and pointed out
that they are not subject to the vicissitudes of concrete things. To
him someone in your state of mind as described above was mistak-
ing the beautiful this and that for 'the beautiful'. Plato insists that
the two need distinguishing, and Glaucon admits that anyone
unable to distinguish them might as well be dreaming; 'the beautiful' is *not* just a collective, and indeed in ordinary Greek it can
mean 'beauty'.

Conventionally the word 'beauty' figures much more prominently.
The actual abstract noun, however, does not crop up, despite the Penguin translator, until 476c2, by which time the expression 'the beautiful
itself' is well established; 'beautiful itself' returns at 476c9; and 'beauty'
receives only one further mention, at 479a1-2, and that in tandem with

'beautiful itself'.[3] The significance of this lies in the linguistic facts which make 'the beautiful itself' etc. more difficult than 'beauty' for the sight-lovers to distinguish from beautiful things or properties, and at the same time harder for them as a task in abstraction. 'The X' in Greek, where X is a neuter singular adjective, can, as scholars know well, function as an abstract; it can also function as a collective, much as in English, e.g., 'the poor' can (see Stokes 1986: 132ff.). An expression for an abstract such as 'beauty' which can also mean 'the collection of beautiful things' (whether 'things' be objects or properties) rather readily permits confusion of the abstract with the things. At the same time, one accustomed to thinking of 'the beautiful this' or 'the beautiful that' might indeed find difficulty in conceiving 'the beautiful' 'by itself' without the possibility of adding any word for a 'this' or a 'that'. The abstract noun 'beauty' and its like scarcely present in Greek any such problems.

So much for the red corner. In the blue corner opposed to the sightlover stands the philosopher. Before the bell sounds, the philosopher stands stripped, revealing not yet a metaphysician, not a two-world theorist, not a devotee of Plato's *Phaedo* and *Symposium*, but a lover of truth. (S)he is a person curious about more than (s)he can see or hear; (s)he is prepared therefore to acknowledge that one can talk about such non-perceptible things as the beautiful, the tall etc. in the abstract, and (s)he is interested in them. Such a person cannot (according to Plato elsewhere) afford to neglect particulars in his/her account of the F itself — witness Socrates' constant counter-examples in the definition-dialogues; but a concern with 'the F by itself' is apparently what differentiates most radically between him/her and the sightlover. The connection between his/her initial love of truth and the following talk of 'the F by itself' emerges in the discussion.

What truth(s) does the philosopher seek to contemplate? Socrates enters the subject of 'the F by itself', we recall, to explain (475e5ff.) what he means by calling the philosopher one who seeks to behold the truth. Contrasting the unity of the F itself with the plurality of its appearances, Socrates makes this contrast the basis of his distinction between sight-lovers and lovers of wisdom. The lovers of sights and sounds welcome

---

3   One may compare the *Hp Ma*, in which according to Brandwood (1976) *kallos* (beauty) occurs only at 289b5 and 292d3. On the other hand, in *Smp*, where Plato has Agathon rather than Socrates introduce the word 'beauty', it occurs 15 times in all.

beautiful sights and sounds but their intelligence cannot see and welcome 'the nature of the beautiful itself'. It is needful to determine the force of the phrase 'the nature of'. 'Nature' here is not 'essential nature' as in Lee's Penguin translation and by implication in Adam's note: Plato especially uses 'the nature of X' as a mere periphrasis for 'X' (cf. LSJ: s.v. *physis* II 5), and this is borne out by the sequel which says nothing of the peculiar essence of 'the beautiful'.

For Socrates and Glaucon distinguish from the sightlovers at 476b10 those few who are 'able to go to the beautiful itself and to see [it] by itself'. The sightlover, at 476c2 one who accepts as established (*nomizōn*) beautiful things but not beauty itself, is further characterized as one who cannot follow a lead to the knowledge (*gnōsis*) of beauty itself. This is not knowledge of the peculiar essential nature of 'beauty'; the question Socrates is asking is simply whether the sightlover spends life awake or dreaming. Dreaming is indeed here the state in which one mistakes X resembling Y for Y itself; and Socrates at 476c9ff. makes clear that X and Y here are (either way round) 'beautiful itself' and beautiful things. Clearly the 'knowledge' differentiating at c3 between waking and dreaming concerns no essential nature, but the distinction between 'the beautiful itself' and the things 'partaking of' it. The philosopher is awake in that (s)he recognizes that there is such a thing as 'beautiful itself' and can inspect both it and the things partaking of it without confusing the two.

This judgement on the reference of 'the knowledge of [beauty itself]' has important consequences for the basic concerns of the rest of Socrates' argument. One step is left of the discussion with Glaucon in his own person, and that is agreement that the philosopher's state of mind should be called 'knowing' (*gnōmē*) because (s)he 'knows' (*hōs gignōskontos*), whereas the sightlover's is to be called 'opinion' (*doxa*) because (s)he is opining (*hōs doxazontos*). Scholars have insufficiently observed that if this is a reasoned step rather than a shot in the dark, the knowledge attributed to the philosopher here must be the same as the 'knowledge' unattainable to the 'dreaming' sightlover at 476c2-4 and by contrast presumably available to the philosopher who is 'awake'. In contradistinction to the philosopher who thus 'knows' as well as 'sees' and 'thinks' in the preceding passage, the sightlover has been accorded no knowledge but only 'thinking' (*hēgētai* 476c6) seeing and confusion. Glaucon after this may reasonably accept that by contrast with the 'knowing' philosopher the sightlover achieves only opinion — what else would one naturally call confused belief? Two consequences flow from this: first, the knowledge in point here is that of a thing, namely, 'beauty itself'; secondly, one would expect precisely here a vigorous protest from the sightlovers, refusing to accept that they have no knowledge of the things they do believe in and recognize, and asserting their right to more than mere opinion in the matter. They would dissociate themselves from Glaucon's too ready agreement with Socrates.

Thus revealed, Socrates' philosopher has to convince his sightlover of the error of his protest. The contest clearly lies between these two, as some interpreters have seen,[4] and not just between a manipulative Socrates and a too pliant Glaucon. The philosopher must find gaps in the defence not of some generalized patsy, but of this actual opponent fighting for this actual type of attitude and belief. The 'philosopher' cannot legitimately employ premises of his own, let alone those of Socrates or Plato; he should base his argument on premises acceptable to his opponent. The following account of the battle assesses the points scored by a Socrates who is trying to fight by the Queensberry rules of dialectic.

Socrates sets the fight going by his next question at 476d8:

> What if he raises an objection, this man who, we're saying, has a belief and not a proper recognition of an actual difference? What if he disputes the truth of what we say? Can we soothe him and tactfully persuade him, without mentioning his unhealthy state of mind?

On Glaucon's agreement to do this, Socrates puts a question on their joint behalf to the now recalcitrant sightlover. Having put it, he says to Glaucon, most importantly, 'You, then, answer me on [the sightlover's] behalf'. There is no textual evidence, nor antecedent probability, that in the sequel Glaucon shifts from answering on the sightlover's behalf to answering for himself. Indeed, the imperative 'answer' is present or continuous in aspect, but that proves little. Simply, without contrary hint it would be normal to take Glaucon as replying always in the person of the sightlover.[5] We should scrutinize his answers not as those of someone convinced in advance and determined to let Socrates have his way, but as the work of a man doing his best for the opposition while

---

4 Notably Gosling 1968: 120f., Fine 1978 and 1990: 85ff., Cooper 1986: 233. Fine in particular is laudably explicit on the 'dialectical requirement'.

5 See on *Socrates* as a representative of two old men in the Laches and of the young Hippocrates in the *Protagoras* Stokes 1986: 65ff. and 203ff.

accepting that their beliefs might put them in some strange positions. Glaucon ought to be accustomed from Book 2 on to standing up for other people's opinions.

We should, then, examine blow by blow the bout which follows. First, using 'gnow' for the recognition with certainty of a thing's distinguishable existence, 'Does the man who gnows gnow something or nothing?' (476e7). Is Socrates entitled to use this verb at all? Yes. The sightlover has (reasonably) denied the statement that (s)he only believes and does not gnow; and to deny one's failure to gnow entails one's admission to the discourse of the word 'gnow'. So is the question in any deeper sense impermissible? Could the sightlover say that when denying any failure to gnow (s)he was only asserting the absurdity of requiring him/her to gnow when there was no such thing as 'gnowing'? Perhaps; but there seems to be no good reason for making such a retort compulsory. A normal sightlover will claim to have gnowledge enough through the senses.

So the point stands: if you gnow, you gnow *something*. Is this in turn reasonable, and what does it mean? The course of the conversation so far, mentioning the 'gnowledge' only of 'the beautiful itself', 'beauty itself' etc., suggests strongly that Socrates and Glaucon have in mind the gnowledge of things, rather than of propositions. The sightlover has denied the distinguishable *existence* of 'the beautiful by itself' and of 'beauty itself', not the *truth* of any proposition or predication except (if it be such) that 'the F by itself' exists. The context thus imposes what (among others) F.C. White (1981: 87 n.1 and 1984) argued for, that 'being' in this bit of *Republic* 5 means, by and large, 'existence'. Glaucon as sightlover may very naturally accept that 'everyone who gnows, gnows something', and that that something exists. He may do so because the existence of something claimed to be 'gnown' is common ground to sightlovers and philosophers: to the philosophers because they claim to 'gnow' 'the F itself', and to the sightlovers because they claim to 'gnow' what they see around them; and both insist on the distinguishable existence of what they 'gnow'. One could not recognize with certainty the distinguishable existence of the non-existent.[6]

---

6 One cannot therefore with Gosling (1968: 121) use in favour of the veridical interpretation of 'be' here the point that it offers an easy 'common ground' for sightlovers and believers in Forms.

This point has needed such lengthy exposition because several interpreters, using the veridical sense of the Greek verb 'to be', have explicated 'How could something not being be known?' (477a1) as 'How could anything not true be known?' (Gosling 1968: 119-130; Fine 1978 and 1990). They then continue applying this sense of the Greek verb to the rest of the argument. This procedure tends to eliminate degrees of existence from *Republic* 5. If the conversation began at 476e one would grant the possibility of this 'veridical' interpretation. It has Socrates ask a sensible question, and Glaucon as sightlover give a sensible answer; one does find it difficult to conceive seriously of a false proposition being known. Glaucon even produces at 477e6 below the answer here given him by 'veridical' interpreters, saying that knowledge is infallible and opinion not. If they were talking about propositions, there is no reason why sightlover and philosopher should not find common ground in accepting that all known propositions are true. But such interpreters seem in expounding 476e-477a to have paid insufficient attention to the precise context in which the argument with Glaucon as sightlover lies embedded. The context deals with existence.[7]

One place in that context deserves re-visiting. The philosopher was described at 475e4 as one who loves to look at the truth. Can the 'existence' interpretation supply a truth for the philosopher to enjoy contemplating? It can. The 'dreaming' sightlover, on Socrates' account, confuses 'the beautiful itself' with the many beautiful appearances; the wakeful philosopher endeavours to see 'beautiful itself' etc. as distinct from those appearances. There is no need to look further for the truth that the philosopher desires to look at: it is the clear distinction between, in the case of each class, the numerous particulars and the single appropriate thing 'by itself' that they share. The distinct things such as 'the beautiful itself' are what the philosopher 'gnows'; the truth he likes to inspect is that of their distinctness. One might wish to equate that which the philosophers at 475e4 love to contemplate almost visually with 'the beautiful by itself' which they have the ability to see at 476b6-11, and, together with the things partaking of it, at 476d1. But that these abstract things are propositions has not recently to my

---

7 Annas' view (1981: 198) that the 'is' of Plato's argument is predicative tempts me not at all. It is not clear why Plato should be so elliptical as this makes him and yet fail to illustrate his meaning at the outset; nor how he expected the poor sightlover to understand.

knowledge been maintained, and seems a difficult notion; and the word for 'truth' at 475e4 seems not to be used for 'genuinenesss' or 'realness' or any other property one would readily attribute to 'the beautiful itself'. The 'truth' of 475e4 is therefore the major truth which emerges in the course of Socrates' explanation; and that is the proposition that 'the beautiful itself' etc. are distinct from the totality of things collected under 'the beautiful' etc.

We may now, then, distinguish as the first proposition of Socrates' argument with the sightlovers Glaucon represents:

   (1) 'Everything gnown exists'.

Socrates' next question (477a2-5) is perhaps rather devious — almost a low blow. The proposition suggested is:

   (2) 'Therefore ... (a) what completely exists is completely gnowable, but (b) what doesn't in any way at all exist is completely ungnowable'.

From 'All gnowns exist' (previously agreed as (1)) to (2)(b) 'All non-existents are ungnown' is a short step. To 'all non-existents are ungnowable' is a longer one, perhaps needing a confusion of the *necessitas consequentiae* with the *necessitas consequentis*. But Plato has arranged for Glaucon for practical purposes to give this one away with his impetuous but very understandable rhetorical question at 477a1, 'How would something non-existent be known?' However, from either (1) or (2)(b) to (2)(a) 'All existents (*or* 'All absolutely existents'[8]) are gnowable (*or* 'absolutely gnowable')' is a long and seemingly impossible step, indeed an unwarranted conversion. But it is one which the sightlovers can reject only as part of an inference marked by *oun*, therefore, and not as a proposition in its own right. For (2)(a) is equivalent to 'If it is absolutely existent it is absolutely gnowable'; and that means to the sightlover, 'If it's material, visible and/or audible then one can gnow it'. Since for the sightlover and soundlover existence is limited to material existence and gnowledge or discernment to the employment of their

---

8 Cooper (1986) and Annas (1981: 196) make too much of 'absolutely' here; the expression is one the sightlover might find obscure but hardly menacing; it could mean 'wholly', but Socrates uses it to contrast with what follows about that which 'both is and is not'. Gosling (1968: 121f.) also regards it as preparatory.

senses, it will be hard on them if they cannot rely on the equivalent of (2)(a). For they will then be reduced to supposing that some material things are not gnowable. Their one mode of knowledge will not stretch to all members of the class of things they maintain exist. This seems enough to reduce the conscientious sightlover to silence in the face of Socrates' inference; even if (s)he distrusts the argument, (s)he cannot easily deny the conclusion. The sightlover might even think rather similarly about (2)(b): (2)(b) was that all non-existents are ungnowable; and if something non-existent (that is, for the sightlover *et al.*, something non-sensible) is gnowable, then the sightlover's obdurate denial of the philosopher's favoured abstracts collapses.

Satisfied that Glaucon's acceptance at 477a5 is not too outrageous, let us pass to his next assent, to the following:

> (3) 'If there is a thing such that it both exists and does not exist, it would lie (wouldn't it?) between the purely existent and the utterly non-existent'.

Since the antecedent of this conditional is a contradiction, it should not matter much what the consequent says. But if this strange antecedent were to be true, there is nothing counter-intuitive about this consequent of Socrates'. A combination of two extremes can easily be thought of as lying between them. One might fault Glaucon's lack of logical sophistication here, but that for the early fourth century B.C. is a venial sin. It would not help from Glaucon's sightlover's point of view to read 'true' for 'existent' here and 'untrue' for 'non-existent': a proposition both true and false, however well it might fit Socrates' or Plato's purposes later, would strike a sightlover at this stage as a riddle no more acceptable than the non-existent existent. But on either interpretation the sightlover can, (s)he might suppose, afford to accept almost anything Socrates offers as a consequence of so seemingly impossible a hypothesis.

Having forgiven the venial, we deal next with something quite hard even to understand. 477a9-b1 submits for Glaucon's assent:

> (4) (a) Gnowledge has for its object that which exists, but (b) ignosance [*sic*] (or 'non-gnowledge') necessarily has for its object that which does not exist; but (c) what has for its object that which lies between [existence and non-existence] must be looked for between ignosance and gnowledge — if there is such a thing.

Here, doubtless, 'if there is such a thing' means 'if there is something between ignosance and gnowledge.'

(4)(b) is at first sight obscure. It could, if we temporarily abandon ignosance for ignorance as Plato abandons it in (4)(c), mean *either* 'All and only non-existents are the objects of ignorance' *or* (*merely*) 'All non-existents are the objects of ignorance'. The former is hard to swallow: it is quite unacceptable to a robust sightlover to say that the field of objects of ignorance is confined to non-existents. I cannot be other than wholly ignorant of the non-existent present Emperor of China; but I am also wholly ignorant of the presumably existent Chinese word for 'Emperor'. Another difficulty is that if 'all and only ...' is what Socrates means, he looks to be wrongly converting (2)(b) 'All non-existents are ungnowable' to 'Only non-existents are the objects of ignosance'.

The second possible interpretation of (4)(b) must be inspected. This says merely, 'All non-existents are the objects of ignorance'. This not only makes sense in itself; it also fits the context better. The sentence embodying proposition (4) as a whole refers to knowledge in relation to being, to ignorance in relation to not-being, and to a perhaps hypothetical something between ignorance and knowledge in relation to a hypothetical something between being and not-being. In its first clause 'Gnowledge *was* set over being'. This is clearly the past tense used especially in Plato when a speaker re-asserts a previous assertion (Goodwin 1875; repr. 1965: 13); this one was asserted, in effect, at 476e9–7a1. Since the non-knowability of the non-existent was also previously asserted, at 477a3–4, the verb to be supplied in the Greek of (4)(b) is presumably still the past, 'was'; the *new* part of (4), with which the past tense is no longer appropriate, is then only (4)(c).[9] Then all the clause in (4) about ignosance ought and needs to say here, is (2)(b), that everything not existent is not gnowable. The addition of 'necessarily' emphasizes that it is not *possible* for us to know anything about the non-existent.

Now we have heard nothing yet about *dunameis* (variously rendered as faculties, capacities, capabilities etc.). We should therefore perhaps

---

9 Those who might object to a shift within a single Greek sentence from supplying the past tense of 'be' to supplying the present tense may take comfort from the possibility of starting a new sentence in the Greek after the clause on ignorance; the second *de* (and), in 477a10, need not be linked in close parallelism with the *men* and *de* (on the one hand ... on the other hand) preceding; starting a new sentence removes to another sentence the supplied present tense.

avoid here the difficulties, which will crop up later, of conceiving ignorance as a positive capability. Perhaps here ignorance or ignosance (*agnōsia*) is simply non-knowledge or the lack of the capability of knowledge. Before Glaucon took up a representative stance the sightlovers were described (476b7 and c3-4) as *not able* to grasp the beautiful by itself, whereas the few philosophers *can* attain the beautiful itself (476b10 and d1). The sightlovers' ignorance is a lack of ability. If this is right, and 'ignorance' is here just the negative of 'knowledge', it is not surprising that Socrates adds at the end of (4) the saving clause 'if there is such a thing'; for he has just suggested the possibility of a *tertium quid* between knowledge and non-knowledge to balance (!) the suggestion in his immediately previous speech of a contradictory thing which both exists and does not exist.

Next comes a brief cut-off torso of an argument. Plato may be stating what he has to prove (Fine 1978: 126); but that does not absolve us from the task of interpreting it as plausible conversation. As a preliminary, in the sentence at 477a9-10 which we have been analysing, Socrates sneaks in a shift in terminology from 'gnowledge' to the ordinary word for 'knowledge'. *Epistēmē* (knowledge) is the natural opposite of *agnoia* (ignorance) which is in the same sentence substituted for *agnōsia* (ignosance). Plato may be pulling a fast one. 'Gnowledge' is discernment, realisation, recognition, and there is nothing obviously infallible about any of these. Plato needs something infallible for a later step (477e4-7). So he imports 'knowledge', in place of 'gnowledge', which was more appropriate and closely linked to what precedes. Venial or mortal offence? The importation would not shock average sightlovers, who believe that their recognition of sensible objects and/or properties affords them the only kind of knowledge there is. Would the sightlovers attribute certainty to what they see? Two obvious candidates for uncertainty are illusions, such as the straight stick in water looking bent, and value-judgements, such as 'this action is fine'. The first of these is unusual and, whatever philosophers of Plato's time or later might say, seldom troubles the ordinary person's belief in the senses as a guide to what exists.[10]

---

10 There is no reason whatever to suppose that the sightlovers are an actual philosopher in disguise, whether Protagoras or any other. Protagoras in particular Plato felt able to name when he criticized him, and Protagoras would not be rightly characterized (by analogy with the soundlover) as eagerly and insatiably looking at sights. To suppose the sightlovers 'put forward ... as those whom Socrates might mean as

The second, judgement of value, is trickier; its status is one main theme of the whole argument, but the average unphilosophical person is subjectively pretty certain of his/her judgements. The sightlovers' original protest at being allowed only opinion and not gnowledge was no doubt grounded in the imputation of confusion and fallibility to their central belief in the senses as the fount of gnowledge or knowledge, a fallibility they are disposed to deny while claiming what they naturally take to be the certain clarity of gnowledge. The more certain they are of their beliefs the less they are going to mind Plato's Socrates substituting 'knowledge' for 'gnowledge'.

The torso of argument continues:

> (5) There is such a thing as belief (or opinion).

This is a hard thing for the normal person to deny, and the sightlover is not abnormal in any sense which seems relevant. Next comes:

> (6) Belief is a different capacity or *dunamis* from knowledge.

Dunamis is a polysemous word whose discussion is best left on one side;[11] but the innocent sightlover has no good reason for supposing that anything untoward will come of its admission to the conversation. The sightlover is obviously quite clear that opinion is a different *something* from knowledge; and the question 'a different *what*?' is unlikely at this juncture to strike him as important. We come now to:

> (7) Each of the two therefore has a different object over against which it is placed, each according to its own capacity.

More important is the vagueness, noted by J.C.B. Gosling and others, of the preposition 'over against' (*epi*), in virtue of which I use the English 'object'.[12] The word needs looking at in its context. Plato used it earlier for the relationship of knowledge to what is, and the relevant sentence (477a9-10) picked up the previous agreement about 'what is' being

---

possible rulers' (Gosling 1960: 120) flouts the text, which has *Glaucon* introducing them as absurd (*atopoi*) candidates for 'philosophers' at 475d1.

11 Gosling (1968), though I dissent from his conclusions, supplies the best brief discussion of *dunamis* (capability etc.) here known to me.

12 E.g. Gosling 1968: 124; but see Santas 1973: 38.

knowable, being indeed the only object of knowledge according to the implications of Glaucon's rhetorical question at 477a1. Accordingly, 'is placed over against' in (7) at 477b7 must also stand for the relation of a *dunamis* or capacity to its objects. 'Objects' here are not 'internal' or 'cognate' but external, since they are things which exist or do not exist or combine the two rather than propositions which are true or false or both.

Why should the sightlover accept that opinion has (a) different object(s) from knowledge? The proposition put to him looks unproved and objectionable. The answer must be that there is *as yet* no rigorous argument to justify Glaucon's incautious acceptance. He accepts, doubtless, partly because Plato wishes to state his demonstrand(s). But the conversation is not wholly unrealistic in consequence, and Glaucon, though not super-vigilant, is not weak or stupid: the discussants have accorded a different object to each of knowledge, ignorance, and something unspecified between them; opinion looks like the same order of thing as knowledge and ignorance; and the term 'opinion' springs to mind as falling between knowledge and ignorance. It is not unrealistic that Glaucon should slip into allowing opinion also a distinct set of objects. But Plato, even if Socrates could have got away with this in conversation, does not want or need him to do so without further analysis.

Then Socrates, before he cuts off this torso, suggests (477b10) that knowledge is by [its] nature set over what exists, to recognize [according to the meanings of *hōs* and *esti*] how it is, or exists, or that it is, or exists. This sentence, painfully ambiguous here, may be postponed till we meet it again at 478a6 (so Kahn 1981: 113). Socrates does not stop to elucidate. We should return to (6) and to its sequel (7). To judge from the sweeping *ara* (therefore) at 477b7 connecting the two, each *dunamis* there must have a different object. This in particular Socrates now clarifies.

The clarification has attracted perhaps more furious criticism than any other major argument in Plato. It appears so fallacious that scholars and philosophers have either recoiled or tried more or less special pleading. I hope what follows is not also special pleading. Here, briefly, is the familiar course of the reasoning from 477c1 on:

(8) *Dunameis* (capabilities) are a class of things by which we and everything else can do what we/it can do.

For example,

(9) 'I call sight and hearing *dunameis*', says Socrates, 'if you understand the type I mean'.

Now one can justly be surprised at the sight- or sound-lovers accepting the notion of a *dunamis*. One cannot see, hear, or otherwise sense a *dunamis*. Why should the sightlovers gag at the 'beautiful by itself' but gulp down the notion of a *dunamis*? Socrates' addition at the end of his sentence, 'if you understand the type I mean', is no idle one; the sight- and sound-lovers could reply: 'No, Socrates, we do not understand this curious way of expressing yourself in general terms which mean nothing to us.' And yet Glaucon says meekly at 477c5: 'But I do understand'. Black though things seem, there is a ray of light. With what *dunameis* does Socrates exemplify and explain the general notion? Sight and hearing. Who are his opponents? The sight- and sound-lovers. If they are going to admit *any dunameis*, they must admit sight and hearing. They cannot doubt, further, after what they said earlier, that we 'can' know (or gnow), believe or be ignorant. If they are going to admit any general terms at all then these, sight, knowledge etc., will be they.

There is a crucial difference between the general term *dunamis* and the general abstract 'the beautiful by itself', because of which one might strike the sightlovers as admissible and the other not. *Dunamis* does not demand a complement in the same way as 'the beautiful'. A *dunamis* must be a 'capability' *to do* (or *be*) *something*; 'the beautiful' may be a collective or an abstract, but as an adjective by itself is grammatically incomplete, needing a noun. *Dunamis* is not a collective nor is it grammatically incomplete; and it is not an abstract in the same sense as 'the beautiful by itself'. For the latter is abstracted in a way which makes talk of it difficult to follow, as talk of a *dunamis* is not. Yeats' 'A terrible beauty is born' speaks, prosaically, of beauty instantiated; 'a terrible *dunamis*' would instantiate not *dunamis* but *dunamis*-hood. Does this imply a mis-statement above of the original objection to 'the beautiful by itself'? Over-simplification, perhaps, rather than mis-statement: when faced with a genuine difficulty of language such as 'the beautiful by itself' presents, *then* the sight- and sound-lovers are unable to acknowledge anything so curious and obscure unless they see hear or sense it; the rest of the time they behave, linguistically and doctrinally, like the ordinary people they essentially are.

Taking this way out, however, might run counter to the belief that mention of 'the beautiful itself' was not so out of the ordinary as to need a person knowledgeable in Socratic dialectic to follow it; it is now being called linguistically obscure. Was Socrates' choice of his friend Glaucon at 475e, as one who would agree where others would not, a suggestion after all that only Socrates' or Plato's intimates could take on board the argument of *Republic* 5? Probably not (see p. 104 above): one could reasonably expect ordinary sight- and sound-lovers both to understand in a limited way what kind of abstraction-process Socrates had in mind to perform, and to refuse without concrete evidence to follow him.

Socrates is honest with the sightlovers in his next speech, from 477c6. He admits that he cannot see any colour of a capacity (*dunamis*) or its shape or the like. So he cannot tell one capacity from another by any of these. But there are ways in which he can tell them apart. He can look at the province of a capacity and at its effect, both of them presumably accessible to normal sightlovers:

> (10) A capacity which is set over the same things *and* produces the same effect is the same; one with a different province *and* a different effect is different. 'What about you?' asks Socrates at 477d5, 'how do you distinguish?' Glaucon replies: 'In that way'.

As it stands this proposition Socrates puts to Glaucon is true: if both effect and province are identical the capacity is identical; and if both differ, then the capacities differ. But Socrates omits to mention that a difference *either* of province *or* of effect would suffice to differentiate capacities. This would not necessarily matter; but in the succeeding argument, especially at 477e8-8b5, Socrates' omission is notoriously damaging. Why, critics ask,[13] should one not exercise a single capacity in more than one field? Why not exercise two different capacities in the same field? Why should we not exercise knowledge in the area of belief? Or belief in the area of knowledge? Why does Socrates say 'province *and* effect' when 'province *or* effect' would suffice? Why bring in provinces at all? The field of cognition is not an empire divided into provinces each with its proconsul assigned by a Socratic Senate.

The following answer to all these points is basically simple; its straightforward simplicity constitutes the major reason for reading the whole passage as aimed specifically and exactly at the sight- and sound-lovers. The answer is that the primary capacities which the

---

13 Most fiercely, perhaps, Crombie 1969: vol. II, 57f. ('fatal flaw' and 'very gross'). It will be clear, despite Crombie's talk, similar to mine, of seeing sights, that I do not take the objects of capacities as internal accusatives in Crombie's sense — that is, if I have rightly understood what Crombie means by 'internal accusatives'.

sight- and sound-lovers *must* recognize and start from are those of seeing and hearing. So we saw at 477c3, where Socrates chose these two to illustrate *dunamis*. Now sight, hearing and the other senses are capacities each distinguished from the others by both province and effect. Notoriously you cannot see sounds, smell colours, hear tastes, touch smells; each sense has in that way its own province; so Santas 1973: 42. Of course their effects are different too: to see is not the same as to hear, and so on. Once we set Socrates' point in its original context of an argument against the sightlovers, it becomes clear. When Glaucon says at 477d6 that Socrates' dual method is the way he distinguishes capacities he is still answering as representing the sightlovers; and Socrates' question to him, 'What about you? How do you distinguish?', is directed to him still as a representative. Glaucon is not a free agent hereabouts, but he is not being manipulated into meekness by an arbitrary author while Socrates gains a spurious triumph. For Plato's purposes Glaucon is a sightlover since 476e7-8. The question is, do his constituents the sightlovers have any grounds for a vote of no confidence in their representative?

They might complain that Glaucon has allowed a misleadingly incomplete induction — that not all capacities necessarily resemble the senses in all respects. When asked how he distinguishes *dunameis*, whether he distinguishes capacities in Socrates' proffered way, Glaucon's simple affirmative was incautious. He ought to have said: 'Socrates, I distinguish one sense-capacity from another in the way you mention, but I am not yet sure whether I wish to commit myself, as representative sightlover, to distinguishing *all* pairs of capacities in this dual way. Let us debate the matter.' The complaint is reasonable. Was Plato aware of it and its reasonableness? To that question, it is hard to give any firm answer.

If Plato was aware of this complaint he might have argued that the induction looks as if it ought to be possible to take a stage further. Knowledge is a capability or capacity in the required sense. It has a restricted, though wide, field of objects, namely things which exist. Its field need not overlap with those of (say) sight and hearing, in that it could cover things which exist as existent, just as sight covers them in so far as they have visible properties, and hearing in so far as they produce audibles. For the sightlovers, knowledge and sensory capabilities are closely related, because they base any claim to knowledge on perception; if they do not, why are they unable to grasp what Plato offers them by way of non-sensibles? If they have an answer to that question, and can say what the difference is between knowledge and the senses which makes the former behave differently as a capacity, then they ought to be able to say what it is; the onus of proof is on them. Aristotle (*Topics* 157a34ff.) enjoined still the actual production of an objection to an induction; and he forbade the objection to consist of the particular example under discussion. But it might not be easy to put such objection into words familiar to an unphilosophical sightlover. 'When', Plato might say, 'you have pondered the difficulty of doing that, consider whether you still want to accuse me of unfairness, of deliberately pulling my opponents' punches while letting rip those of my own man in the ring'.

This defence is certainly not entirely successful, and it is not my claim that it is. Plato's sightlovers might feel let down, and a modern sightlover certainly would. But conventional accounts of the argument do not take proper cognisance of the point that an inductive conclusion based on an insufficient and unprobative set of examples does not represent so gross a betrayal by Glaucon as people tend to think, *because* Socrates mounts inductions elsewhere which are misleading by their incompleteness, or paucity of examples, and Plato shows very little awareness of the problem. Richard Robinson (1953: 33ff.) pointed this out. Individuals who protest directly at an inductive series in Plato have a strong motive: one thinks of the young Hippocrates' blush at *Protagoras* 312a. Meno's embarrassment at 73a is hardly in that class; but then Meno is expected to make good his objection, which tacitly falls when he cannot. Glaucon is no worse than other Platonic respondents to Socratic questioning.

We may appeal to Aristotle again (*Topics* VIII 1) for the importance in dialectic as it was then understood of the order in which questions were put. In *Republic* 5 Socrates floats before Glaucon the examples of sight and hearing at 477c; and it is a serious under-estimation of the sheer cleverness of Socrates' subsequent line of questioning to suppose that a sightlover ought *at this stage* to foresee any possible detriment to his case in giving him a quick affirmative based on those examples and the similarities noted above between them and knowledge. To expect caution in these circumstances is to expect too much.

Critics might concede that the sightlovers' representative is not bludgeoned into giving Plato's Socrates the answer he wants, but continue to protest that he is cozened. In that case, however, protest should not be directed specifically at this particular argument, but at Plato's whole practice of purveying Socratic dialectic. Objection to the whole practice would require lengthy discussion. Questions to discuss would include how far Plato was aware in middle age of any rigorous form of reasoning not dependent on any assumptions offered by a second party; how far, that is, he could distinguish logic from dialectic. There follows the question how far geometry had progressed in rigour and self-validating independence a generation before Euclid's codification; another question would ask how far mathematics seemed simply a special case in which the premises looked undeniable by any sensible respondent; a subsidiary one could inquire whether it was the arrival of Eudoxus' mathematical expertise in the Academy c. 367 which caused Plato largely to abandon 'Socratic'-style dialectic in his later years. In the meantime we should reflect that at *Gorgias* 508e-509a Socrates describes an essentially dialectical argument as binding with fetters of adamant; and that *Republic* 2 does not necessarily start with a wholesale denigration of the arguments of 1 as dialectical, but may with equal plausibility be read as opening with a wish for an argument to refute sets of views opposed to justice which are less idiosyncratic than those of Thrasymachus. Much is at stake here; and protest at one particular manifestation of dialectical argument will carry no weight by itself.

Other defences of Plato's argument seem to me (but then they would seem to me) less satisfactory. There have been attempts to regard the effects and the field of a capacity (*dunamis*) as, in effect, the same thing. The most elaborate attempt of this nature was mounted by Jaakko Hintikka;[14] this argued that passages in Plato, Aristotle and elsewhere confounded a *dunamis* and its goal. But as Santas (1973: 38ff.) at once replied, there is no special reason to believe, and some fairly clear reason for not believing, that Plato in this particular passage was committing this type of confusion, whatever one may think of Hintikka's other passages. Santas' own way out of the difficulty in some features anticipates mine, though it results from a very different attitude to the whole context. He argues from many passages that: 'They [sc. sight and hearing) are probably, *for Plato,* [italics mine] closely analogous faculties or powers to those of knowledge and belief.' Santas (1990: 52ff.) appeals rather similarly to other passages, namely, to a later stage of this argument and to Book 6, both of which appeals violate the

---

14 Hintikka (1973: 7f.) did not notice that *ekeino monon* (that alone) at 477d1 contrasts with colour, shape etc. in the previous sentence, and *hence* does not necessitate the identity of object and effect as a single thing (as Santas [1973] saw in his reply but did not make wholly explicit).

normal requirements of dialectic. To this sort of expedient the answer is that what is true for Plato is irrelevant in an argument designed to convince the sightlovers. It is not what views of his own Plato can surreptitiously foist or inadvertently pin on such people but what an honest sightlover might think which ought to be relevant, and should be regarded as relevant until Plato has been *proved* guilty of such foisting or inadvertence. Gosling had already in 1968 advanced a view in some respects like Hintikka's, in that he supposed the effects and field of objects of a *dunamis* to be closely connected Platonically. But his version of the argument's course leaves one wondering why Plato bothered, if he could proceed as directly as Gosling supposes, to detour round the notion of a *dunamis* at all.

Fine has written two versions of the argument: the second has the serious defect that it treats the association of opinion with an intermediate between being and not-being as a fundamental premise (1990: 87ff.), whereas it clearly functions rather as a conclusion to an argument stretching from 477b11 to 479d, and is not used as a premise before 479d despite being hinted at as early as 477a-b. Both versions champion and rely upon the veridical sense of 'be' in Greek which we have seen to be alien to the context. The second also violates, as Fine virtually admits in two footnotes (1990: 92 n.13, 93 n.15) the dialectical requirement (1990: 87), that the argument should use only claims acceptable to the respondent. The key point that has passed inadequately noticed by her and others is the dialectical relevance of the distinct fields of sensory faculties.

Before we proceed to ignorance, some questions need airing about the capabilities (*dunameis*) concerned. Socrates makes a fresh start, but with Glaucon still playing the sightlover, at 477d7, asking: 'Is knowledge a capability?' The reply is, plausibly, 'Yes, and the strongest of them all'. And belief/opinion (*doxa*)? 'Yes, for that by which we are able to believe is nothing other than belief'. The question whether knowledge and belief are capabilities or capacities in the required sense is now out in the open. It can be seen to turn on a simple but hard point: the meaning of the Greek dative case, the case of the relative pronoun in the locution 'by which'. It is true that we can see 'by sight'. It is not blatantly false that we can know 'by knowledge' and believe 'by belief'. That does not remove suspicion that, whereas sight is indeed a capability — for when you give 'the gift of sight' by paying to a suitable charity you are indirectly giving a capability — but that if you give me belief or knowledge you confer no such capability. If you confer upon me the capability of believing, it is not belief you give, but faith, trust, or the like. Did Plato see this or not? As usual where Plato deals with slippery linguistic phenomena, it is difficult to be sure; but he and his contemporaries might have found it rather hard to explain and distinguish those datives.

There is one further difficulty, fortunately not serious, about 'belief' or 'opinion' as a capability: the Lexicon suggests the absence of any external object for the verb 'opine' (*doxazein*) in normal Classical Greek. One can know, but apparently not 'opine' something externally. Parallels from the *Theaetetus*, quoted by Cooper (1986: 235), do not help this problem, being suspect of philosophical excogitation as opposed to natural speech. This might seem a solid obstacle to taking the things opinion stands 'over against' in this argument as external rather than internal objects. But the obstacle is more apparent than real. Having accepted on the basis of the senses the principle that capabilities are differentiated by effects and by external objects, the sightlover is caught: if he gives opinion as a capability no external objects he cannot, after accepting Socrates' induction, distinguish it from other capabilities. Is it then a capability at all? In English the matter might be one for grave doubt, but the Greek Lexicon offers two prose passages using *doxa* (opinion) in a relevant sort of dative, Herodotus VIII 132. 3, and Thucydides V 105. 'Opinion' therefore satisfies Socrates' rather loose requirements for a capability or *dunamis*.

Perhaps even more difficult than the individuation of capabilities is the case of ignorance. 477a-b hinted, but no more, at its treatment as a capability on all fours with knowledge and opinion. We saw that Plato's language there allowed, but did not require, the reader to entertain the proposition that necessarily all the things we are ignorant of are non-existent. The vagueness there and elsewhere of the preposition *epi* which Socrates uses to mark some necessary connection of ignorance and the non-existent, even though in context it must refer to external objects, might give rise to suspicion of skulduggery: one might suspect Plato of preparing the sightlover or the reader by means of an ambiguous version of an acceptable proposition for another, less acceptable to sightlovers.

This is a necessary preamble to discussion of 478c2-3, where less acceptable propositions do appear. By now the sightlover has succumbed to Socrates' incomplete induction and agreed that knowledge and opinion operate in separate fields. The argument then runs first, that every opinion has an object; and secondly, by elimination it seeks to identify the objects of opinion. They cannot be what is, which is the province of knowledge. They cannot be what is not, for 'We assigned ignorance by necessity to what is not' (478c2-3). This argument by elimination does assume that ignorance is a *dunamis* or capability and not a mere absence of capability — for otherwise the argument would supply no reason for the strict separation of the fields of ignorance and of opinion; it also assumes that the field of ignorance is exclusively what is not, the non-existent; otherwise one would have to determine exactly what ignorance did cover before eliminating all it covered as a field for opinion.

Noting these two difficult and surprising assumptions, let us ask how sightlovers might feel about certain classes of object. We would find them with no doubt of their own knowledge of some things. Seeing a colour they could feel unphilosophically sure that the colour and the thing showing it exist. In normal state the sightlovers would of course have opinions about what colour the dress was that they saw yesterday; and they would know that the dress they were looking at now was the colour they saw and that it was there. But here in *Republic* 5 previous agreements forbid them to assign overlapping fields to knowledge, opinion and the senses.

What the sightlovers do not need any faculty for are things they have never heard of or contemplated: the paintings of, say, Monet. We should attend rather to things they cannot acknowledge, the beautiful by itself and the like. These they do not just happen not to know; they do not recognize or even cognize them. They do not 'gnow' them, but confuse them. Non-gnowledge or ignosance, *agnōsia*, is a fair description of their state; the substitution of *agnoia*, ignorance, we already discussed. But why should either of these turn at 478b-c into a positive capability?

One can put up some verbal defence for this. Nowhere in the argument does Socrates describe ignosance or ignorance by a separate negative and a noun for 'knowledge'; he uses single words beginning with the negativing 'alpha privative'. There is a Greek verb (*agnoein*) for 'be-ignorant' formed in the same way. If the sightlovers stick to the definition of a capability (*dunamis*) as that 'by which' one can do something, one could sneak ignorance past them as that 'by which' one can be-ignorant. The defence limps. It would be stronger if one could read the rarer word 'ignosance', and thus at a pinch 'ignorance' as the *unwillingness* to acknowledge or recognize certain things. But despite R.E. Allen (1962: 330; *obiter dictum*) the text warrants only doubtfully this interpretation of the sightlovers. The question was one of ability, not unwillingness, early in the argument. Unwillingness enters only with the sightlovers' refusal at 479a4 and 480a4 to countenance the view that the F itself exists. How their unwillingness to put up with this relates to their inability to follow it is not clear. So far as they do display a refusal to countenance the distinct existence of the F's, one might dragoon their unwillingness into forming a positive aspect of the ignosance of the sightlovers, enough to rescue it from being a mere negation. But too much cannot be made of this, as their refusal to tolerate talk of 'the beautiful' as a single existent may result from pure intellectual confusion.

So far it seems that Plato's Socrates has only a limping or a dubious defence. He seems to be sowing confusion in order to further, in Gilbertian terms, his felonious little plans. But are those plans felonious? And if so, in what degree? It is time to experiment a little with the sightlovers' commitments so far. The characteristic sightlover is committed to:

(11) I gnow visible things; I know they exist and that in principle I can find out and know about them if I am in the right place at the right time.

(12) I claim not, and I am unable, to gnow non-visible things such as your 'the beautiful by itself' etc., because they do not exist.

[(13) Of course I don't know about the paintings of (who was it?) Monet.]

(10) Different faculties/capabilities have different objects and different effects.

(6) Knowledge and belief are different capabilities.

Experimenting with these commitments means analysing what happens if the sightlover starts to allot capabilities to objects. Knowledge (s)he need have no qualms about; (s)he knows the existence and the significant properties of the kind of things (s)he is interested in, visible things which have colours etc. His/her commitment to (11) is clear. But commitment to (10) and (6) starts to give trouble over belief. The field of belief cannot be sensible objects or their properties, unless (s)he is prepared to give up knowledge of them and leave the philosopher victorious. This rules out the sightlover's believing things about the objects of the senses which (s)he is told by other people from *their* knowledge, for presumably their knowledge and his/her belief cannot operate over the same field. Nor can (s)he offer any *beliefs* about the paintings of Monet, though (s)he might be able to offer conjectures. So what is the field of belief? (S)he cannot reply 'those things I hear of from you, "the beautiful itself" etc.'; for (s)he has denied any separate existence to such abstracts and cannot therefore claim to hold any sense-making opinions about them any more than I can about the present Emperor of China. Can (s)he believe simply that 'the beautiful itself' etc. do not exist? As a proposition that might seem to fit the bill for an object of belief. But Plato's argument is not, as I see it, conducted in terms of propositions at all, but simply of objects one knows, believes in or is ignorant of. Neither party to the argument is talking of propositions, and if they started to do so the sightlover, who has never seen a proposition, as opposed to its written expression, and the soundlover who naturally has never heard a sentence's meaning, as opposed to its sound, are likely to retire baffled. So when the sightlover is eventually offered a field of belief by Socrates, the reaction ought surely to be a sigh of relief and a look of thanks. The bizarre things (s)he is called upon to believe in are at least better than nothing; (s)he *cannot* have a capacity which is incapable of exercise because it has in principle no object (see 478b).

If the sightlover has a capacity, namely belief, looking for a field, (s)he also has a field searching for a relevant capacity. What capacity can (s)he assign to those objects such as 'the beautiful itself' which (s)he does not recognize as existent? Knowledge, clearly not; belief we have ruled out. (S)he might ignore them? But (s)he cannot do that with the philosopher, as Socrates says at 476c3, leading him/her towards the gnowledge of them. Being unable to conceive of their distinct existence, (s)he admits to knowing nothing about them; 'Ah!', one imagines him/her saying, 'some kind of ignorance is what I have about these special things (quite different from Monet paintings) whose distinct existence I deny'; and some kind of ignorance or ignosance is what Socrates offers at 478c, picking up 477a-b. Since the sightlover knows indeed nothing about these entities, which (s)he deems mere philosophical imaginings, (s)he will not dourly resist the transition from one kind of ignorance, ignosance, to another kind, opposed to 'infallible' knowledge.

Now only bits of this appear in the text, rather like the tips of icebergs sticking out of the sea. And one cannot be sure that Plato himself followed every step given. But if something like these ideas were in Plato's mind, I believe things become clear in this stretch of dialogue which were unclear before; and now of course it can be read as a dialogue.

At 477e6-8 knowledge is infallible, belief is not: N.P. White (1979: 158) says, 'There is no such thing as knowing mistakenly, whereas there is such a thing as believing mistakenly'. Glaucon as sightlover may accept this difference between knowledge and belief; he may regard it as a 'difference in effect' in terms of the earlier dual way of distinguishing capacities and (Santas 1973: 45) if that way persists this far, then since 478a3ff. deals with objects we must have a difference of effect here. In the matter of objects, knowledge is set over what is, to gnow *hōs ekhei*, how it is or that it is. Here 'How it is' avoids tautology and matches Greek idiom better. It presumably means 'What its properties are'. But belief is not set over what is gnowable, and hence not over what is or exists; and not, again, over the non-existent. A few tips of icebergs become apparent hereabouts. If belief is not set over the existent or the non-existent, then it must be — or rather, is plausibly — set over what neither exists nor not-exists. This conclusion is reached at 478c6, but not before ignorance has entered the argument again (478c3-4).

On ignorance in the revived argument, a point needs elaboration: Plato's characters set out at 477a-b on the way, clearly, to formulating a correspondence between belief and objects of intermediate ontological status. On that way they assigned ignos/rance to the non-existent. So the assignment of ignorance came before that of belief, whereas in my exposition the quandary over belief, ruling belief out as the capability set over 'the beautiful itself' etc., preceded in the argument the necessary assignment of ignorance to the non-existent. The same order, not mine, recurs at 478b-e. We need to distinguish here between the positive and the negative points Socrates is making about belief; it is, I think, taken as evident without saying that the sightlover can*not* assign knowledge or belief consistently to 'the beautiful itself' etc., whose existence he cannot accept, and is left with nothing but ignorance to assign to such things. The assignment of belief to the ontologically intermediate then comes much more easily: it is convenient to say at 478c10 that belief is neither more obscure than ignorance nor surer than knowledge; and Plato needs all the dialectical conveniences he can lay hold of to persuade a normal sightlover that his beliefs are assignable either to a contradiction ('both are and are not' at 477a6) or to an *in*cluded middle ('neither are nor are not' at 478c6). Anyway, Socrates ploughs relentlessly on, to the effect that belief lies between knowledge and ignorance, and *should* accordingly have a set of objects between their sets; its set, though located between being and not-being, has still to be identified.

At this stage (478e7) the argument explicitly brings back the sight-lover. (S)he is repetitively said to think there is no such thing as 'the beautiful by itself' etc., remaining the same in the same respects. (S)he acknowledges the many fine things, but forbids anyone to say that e.g. 'the beautiful' is one. But Socrates has one more nail for his/her coffin. This is an argument that the things the sightlovers perceive and/or pursue are actually qualified, as 'both being and not-being', to be the objects of this 'capacity' between knowledge and ignorance which they have called 'belief' or 'opinion' and excluded from being set over either 'being' or 'not-being'.

This argument too is controversial.[15] Its point *ought* to be to establish the 'being and not-being', that is to say in this context the existence and non-existence of the things sightlovers see. Critics recognize that the argument establishes no such thing. Two issues will arise: whether Plato thought the argument established the above point, and whether he needed in view of the argument's place in the dialectical sequence either rightly to establish the point or to believe he had.

The things the sightlover recognizes, the many beautiful, just and holy things, will they appear, as appropriate, ugly, unjust and unholy? Yes, says Glaucon. Similarly things double appear half; and things large will be called small. On this again incomplete induction the sightlovers agree by Glaucon that each of the many opposed things they say 'are' (i.e. exist) both are and are not.

This raises questions: first, why does this induction's conclusion talk about 'being' when its premises talk, in various tenses, about seeming and appearing, or being called? Secondly, why the leap from the 'being' of predication, which alone seems to be at issue in some at least of the examples, to a conclusion which in the wider context ought to be about existence? On the first, the sightlovers are in a weak position on the whole to distinguish between appearance and being; knowledge or gnowledge comes for them through the senses. They cannot fall back on straight sticks looking bent in water or the like, because these are special cases only; in practice the sightlovers must accept the general equivalence of appearing and being. They cannot say appearances *systematically* mislead without ending in an alien total scepticism. On the second question, one can defend Socrates and Glaucon in this

---

15 I am indebted especially to the exchange between Gosling (1960), F.C. White (1977), Gosling (1977) and F.C. White (1981); but 1 have not thought it necessary here to document precisely their views on individual points.

section of the argument much as G.E.L. Owen (1960: 94 n. 1) defended Parmenides against a charge of confusing predication with existential being. Predicating expressions can be re-formulated existentially: if 'this is beautiful' ceases to be true because 'this is now [or in some respect, or from some viewpoint] ugly', then 'there exists now [here, etc.] an ugly thing' and 'there existed or exists [here, now etc] a beautiful thing', so that there no more exists a beautiful than an ugly thing wherever sightlovers look.

The reader (Plato's or mine) may find this unconvincing. But it is questionable whether (s)he need or need not be convinced. For, first, the conclusion to which the argument arrives exhibits a tentativeness not always noticed but still noticeable. Socrates does not, at 479c6-7, ask Glaucon directly to accept that the sightlover's sights are correctly placed as the objects of opinion or belief. He asks rather if any better position can be found for them than between the things which exist and the things which do not; the sights are not, he confirms, more obscure than the non-existent, nor are they clearer than the existent with respect to being to a higher degree existent. Secondly, the sightlovers, whether satisfied by the preceding argument or not, might find this offering hard to refuse. For, as we saw, they need an object for opinion or belief; they cannot leave a faculty without object. The object cannot be the non-existent; nor can it be coextensive with the existent, unless they surrender by agreeing to do without knowledge. Things between existence and non-existence are in short supply. In this bind it is hard for the sightlovers not to put at least some things they believe in into the limbo between existence and non-existence. This forces them to admit propositions they do not really believe; if this whole passage came up in an earlier dialogue more people would regard it as what it is, a not uncharacteristic Socratic elenchus, complete with the normal Socratic use of the respondent's own explicit or implicit premises and with incomplete Socratic inductions.

But what about knowledge and its objects? The sightlovers have laid claim to knowledge or gnowledge. They are now left with ignorance for Forms or other things in their view non-existent; and with opinion for the things between being and not-being, that is, the sensibles; and with no object for knowledge.[16] Surely they can object? But the philoso-

---

16   The finger etc. of *Rep* 523a-b (cf. Annas' Man [1981: 210]) are left out of 5. To admit *knowledge* of them would ruin the philosopher's distinctiveness at any time; Plato

pher would retort that in his view they do not have knowledge, and hence he is not obliged to supply them with a distinct field of objects for it. They could respond that they now want to retract some admissions and shift to a position with knowledge for the sensibles, and with no object for opinion (which they would then abandon). But this too would be uncomfortable; sightlovers with knowledge but no opinion would be rare and incredible specimens. The philosopher has them in his dialectical toils.

The desired effect of the whole elenchus appears to be the showing up, or at least the manufacture, of an internal incoherence in the position of those who deny in their confusion the existence of 'the beautiful by itself', 'beauty by itself' and the like — what we now call the Forms. The incoherence consists in the inability to maintain the initial position that they know the beautiful, the just, and the like. This is due to the necessity of finding the object of the capacity intermediate between knowledge and ignorance. This object turns out to be the collection of beautiful etc. things. The total effect is not a direct proof that the Forms exist, let alone that they possess certain properties, such as being forever the same; such properties of Forms are indeed introduced only casually at 479a1-3, without any proof in Book 5. The objects of the philosopher's knowledge are taken for granted in that their existence is not directly proved and their properties are entered without argument. Book 5 attempts rather to prove or persuade us that the claims of the dwellers in what will become Plato's Cave are incoherent. At best it uses that incoherence to point to the way out of the Cave. The alleged incoherence is used immediately in Book 6 to show the unfitness of the Cave-dwellers to rule. Sightlovers they may be; but they are, as it were, 'blind' (484c).

As in all Plato's Socrates' dialectical arguments, the question arises how far Plato himself believed the individal steps along the way. Scott Berman (1991: 126 n. 18) refuses to accept, *à propos* of Socrates' alleged hedonism in the *Protagoras*, that Plato would use any premiss he did not believe to support a position he did believe in. But argument from one's opponent's premisses was established practice in the ancient

---

might reasonably not have Glaucon as representative sightlover make a point, distinguishing fingers etc. from relative terms, which is one of his own more subtle ones.

world, plausibly deriving from Zeno of Elea. Berman's refusal is out of place. If even a conclusion is reached on the way to refuting an opponent, Plato's Socrates is not committed to it, and *a fortiori* Plato himself is not. Based on premisses Plato need not accept, such a conclusion may be no more than a tool for the easier demolition of someone else's edifice. The conclusion towards which *my* argument is tending is in line with some other scholars' views; it is that the separation of the provinces of belief and knowledge in the *Republic*, which contrasts so strongly with the permission in the *Meno* for knowledge to supervene on belief in the same proposition or other object of cognition, need not be accepted as an item in Plato's own stock of philosophical beliefs on the basis of *Republic* 5, whatever may go on in other parts of the *Republic*.

With those other parts of the *Republic* I have no space to deal properly. Fine (1978: 121) has pointed out that the introduction of the Form of the Good at 506 presupposes *opinions* about that Form, or about 'the good'. We may observe that the simile of the Sun could not be better adapted for helping a sightlover to understand; and that the Cave reaches the conclusion by a sleight of hand one may perhaps call rhetorical that the equivalent of the sightlovers in 5 spend their lives looking not at objects but at shadows. The Line is more debatable. It would not necessarily be surprising if Plato liked at times to keep up his dialectical position against the sightlovers, but sometimes liked, or even by inadvertence happened, to fall into his own, or perhaps one should say his own *earlier*, position on the matter of the fields of opinion and of knowledge.

Parts of this conclusion are not new; but I hope the reader will have found the way there of some interest.

Unifying the Protagoras

Richard Rutherford

Since the interpretation of Plato's dialogues is a controversial and difficult business, I should begin by giving some account of my own working assumptions and approach to Plato. First, and fundamentally, I am coming to Plato from the literary side; I am not a philosopher, and do not believe that the study of Plato can or should be pursued only by philosophers. My interest in Plato as a great literary artist leads me to examine the use he makes, in all of his works, of *dialogue* form; and with that comes consideration of the characters or personalities in the dialogues, and of how they interact with each other.[1] Secondly, I take it for granted that in many of the dialogues there is as much emphasis on the questions and problems raised as on the answers offered. This is most obvious in the early, so-called aporetic dialogues, works such as the *Euthyphro* or the *Laches*, in which the only conclusion reached seems to be that the proposed answers so far are unsatisfactory. We shall see that this critical spirit continues in the *Protagoras*. Thirdly, I would reject the simplistic view that Plato is simply putting forward his theories and philosophy through Socrates, that Socrates is simply the mouthpiece of Plato and is propounding a set of theories which we can label Platonism. Extreme versions of this approach will claim that everything Socrates says is endorsed by Plato and that everything anybody else says is wrong and misguided and to be rejected. To adopt either of those assumptions leads to considerable difficulties in interpreting the *Protagoras*. A valid approach to Plato's dialogues and to Socrates' role within them must, I feel, give proper attention to the hypothetical, often paradoxical, nature of the argument, and to the constant presence of

---

1 See further Laborderie 1978: esp. 409-22.

irony and humour in the character of Socrates. Fourthly, I would lay emphasis on Plato's interest in the *way* in which an argument is conducted: the dialogues reveal a concern with the proper form and manner of discussion, and the behaviour of the participants is viewed in moral terms. Socrates insists, for example, that their primary concern should be to find the truth, not to score points off one another, nor to win applause and impress an audience (e.g. *Grg* 457c sqq.). Cheating, concealing one's real opinion, or changing one's ground is unfair and illegitimate; abuse, invective or mockery do not constitute a proper refutation (e.g. *La* 195a, *Grg* 473de). But although the discussion is between friends, and honest cooperation is the ideal, that does not mean that we should flatter each other or smooth over differences: it is necessary, and right, that errors should be revealed, and above all in matters concerning morality and the proper way to live. In short, philosophic discussion should be conducted in a morally right way.

I want now to consider the more specific problems of the *Protagoras* with these general principles in mind.

Whereas in the *Euthydemus* Socrates had encountered a pair of sophists acclaimed by their immediate hearers but dismissed as nonentities by the listening Crito and the figure of 'Isocrates', in the *Protagoras* he faces one of the most distinguished of the profession, and the level of debate is on an altogether different plane. It is also probably relevant to recall that later in his career Plato took Protagoras seriously enough to devote a great part of the *Theaetetus* to the examination and exploration of his most famous saying 'man is the measure of all things' (fr. B1, *Tht* 151-2, 161-79). It would be surprising, then, to find the sophist a straw man in the dialogue which bears his name. Moreover, it is longer and more intricate than the *Euthydemus*, and the issues raised do not depend on trivial wordplay or on obviously outrageous false reasoning.

Nevertheless, the dialogue has often puzzled and irritated students of Plato. Much of the uncertainty felt by readers concerns the unity of the work — not that anyone has ever seriously doubted that it is indeed entirely a work of Plato, and wholly characteristic of him, but there is undoubtedly room for discomfort on the level of conceptual unity: what is the *subject* of the *Protagoras*, what is it about? The main discussion seems to wander bewilderingly, some would say perversely — from the nature of Athenian democracy through the evolution of human society, the unity of the virtues, the analysis of a poem by Simonides, back to the virtues and particularly courage, and then on to a refutation of the popular view of the power of pleasure and emotion over reason. At the end, very little seems to have been settled. And what is the relevance of the introductory scenes, first between Socrates and an unnamed friend, then between Hippocrates and Socrates at the beginning of the narrated part of the dialogue, before the two of them arrive in the presence of the great sophist?

The other great area of uncertainty concerns the last phase of the dialogue, in which Socrates extraordinarily defends the principle often called the hedonic calculus: that is, he supports the argument that pleasure is the good, and that the function of the intellect is to weigh pleasures judiciously against one another, practising an art of measurement which will enable one to weigh up present discomfort or pain against future pleasure or profit. By this means, Socrates makes an ingenious transition to a doctrine found elsewhere in Plato, that no man does wrong voluntarily; it is only that he has made the mistake of miscalculating the relative amounts of pleasure which he will derive from an action. Could Socrates ever really have held this 'hedonic' view of virtue, and if he did not, what does Plato mean by presenting it with Socrates as its advocate?

It may be helpful to approach these major issues indirectly, by looking at the dialogue as it unfolds, and considering, as I've already suggested, some of the more dramatic and verbal aspects of the *Protagoras*, including characterization, interaction, tone, rhetorical style, and so forth.[2] One aspect which clearly merits attention is the personality of Protagoras himself, and in particular how conscious he is of his own status and prestige (not least in rivalry or opposition to the other sophists present). The narrative comments by Socrates regularly lay emphasis on his *amour-propre* and his reluctance to be proven wrong (333d, 335ab, 338e, 348b, c1). As elsewhere in Plato, the personalities and the reactions of the participants are relevant to the way the discussion progresses. We need only consider the way in which Socrates comments on Protagoras' unease and displeasure, and how often the inconclusiveness of an argument is due to Socrates' tactful restraint, to his willingness to refrain from driving his point home all the way (332a, 335a9ff.; cf. 362a). There is a contrast to be drawn here with the *Gorgias*: in the latter dialogue, and especially in the conflict between Socrates and Callicles, there is no concession or compromise: antagonism is

---

2 Cf. in general Stokes 1986: 32-3.

open, tempers are hot, and the polarization of views is taken much further. Arguments and propositions in Plato cannot readily be divorced from their original setting: we must be cautious about ignoring the occasion, the personalities and the method, which lead a speaker to adopt a certain position.

We begin in a sense at the end. When the dialogue opens, Socrates has just come from the discussion which the dialogue contains, and narrates the whole episode to an eager friend. Part of the point of this 'framing' device seems to be to show that Socrates is not an out-and-out opponent and critic of Protagoras. We do not find him, now that he can speak openly, pouring forth an indictment of Protagoras' ignorance, the futility of his method and aims, or the like. Rather, Socrates is still admiring and interested by all that he has heard and seen of him — not without qualification, however, as is suggested by the following exchange:

> 'And the stranger really seemed so beautiful to you that he appeared more beautiful than the son of Cleinias?'
> 'How can what is supremely wise not be more beautiful, my dear fellow?'
> 'Then you've just been in the company of someone wise, Socrates?'
> 'The wisest of all those of our time, if Protagoras seems to you to be the wisest.'
> 'What's that you say? Protagoras is in town?' (309cd)

Protagoras' name has so far been held back: this is the moment at which Socrates reveals the name of his recent interlocutor, and we note at once the eloquent 'if' clause, which throws the evaluation open for discussion. It would be wrong, however, to assume that Socrates is being ironic in a crude way here (as if he were inwardly scoffing 'Ha ha, wisest of men today — *that's* a laugh!'), and that is certainly not how the unnamed friend interprets him. Rather, the friend is as excited as Hippocrates was when he learned that Protagoras was back in Athens. Socratic irony is richer and more complex than 'the customary conception of irony — i.e. the mere exchange of a yes for a no';[3] it does not convey outright dismissal or condemnation of its object, but arouses doubts and questions, as Socrates is already doing here. So too his

---

3 Friedlaender 1958-69, vol. 2: 13. See further Vlastos 1991: ch. 1.

equation of beauty and supreme wisdom is put in the form of a question, one which his companion fails to meet. Instead he rushes on with a counter-question. Socrates' challenging equation of beauty and wisdom, which would be true only in an ideal world, is left hanging; as a result, Alcibiades' beauty and Protagoras' wisdom are both called into question.

Socrates' qualifications, then, are lost on the anonymous friend; he is another Hippocrates. Recent critics have already noted (and we can see this again in the *Gorgias* and the *Phaedrus*) how often Socrates' conversation and personality are ineffective, having no lasting influence on the listener. In the present case, we never return to the frame and therefore do not know how the friend reacted at the end of Socrates' narration (contrast the *Euthydemus*); nor are we given any hint of Hippocrates' verdict on the dazzling exchange which he has actually witnessed. The reader is left to evaluate Protagoras' performance for himself.

It is notable that the opening dialogue concludes by stressing the enjoyment that the friend and Socrates will derive from the latter's recapitulation: the point is emphasized by the repeated use of the word *charis* (310a). This may be unimportant, but a possible explanation might be that it points forward to a recurrent theme of the dialogue as a whole: pleasure in the discussion and in Protagoras' rhetorical prowess; good and bad pleasures in the view of the common man and in the more sophisticated and paradoxical version of this view put forward by Socrates. It is common for Plato to introduce a dialogue with key words or word-play or half-serious ideas which gain in significance and seriousness as the argument advances. A very obvious example is the opening of the *Hippias Major* where Socrates remarks 'Ah, it's Hippias, the handsome and the wise' (281a): as in the initial exchange of the *Protagoras*, a question mark is raised about whether these two attributes do go together, either generally or in the case of Hippias (cf. Woodruff 1982b: 36).

Socrates' narrative begins at night, with himself sound asleep in bed, when the youthful Hippocrates arrives to bring him the news of Protagoras' arrival in Athens (which in fact is not news to Socrates), and to demand that Socrates escort and introduce him to the great man. Humour and implicit comment are at once apparent: Hippocrates heard about the sophist's presence in Athens late the previous night, and nearly came dashing to wake Socrates up at once; Socrates has known about it for longer, and appears unmoved and disinclined to lose sleep over it. What emerges clearly from the episode is Hippocrates' naïveté. He is scatter-brained in general (310c 'I meant to tell you I was going after my slave, but something else put it out of my mind...').

He is all-a-twitter (cf. 310d3) with the great news, desperate to gain access to Protagoras, but he admits he has never seen the man or heard him speak. In terms of Socratic dialectic this is a warning sign: in the *Gorgias* Polus sarcastically asks Socrates if he would say that Archelaus of Macedon, or the great king of Persia himself, was a happy man or an unhappy one, and Socrates replies: 'How do I know? I've never met the man' (470d). Similarly though more indirectly here, Socrates is kindly but sceptical. The earliness of the hour gives him an excuse to chat with the boy before they actually go to Callias' house, where Protagoras is residing, and in that conversation Socrates takes the opportunity to sow some doubts. These doubts focus on the central questions which Hippocrates in his enthusiasm has failed to consider: just what kind of a man is Protagoras, what is his teaching; what does he do to people? Similarly in the *Gorgias*, when Gorgias agrees to converse with Socrates, the first question the latter puts to him is deceptively simple, yet momentous: 'who he is' (447d).[4] The questions of who Protagoras is and what he teaches remain important throughout the dialogue and arguably unanswered by the end, because Protagoras does not have a single, adequate, clearly formulated answer to give.

The exchange with Hippocrates also serves to show the contradiction in his position, a contradiction which reflects the ambiguity of Athenian attitudes to the sophists,[5] exemplified by Callicles' sneer in the *Gorgias* (520a), Anytus' abuse in the *Meno* (91), and of course the views of conservative thinkers as echoed in Aristophanes' *Clouds*. Hippocrates is eager to meet and learn from Protagoras, but when it is put to him that he will become a sophist himself by so doing, he blushes violently ('for', remarks Socrates, 'it was just then becoming light enough for his face to be seen').[6] He admits that he would feel ashamed to turn himself into a sophist, and Socrates kindly suggests that perhaps what Protagoras teaches is not so much the trade of sophistry (a *technē* of such a kind that if you learn it you become such an artisan yourself — like someone

---

4 Cf. Sophocles, *Oedipus the King* 413-15; Euripides, *Bacchae* 506f. All three passages play on the apparent simplicity of the cornerstone precept of Greek morality, 'know thyself'.

5 Cf. Guthrie 1962-81, vol. 3: 32-4, 38ff.; Kerferd 1981: 20-2.

6 Friedlaender 1958-69 vol. 1: 159-60 suggests that this is a form of symbolism ('came the dawn ...').

learning carpentry); rather, perhaps it is something that you learn for the
sake of general culture, as befits a private citizen and a free man (312b).
This calms Hippocrates' embarrassment for the time being; but it is also
intended to suggest how vague and suspect Protagoras' claims are,
when his aspiring pupils cannot be sure what benefit they will derive
from their instruction. At this point Socrates takes the opportunity to
give the young man a lecture on the danger of willingly and ignorantly
submitting his soul, the most precious part of himself, to an unknown
foreigner. How much more careful he would be with his body!

The naïve and uncritical attitude of Hippocrates *is* blameworthy, and
it would be wrong to label Socrates as priggish, or to suspect that he is
carping at Protagoras out of jealousy or rivalry. His aim is rather to
awaken Hippocrates to a properly questioning attitude: instead of
accepting Protagoras' reputation on trust, he should consider for himself the significance of what he is doing and judge whether Protagoras
is the right teacher to choose (cf. *Laches* 180a-b). In other words, Socrates
wants him to cut loose from Athenian fashion and think for himself.

One other passage in this introductory scene merits comment, again
for its moral implications rather than for any strictly philosophic content. 'When we arrived at the forecourt', explains Socrates, 'we paused
and went on talking about something which had occurred to us on the
walk. In order that this might not be left unfinished, and so that we
could go in having settled the topic, we stood there in the forecourt and
talked on until we came to an agreement' (314c). This finds a close
parallel in the *Symposium*, when Socrates gets left behind on the way to
Agathon's, and falls into a trance, meditating on an unspecified subject
until he has reached a conclusion (174a sq.): this practice, according to
Aristodemus, is habitual with him (175b). In the *Gorgias*, Socrates more
than once expresses anxiety that they should not leave the argument
unfinished, or 'without a head', as he puts it in one speech (505cd).
These passages seem to contrast Socratic determination with the more
relaxed or uncommitted discussion techniques of lesser men. In the
Protagoras, the decision to conclude the subject which had occurred to
them *en route* should be contrasted with the rambling inconclusiveness
of the subsequent debate, and with the notable tendency for the discussion to change course or method. Once Socrates and Hippocrates are
inside Callias' house, variety and disorder become the keynotes, and
there is a disturbing readiness to give up half way. Socrates expresses
his anxiety about this more than once (347c1-2, 348a9); at the end of the
dialogue he is still eager to go on further (361d), but it is Protagoras
who is reluctant and would prefer to postpone (*ibid.* e, 'till another

time'). Perhaps the setting too may contribute to this contrast. Socrates and Hippocrates conclude their discussion privately, just the two of them (the ideal dialectical situation) in the open air; contrast the indoor confusion and hubbub, the division of the company into a series of cliques within, as described in the entertaining passage which follows (314e-16a). Callias obviously regards it as a major coup to have as many sophists as possible under his roof (he is supposed to have spent more on sophists than all their other Athenian patrons put together; see *Ap* 20a). As one would expect, however, the result is absurd and chaotic, with each of the sophists holding forth independently; it is, as Socrates remarks, impossible to hear them indoors in competition with one another, especially Prodicus with his booming, resonant tones (316a1). This initial impression is borne out by subsequent developments, for the sophists compete with one another in other, less likeable ways, to score points off one another or to show off: we see this at 317c and 318e, and again later, in the way in which Prodicus and Hippias back up Socrates against Protagoras. Socrates in his account of the scene quotes a number of phrases from Book 11 of the *Odyssey*, comparing the three great sophists with the three great sinners in Hades (315). This is jesting and relatively casual, it is clearly not portentous denunciation; nevertheless, it plays a part in guiding our expectations of and our reactions to what follows.

Once Socrates has presented Hippocrates to Protagoras, and offered him the choice of private or public discussion (a choice which may prove significant for the progress of their discussion), Protagoras gives a general account of himself, explaining that he is not, like some, ashamed of professing the sophistic art, nor does he regard dissimulation as the best defence against those who might disapprove of him. In the course of this speech he names various poets and priest-like figures, sages of the past, who have concealed their sophistic status behind other labels — *poïesis, mousikē* and so on. He himself, however, is quite ready to proclaim himself a sophist and a teacher of *aretē* (loosely, 'excellence') (316c-17c). The declaration is interesting, as it aligns the sophists, and especially Protagoras himself, with the poets. The analogies are clear: the poets too were considered figures of wisdom and authority; they were often seen as teachers of virtue and morality (Protagoras alludes to this use of poetry in schools later, 325e); and of course they gave pleasure through their performances. The sophists inherit something of their role as entertainers and myth-makers, as Protagoras' speech will show. The reference to Simonides also paves the way for the critique of his poetry later in the dialogue: there, however, the sophist acts as critic, and therefore assumes a position of superiority to the poet (though ambiguously, since his own criticism is then challenged). Protagoras' speech thus sets his profession in a distinguished tradition, but also suggests that some of the uncertainties concerning the interpretation and evaluation of poetry may be applicable to his own teachings. In what sense poets do teach their audiences and listeners has never been a simple question, and was the subject of active debate in the late 5th and early 4th centuries,[7] by Plato and others; as will emerge, some of the same doubts can be raised about Protagoras' exposition of his principles.

I move on now to the major speech of Protagoras, in which he most fully and most convincingly presents his view of human society and of his own role as a teacher. I take it for granted that, although no doubt it bears *some* relation to the historical views of Protagoras, this speech is not straightforwardly lifted out of a published work of Protagoras, whether his *On the original state of things* or another,[8] any more than the speech ascribed to 'Lysias' in the *Phaedrus* is likely to be an authentic speech by Lysias. Even if these were authentic and un-Platonic, however, the important question would still be how they play their part in the Platonic context: in the present case, what place does the speech of Protagoras have in the dialogue *Protagoras*?

The speech is an epideixis or 'display-piece', of a particularly sophistic kind. It is very clearly signposted and structured: as in Gorgias' *Helen* or Agathon's speech in the *Symposium*, there are clear divisions when a new argument is introduced (323c, 324c5-9, 326e6f., and the final summary, 328c). In the preliminaries, Protagoras offered his audience a choice between a *mūthos* ('story') and a *logos* ('argument'); when his audience leaves the choice to him, he says that perhaps a *mūthos* will be 'more pleasurable'. Again we observe the stress on pleasure as the aim, typical of epideictic rhetoric. Furthermore, the choice is not, as is customary with Socrates, a choice of the necessary and appropriate form, but seems arbitrary: either will do, the form is not integral to the message. And indeed Protagoras demonstrates his versatility (or his lack of consistency?) by switching to a *logos* or more 'modern' style of argument for the second part of his speech (324d).

---

7 Cf. Aristophanes, *Frogs* etc.; Pohlenz 1920; Flashar 1958.

8 For discussion see Taylor 1976: 77-9.

The speech is intended to show why the Athenians are right to suppose that political intelligence is common to all citizens and also why, despite that, it is teachable, and Protagoras is a suitable and indeed an exceptional teacher. That is, it combines social analysis and self-advertisement. The other point Socrates makes, that notable fathers appear unable to teach their sons to excel in politics, is essentially subsidiary, and perhaps does not deserve the space it receives in Protagoras' reply, for, once we grant that such skill is teachable, it is not surprising that (as Protagoras says at the end of his speech) some should be abler teachers than others. The speech needs to be seen as a response to a particular set of questions in a specific place: had Protagoras not been in democratic Athens but (say) in an oligarchy, he might have had an easier case to present, for he could have discounted the proposition that all men possess some degree of political *aretē* and declared Athenian practice misguided.[9] As things are, he is presented with a challenging task and responds firmly and persuasively. Besides the main thrust of his argument, he enlivens his case with interesting and enlightening observations or 'talking points', for instance in his comments on the rationale of punishment (324ab). The impression we receive is of a clever, quick-witted and articulate man.

There are nevertheless problems in Protagoras' speech, not all of which can be treated here. Four of these problems can be isolated, and should suffice to establish that his case is flawed: some of the points made here will help to show how the rest of the dialogue builds on the effect of this major exposition by Protagoras.

1) It is still far from clear at the end of the speech what exactly Protagoras is prepared to teach his pupils. This was only partially settled at 318e-19a:

'With me he will learn about only that which he has come to learn. The instruction I give is sound judgement concerning his own house-

---

9   For such flexibility in different places cf. Pindar, *Pythian* 1. 75ff; Hippias in Plato, *Hp Ma* 285-6; Anderson 1986: 34f. (cf. St Paul's 'all things to all men').
 This argument would be weakened if Protagoras is correctly seen as a champion of democratic theory first and foremost (e.g. Morrison 1941, Farrar 1988); but the evidence for this seems extremely limited. See now Stadter 1991: 113-14, who questions the evidence for both Pericles' acquaintance with Protagoras and the connection Protagoras-Pericles-Thurii.

hold affairs, how he may best manage his home, and concerning the affairs of the city, how he may be the most able [or "powerful"] in word and deed on public affairs.'

'Am I following what you say?' I said. 'For you seem to be talking about the art of politics [*tēn politikēn technēn*], and to be promising to make men good citizens.'

'This is exactly the profession which I do profess, Socrates', he answered.

Even in this short exchange there are plenty of ambiguities: is Protagoras teaching good judgement, social skills, articulacy as a speaker, or 'how to win friends and influence people'? How important is the 'household' side, which drops out of the discussion? Is Socrates in his reply using 'good' in the moral sense, and was that presupposed by what Protagoras said, or is it a significant new point?

If one pursues this question of definition through Protagoras' speech, one finds little further clarification. *Aretē* continues to be the chief term used, with or without the adjective 'political', but in the myth Zeus makes Hermes pass on *aidos* and *dikē* to men, and elsewhere *dikaiosynē* and *sophrosynē* ('justice' and 'self-restraint') are used as components of political *aretē* (322e), *adikia* ('injustice') and *asebeia* ('impiety') as its opposites. In 324d the emphasis looks to be on success in politics (which might, but need not, entail moral authority), whereas in 325d and 326a-c the stress is on moral awareness. In 328b, in his final summing-up, Protagoras declares his talent to be 'in helping someone to become a fine gentleman' (*kalon kai agathon*), a phrase which notoriously suggests social and worldly status rather than moral preeminence.[10] In short, even the single term *aretē* seems to mask confusion between at least three ideas: success (or the capacity for it) in a career, political skill and judgement, and moral awareness as required in public life. These ambiguities are crucial to Protagoras' whole self-presentation as a teacher.[11]

---

10 Cf. de Ste Croix 1972: 371-6.

11 My colleague Dr. R.L. Judson suggests to me that *Protagoras'* general philosophic position may be relevant here: can he, as a relativist, make such distinctions? In other words, what is excellence and success for one person may not be so for another. Cf. Vlastos 1956: esp. liv.

2) The division of the speech into *mūthos* and *logos*, already mentioned, raises problems. Although Protagoras, in the sophistic manner,
modernizes the mythology (introducing, for instance, the conception
of primitive man as brutish, and referring to ecological ideas of survival
of the species at 320e-1b), there remains a considerable mythical resi-
due, and it seems hard, if not impossible, to carry out a full-scale
rationalization, converting the myth into a coherent non-mythical explanation. For example, in the myth Zeus confers the precious gifts of
shame and justice on mankind, and so ensures man's survival; but what
does this mean in non-mythical terms? Where does man's innate potential for morality come from if not from a supernatural source? And
if it was not supernaturally derived, what was the point of telling the
mythical version in the first place? Or again, in the *logos* section, the
reference to the laws, which guide the citizens to walk in the paths of
virtue, as 'discoveries of the good and ancient lawgivers' (326d6) leaves
unexplained where the lawgivers derived their 'goodness' from, and
how they made their special discoveries.

3) Protagoras' central argument in reply to Socrates' doubts is that
everyone who is not merely bestial has some basic level of *aretē*, for
otherwise he could not exist in a community; nevertheless, he can still
claim to be a teacher of *aretē* at the more advanced level (he also asserts
that work in schools, study of the poets and obedience to the laws instil
it). But this argument seems again to slide between different conceptions of *aretē* and very different degrees of it. Which is Protagoras
offering to teach, moral and social virtue or political success, and do
they have any necessary connection with each other? And does not his
argument reduce the concept of political *aretē* as possessed by an
average Athenian to an unacceptably low level? Can such minimal
adherence to social norms really be called *aretē* in anything like the same
sense as the preeminence in society which Protagoras claims to teach?
(Cf. Taylor 1976:92-3) Further, even if we accept Protagoras' argument,
he has reduced his own contribution. He never claims that he can teach
aretē where nothing was there before, only that he can enhance the basic
potential which people already have. (In the *Gorgias* too, it turns out
that the sophist's concern with the fundamentals of moral instruction
is casual compared with his concern with worldly success.)

4) Socrates' initial question concerned the democratic assumption of
the Athenians that any citizen, not just the experts or the elders, was
able and entitled to contribute to political debate in the assembly.
Protagoras in his reply refers more than once to the beliefs of the
Athenians and of men in general (322d, 323a, c, 324d, etc.). The form of

argument is perhaps questionable, for it is not being asked simply what the Athenians can be shown to believe, but whether those beliefs are justified. But more significantly, Protagoras here accepts the argument from majority or universal opinion: the Athenians and everybody think or do X therefore X must be at least probably right. This suits his argument here, but is not his regular position: we may contrast a number of passages later which suggest a more dismissive and contemptuous attitude to 'the masses' (esp. 352e3-4, 353a7-8).

Socrates' reaction to Protagoras' speech provides another nest of significant words and imagery:

> After Protagoras had made a display of such length and of such matter, he concluded his speech. And I sat spellbound, and continued to gaze at him for quite some time expecting that he had more to say and eager to hear it. (328d)

There is a strong implication here that in Socrates' view something crucial has been left out — namely, a definition and coherent conception of *aretē*, its sources and function, and the way in which it is to be taught. The word 'spellbound' picks up the initial description of Protagoras as he was when Socrates and Hippocrates arrived, enchanting his audience with his voice in the manner of Orpheus (315a: there, the same verb, *keleo*). Plato regularly uses such language to describe both the poetic prose of the sophists[12] and their concentration on the emotions, the pleasure-loving elements in their audiences. In both these respects, he has precedent and justification in Gorgias' *Helen*, with its memorable account of the psychology of *logos*.[13] Socrates' reaction to Protagoras, then, acknowledges the sophist's persuasive skill, but at the same time insinuates the suspicion that stylistic and intellectual glamour may mask basic confusion.

It is from this point on that dialectic, and the ethical and methodological issues which it involves, become more important in the dialogue and affect its formal structure. The rest of the dialogue considers the 'one little thing' which Socrates still wants to know after Protagoras' epideixis: namely, how are the virtues related? Are justice and moderation and

---

12 Cf. *Mx* 235ab, *Smp* 198; de Romilly 1975: chh. 1-2.

13 For text and translation see MacDowell 1982; for discussion e.g. Segal 1962.

holiness and courage and wisdom all parts of *aretē,* and does a man who has one of them have them all? But this enquiry into the unity or diversity of virtue does not proceed straightforwardly. The following table shows the structure of the rest of the *Protagoras.*

> 328d - 334c: following up Protagoras' speech, Socrates questions Protagoras about the virtues.
> 334c - 338e: methodological interlude. Long speeches *versus* short, etc. Protagoras undertakes the task of questioning.
> 338e - 347a: discussion of a poem by Simonides. Protagoras criticizes it as inconsistent, Socrates defends and interprets it.
> 347a - 348c: second methodological interlude, after which Socrates takes up the questioning.
> 348c - 360e: resumption of enquiry into the relationship of the virtues, with special reference to courage.
> 360e - 362a: Socrates sums up; conclusion of the discussion at Protagoras' request; farewells.

Even this bare summary should make clear that formally the *Protagoras* is not simple. After the performance by Protagoras, we turn more to question-and-answer, Socrates' preferred form of discussion; first Socrates is the questioner, then Protagoras, then Socrates again. The main subject, the unity of virtue, is abandoned at 334c because of Protagoras' growing dissatisfaction, and not resumed until much later. In between, Socrates, Protagoras and others argue about the merits of long versus short speeches and other aspects of the discussion, and we have a chance to hear something from the other persons present in Callias' house. Eventually Protagoras agrees to continue in brief question-answer style, but only with himself as the questioner and on his chosen subject, poetry: the discussion of Simonides' poem comes in, it seems, *à propos* of nothing, though the fact that its subject is *aretē* gives it a certain specious connection with the rest of the dialogue. It is clear from Socrates' comments at the end of that section that the whole poetic discussion has been, for him, a pointless digression. Only after a further exchange on methods, and after the rest of the company have brought considerable pressure to bear on him, is Protagoras prepared to submit once again to Socrates' interrogation on the supposed main subject; and he makes some difficulties even at that stage.

In short, the structure of the dialogue is intimately related to the characters of those conducting it, and itself serves to illustrate, no less than the *Laches* or the *Euthydemus,* right and wrong ways of approaching a discussion of ethical or any other themes.[14] Like other eloquent or professional speakers in Plato (Callicles in the *Gorgias*, Thrasymachus in Book 1 of the *Republic*), Protagoras has done his set piece, his epideictic combination of myth and argument, and wants to rest on his laurels, or at least remain in control of the discussion; he is much less happy to become the questioned party, the victim of Socratic elenchus, and to have the inconsistencies or oddities in his position exposed to view — above all in front of his fellow sophists, before whom he was previously happy to show off (cf. Socrates' plausible diagnosis at 317cd 'I suspected that he wanted to put on a performance in front of Prodicus and Hippias and show off because we had turned up to admire him ....'). This also helps us go some way towards understanding the problem of the dialogue's unity; for it seems that a unified, unilinear development of the argument is not possible precisely because of the differing views and attitudes of those involved in it. Protagoras' concern for his own prestige prevents him from being as committed to the pursuit of truth as Socrates: he naturally does not want to admit that his original epideixis was radically flawed. Moreover, the dissension among the sophists and others present about how the argument should be conducted illustrates the difficulty of conducting a discussion at all with so many vociferous and self-important personalities present; as already mentioned, we can contrast this with the more intimate, one-to-one conversation between Socrates and Hippocrates while *en route*.

It would be tedious to consider all these episodes in detail, and the general lines of interpretation should by now be fairly clear. I shall comment selectively first on the methodological interlude at 334c-8e, then on the discussion of Simonides, before proceeding to the most puzzling part of the dialogue, the final section on the 'hedonic calculus'.

The exchange on *makrologia* ('lengthy speech') and its opposite, *brachylogia* ('conciseness'), develops a theme found elsewhere in Plato, the concern for the appropriate form. (Cf. *Grg* 449c and Dodds 1959 *ad loc.*) Protagoras wishes to continue with long and elaborate speeches, whereas Socrates complains that he cannot keep up with these and would prefer short dialectical question and answer. The dispute is prompted by a long and largely irrelevant display-speech by Protagoras, which in its style and its generalizations has very much the flavour

---

14 On the ethics of dialectic see esp. Lloyd 1979: 100-101.

of a sophistic set-piece (334a-c; cf. e.g. *Grg* 448c4ff.). When Socrates protests, Protagoras resists, and in the end makes clear his irritation by a refusal to compromise:

> 'Socrates, I have entered into contests of words with many people, and if I had regularly done as you ask, and conversed in the way my opponent told me to converse, then I would never have looked superior to anybody, nor would the name of Protagoras ever have been known among the Greeks.'
> I realised that he was displeased with the answers he had given previously, and that he would not be prepared willingly to converse under my questioning .... (335a)

Later, Socrates himself contrasts Protagoras' conception of how to conduct a discussion with his own: 'I thought that a conversation with people talking to one another was something distinct from a public oration' (336b). Protagoras' references to competition and superiority betray his anxiety to come out on top, just as his preference for elaborate set-speeches belongs more to the combative sphere of oratory than to dialectic.

Again, this is a significant contrast, not a polemical clash of methods or an instance of Socrates simply being difficult. Extended sophistic monologue is subject, for Plato, to both formal and moral objections: exposition in this style may lead to fine rhetoric, but it is harder to follow and allows the introduction of more questionable statements, doubtful transitions and grandiose periphrases (cf. *Rep* 1. 348ab). The comparison with political oratory, like the comparison later of poets and books, is hardly complimentary. Moreover, the sophists claimed to be able to give answers of any length, a point Socrates makes at *Protagoras* 334e (another instance of their carefree versatility);[15] hence Socrates' request is scarcely unfair, even though we can understand Protagoras' feeling that this restriction cramps his style.

The subsequent discussion, as Socrates gets up and threatens to leave, offers a chance for the others present to put their views and illustrate their styles. Callias' amiable intervention needs little comment: he simply tries to smooth things over, and emphasizes how much they are all enjoying themselves — pleasure prevailing over instruction

---

15   Cf. Prodicus at *Phdr* 267b; Hudson-Williams 1950.

again. After him Alcibiades, supposedly the beloved of Socrates, inter-
venes in support of his friend (336b7). This is the first time Alcibiades
has spoken, though he was mentioned as present at 316a (the scene-set-
ting), as well as in the initial exchange between Socrates and his friend.
His participation here and at 347b presumably represent the help
Socrates there says he had from Alcibiades. In both cases he directs the
conversation back on to more Socratic dialectical lines. His is not a
flawless diagnosis of the situation, for he too uses competitive language
(esp. 336c2-4), rightly as regards Protagoras, wrongly concerning Socrates. He hints at Socratic method (336c6-7), and he sees through
Socrates' pretence of forgetfulness, describing it as 'play' (336d3). The
insight of Alcibiades into Socrates' character may not be so profound
as in the *Symposium*, but as in that dialogue he sees more clearly than
the others present.

Prodicus, with his subtle, indeed excessively recondite distinctions,
is one of the most interesting of those intervening (337a-c). His speech,
like many in Plato, is misguided without being merely absurd. His
distinctions and his argument are inadequate to the occasion, but they
suggest truths. Thus his advocacy of common participation but not
equality (337a3) is picked up by Socrates in his speech a little later; his
warning against eristic, that is, quarrelsome and point-scoring argument, resembles many remarks by Socrates elsewhere, for eristic can
be regarded as a kind of parody or travesty of dialectic. That is what
we find in the *Euthydemus*, in an argument where mutual goodwill and
consistency are absent. Prodicus' final comment is also striking, in part
because it takes up the 'pleasure/hedonism' theme.

> '... we who listen would derive in that way the most enjoyment,
> though not pleasure (*euphrainoimetha* as opposed to *hēdoimestha*): for
> one derives enjoyment from learning or the exercise of purely mental
> intelligence, whereas one gains pleasure from eating or some other
> pleasant, purely physical experience.' (337c)

The fact that Prodicus' speech in no way corresponds with normal
Greek usage points to the artificiality of any such antithesis; and indeed
the speakers, including Socrates, are constantly speaking of their pleasure in the actual discussion (e.g. 335c6, 361d6), and enjoyment of
epideictic literature in particular is often compared with or metaphori-
cally expressed as enjoyment of food, drink and sensual experiences
(cf. Bramble 1974: 50-1). Prodicus' speech thus suggests the ways in
which the discussion falls short of the ideal.

Hippias' speech is much more elaborate and stylistically rich: ornate metaphors such as 'the council-chamber of wisdom' (337d6), inversions, pleonasm (e3, 338a8f.), and the unnecessarily florid sailing-metaphor in his finale. Again there is stress on the pleasure derived from the discussion, and flattery too, in the self-satisfied description of the company as 'the wisest of the Greeks'. Hippias finally proposes 'that we select an umpire, chairman or president [pleonasm again] to see that each of you keeps to the moderate length' — whatever that is! This bland advocacy of 'civilized' concessions to one another is accepted by everyone except Socrates, who replies with some sharpness that this will not serve, as there are differences among them in intelligence and judgement; but he preserves the decencies by putting the comment in the form of a compliment to Protagoras (338c2-3). (His remark on their *similarities* (338b7) also picks up and adds a sharper point to Hippias' generalization at 337d1.) This objection is not merely putting Hippias down; it is necessary to remind the company of the crucial differences in the two approaches to debate, rather than having the whole procedure lumped together in a jumble of non-rules such as Callias and Hippias proposed. Socrates concludes that they should not have one single arbitrator, but all act as arbitrators together (338e2). This is a paradox, and perhaps a worrying one: certainly the combined judgement of the audience reaches no very substantial decisions or conclusions in what follows. But Socrates' suggestion differs from Hippias' in that it quietly points to a truth — that all the audience do need to judge the speeches, and the subject matter, for themselves, not just applauding unthinkingly or relying on the authority of a supposedly wiser judge. (A somewhat similar point is made more clearly at *Rep* 1. 348ab: the company must be their own advocates and judges alike.)

The discussion resumes with Protagoras asking the questions; he now embarks on the famous discussion of Simonides' poem on the good man.[16] The way he introduces this is revealing: 'Socrates, I consider that the supreme part of a man's education is cleverness about words' (*not* actions or realities). Thus the sophist shifts his ground on to territory in which Socrates has little interest, as emerges from his comments at the

---

16   See Page 1962: no. 542; translated e.g. in Lattimore 1960: 55f.; discussed by Bowra 1961: 326-36.

end of this section (347c-8a; cf. *Smp* 176e).[17] Protagoras' change of tack is evidently due to his finding Socrates' style of discussion too uncomfortable. In this section he uses the poem as a kind of scapegoat: he has become the questioner, but instead of tackling Socrates directly, he pokes fun at and picks holes in the poem, which cannot answer back. This probably does reflect sophistic methods of literary criticism accurately enough (we know that Protagoras and Prodicus were both much concerned with correct use of words, and that Protagoras found fault with the first line of the *Iliad*[18]), but here it is given a sharper ethical point. Protagoras is not only sidetracking the main discussion, but avoiding being shown up further. Instead he accuses the poet of self-contradiction, the very fault which Socratic elenchus is designed to expose and resolve,[19] and the fault of which he himself seems guilty. As in other dialogues, when the sophists show the way, Socrates is prepared to follow; but characteristically he handles the task of interpretation differently. Instead of denigrating the poet, he defends his consistency, and indeed makes Simonides into a somewhat Socratic figure, one who recognises human limitations and imperfections, and who shows a pessimistic but realistic humanity. One particularly clear analogy betwen poet and philosopher is 344b, where Socrates maintains that the whole of Simonides' poem is an actual elenchus of the saying by Pittacus from which the poem takes its starting point. In other words, according to Socrates, Simonides has been playing a Socratic role, conducting an interrogation of Pittacus, testing his wisdom and exposing his pretensions. Similarly at 345de, Socrates glosses Simonides by attributing to him the characteristically Socratic principle that no one does wrong willingly. The point is not that Socrates' reading of Simonides is any more plausible than others' — indeed, it involves some clearly far-fetched

---

17 It is particularly notable that this form of discussion shifts the enquiry from a direct encounter with moral questions to an investigation of what a poet thought about moral questions — an investigation difficult in itself and unprofitable if we do not accept Simonides as an 'authority'. Cf. the critique of the poets as 'teachers' elsewhere in Plato (e.g. Dodds 1959: 320-22 on *Grg* 501d).

18 Protagoras 80 A 1 Diels-Kranz, etc; Pfeiffer 1968: 32-9. The approach is parodied in Aristophanes' *Clouds* (658ff., 681ff., 847ff.), and especially in the *Frogs*. For a different side to Protagoras' criticism see Oxyrhynchus Papyri no. 221 (tr. Guthrie 1962-81: vol. 3, 269).

19 *Grg* 482b-c, with Dodds 1959; Lloyd 1979: 101 nn. 233-4.

moves. Rather, the difference lies in the kind of lesson he draws from it; whereas Protagoras patronizes the poem, Socrates asks what truths it can be seen to contain or imply.[20]

Protagoras' unease and reluctance to continue once the discussion of the poem is over is very clear: at 348b he keeps a resentful silence, and refuses to be frank about his feelings (348b1-2, 5). Alcibiades again steps in, and shames him into rejoining the conversation (348c1); then, after another digression on method by Socrates, in which he assures Protagoras that he is not trying to cheat or bamboozle him, the last phase of the main discussion, on the unity of the virtues, begins.

The argument which ensues must be seen in context, as an argument between Socrates and Protagoras, in the light of all that Protagoras has claimed or attempted to prove earlier. The central issue of the dialogue, as should now be clear, is what is the nature of the *aretē* which Protagoras claims to teach? With that question come others: what is the relation between *aretē* and knowledge or wisdom? How useful or powerful are they? How effectively can the wisdom (*sophia*) imparted by the sophist govern human nature, and the natural drives of pleasure and pain which, in popular opinion, are constantly dominating and overruling the power of reason?

An important strand in the argument is this theme of popular opinion, the views of the masses. As before with the poet Simonides, so here the general public are brought in as alternative subjects of interrogation, this time by Socrates. In part this is tactful, to ease Protagoras' position; in part it may enable him to achieve some sleight-of-hand with the argument. But the main point is surely to call into question Protagoras' relation to popular ideas: is he above them and operating on a different plane entirely, or is he in fact accepting or entangled in them? Here as elsewhere in the dialogue Protagoras' attitude is ambiguous (cf. Stokes 1986: 353f.). At times he claims to be above paying attention to popular ideas (333c1-3, 352c8-d3, 352d5, 353a7-8), but elsewhere he has appealed to universal opinion as evidence in support of his own case (323a5ff., etc.; see above, pp. 144-5), and in 351b-d, after some wavering, he assents to the popular distinction between good and bad pleasures, being clearly uneasy about agreeing that pleasure in itself is always a good thing. By 359c he is again trying to appeal to — or shuffle off the question on to —

---

20   Cf. his attitude to myth at *Phdr* 229c-30a.

'what people say', but there Socrates insists on bringing the question home to 'you' (*ibid.* d1).[21]

Socrates has cited the view of the masses that knowledge is a weak thing, unstable and easily overcome by pleasure. Naturally, as an exponent and salesman of knowledge, Protagoras resists this view emphatically (352c9-d3: 'it would be an especial disgrace to me above all men not to maintain that wisdom and knowledge is the mightiest of human things.'). But he and the rest of the sophists are much readier to accept the modification of this view which Socrates, by a devious route, presents to them (358a): that men are overcome by pleasure because of ignorance: they simply have not appreciated correctly the relative pleasure-potential of immediate and more remote experiences, and so have made a mistaken choice. But although this meets with their approval, as giving a more prestigious role to knowledge, it is a degraded conception of knowledge, and leaves pleasure as the primary principle, the *telos* according to which choices are to be made — surely the most disturbing feature of the popular attitude.[22]

Socrates' use of the hedonic calculus should not, then, be over-literally interpreted as expressing his own view of the relationship of knowledge and pleasure.[23] Rather, this argument is employed to demonstrate once again the inadequacy of Protagoras' thinking about his profession and its intellectual basis. Protagoras is entrammelled at least partly because he lacks a critical or dialectical approach; that is, he does

---

21 Cf. the important passage in *Rep* 6. 493a: 'Every one of those individual teachers, whom the people call sophists ... in fact teaches nothing but the beliefs of the people expressed by themselves in their assemblies. That is what he claims as his wisdom.'

22 I find attractive the view of Nussbaum 1986 (esp. 106-117), that Socrates would endorse the need for an art of measurement with which to discriminate between different objectives, whereas he is not committing himself to the view that pleasure should be the quantifiable criterion measured by that art. Her additional suggestion (112, 450) that hedonism is in any case ethically respectable strikes me as ill-founded for ancient Greek culture in general and Plato in particular; see further Dover 1974: 124-6, 208-9.

23 Cf. Sullivan 1967; Stokes 1986: 358-70. For the view that Socrates does accept this doctrine see esp. Taylor 1976: 208-10 and Gosling & Taylor 1982: 45-68. (A variant is the position that Socrates or Plato or both really did go through a phase of believing this principle (cf. e.g. Dodds 1959: 21; but see Guthrie 1962-81: vol. 4, 231). If so, however, would the conception be restricted to one dialogue?) More bibliography in Nussbaum 1986: nn. to ch. 4 (esp. 450n.51).

not analyse the terms which he and the populace use in common, for instance 'pleasure', 'knowledge' and above all *aretē*. Throughout the *Protagoras* we lack a coherent rationale of what Protagoras teaches and how he goes about it. For Socrates, the core of his teaching is lacking; for a true morality will guide the choice of pleasures by reference to a *telos* beyond them, and it is that which Socrates is constantly asking for in his dialogue with the people (see esp. 354b7f. '... or can you point to any result by reference to which you call them good, other than pleasures and pains? They would say no, I think'; 354d2, 8; 355a1 'But even now you are at liberty to withdraw, if you can give any other account of the good than pleasure, or of evil than pain. Or are you content to say that good is a pleasant life without pains?'; 355d6, 8; all of these passages leave the question open, but disturbingly imply the inadequacy of the answers being provided).[24]

Like the interpretation which Socrates offered of Simonides' poem, the 'hedonic calculus' theory does not answer every question raised so far, but only brings a particular phase of the discussion to a conclusion which neither Socrates nor Protagoras will find satisfactory. The speech of Socrates after he has brought the sophist to agree that courage is a form of knowledge makes clear that Socrates is not content with this 'victory'; instead he emphasizes the paradoxical aspects of their conclusion, and insists that the quest for a definition of *aretē* has only begun (360e7-8). In this speech he picks up the mythical aspect of Protagoras' long epideixis earlier, perhaps as a compliment to Protagoras, but perhaps also as an indication of the kind of personal lessons or morals that can be drawn from the myths:

> 'For my part, Protagoras, when I see all this in such dreadful upside-down confusion, I feel a total desire for it to be made clear, and I would be ready for us to go through these subjects thoroughly, and investigate the definition of *aretē*, and look again at whether it is teachable or not .... In that story of yours Prometheus appealed to me more than Epimetheus; using him and taking forethought for all my life I am busy considering all these subjects, and if you were willing, as I said at the start, I would have the greatest pleasure in scrutinizing these points in your company.' (361cd)

---

24 Vlastos 1956: xl n.50, seems to me to underplay the significance of these qualifications.

Protagoras' reaction, however, is courteous but uncooperative. After complimenting Socrates on his zeal and his ability, he prefers to put off further discussion for another time. 'It is time now to turn to some other subject' (e6). Socrates' acceptance is equally polite, but we cannot help feeling that Protagoras has failed a test: he lacks the determination, and the concern for truth, which would enable him to ignore his own failures or false moves and concentrate on the enquiry at hand.[25] Socrates, on finding that Protagoras is not willing to pursue that enquiry, immediately remembers an engagement elsewhere and departs (362a2, cf. 335c5-6).

It will by now be clear that the *Protagoras* is well-named; that is, it could not simply be entitled (e.g.) *On political aretē*.[26] The part played by Protagoras, with all his eloquence, prestige, vanity, dignity and tetchiness, is essential to the form and development of the argument; hardly less significant is the constant presence of an audience of patron, potential disciples and trade rivals. It is relevant too that Socrates is presented as still a relatively young man at the time of the conversation (esp. 317c — Protagoras is old enough to be the father of any of those present; 361e). Hence Socrates and Protagoras are not conversing as equals. Personalities influence the discussion; Protagoras at various points avoids interrogation, Socrates makes concessions or tactfully plays along. The consequence of all this is that the dialogue cannot be an ideal model of dialectical argument on *aretē*; it is contaminated by other motives and methods, affected by the agonistic tendencies of the sophists, soured by *philonikia* ('desire to win') on at least one side, and set against a background of spectators who want a good show rather than a philosophically correct solution. It is not surprising that the dialogue then ends inconclusively. I have suggested that the one conversation which we do not overhear, the private dialogue of Socrates and Hippocrates as they approach the house of Callias, provides an ideal model of the purely dialectical discussion, which does reach a

---

25 Dr. Andrew Barker suggests that Protagoras here lacks *courage* to continue, and that this is apt in view of the special attention which the dialogue has paid so far to the place of courage in relation to the other parts of virtue. For a comparable, though more explicit, form of self-reference see *Grg* 505c.

26 Diogenes Laertius, *Lives of the Philosophers* iii. 59 mentions an alternative title 'The sophists' — more acceptable?

resolution. Thereafter, we might say, things simply go down hill. The reader will have guessed the analogy I naturally want to draw, in order to bring my paper in line with the title of this series. When he begins to survey the scene within Callias' house, Socrates compares the vision of the three sophists with the vision Odysseus has of the great sinners in Hades; he thus evokes a descent into the underworld. Just so, the philosopher of the *Republic*, having seen the truth of the world above, must return to the Cave to attempt to teach his former fellow-captives; and just as they resist his efforts to enlighten them, so the company in Callias' house in the end fall short of the dialectical ideals which Socrates offers and endeavours (imperfectly?) to exemplify in his own performance.

Dialectical Drama: The Case of Plato's Symposium[1]

Martin Warner

I

'When the eye of the soul is sunk *en boborōi barbarikōi* [in barbarous swamp], dialectic gently draws it forth and leads it up', Socrates tells us in the *Republic* (533d) as he summarizes that process of thought which enables us to grasp the nature of the good in itself, the source of all that is beautiful (517c), bringing us 'to the contemplation of what is best among realities', a process for which he had used the ascent from the Cave to the vision of the Sun as a parable. In the *Symposium* (211a-e) Socrates endorses Diotima's account of another ascent, in this case to the vision of *auto to kalon* ('the beautiful itself') which above all makes life worthwhile and in the light of which one's concerns before the ascent began may be recognized as 'great nonsense'. The parallels are striking, and are reinforced when one notes that Socrates and his host have agreed earlier in the *Symposium* (201c) that all good things are beautiful, and that Socrates' subsequent dialogue with Diotima has made significant use of the close connection between the concepts of beauty and of goodness.

---

1 My thanks are due to a number of colleagues in the Centre for Research in Philosophy and Literature at the University of Warwick, but especially to Andrew Barker, Christine Battersby, Malcolm Hardman and Martin Wright for constructive questioning when a draft of this paper was presented to the Centre and for subsequent discussion. Also to *The Philosophical Quarterly* for permission to make use of some material from my 'Love, Self and Plato's *Symposium*'.

At least equally striking, however, is the meagreness in the *Symposium* of those procedures of disciplined discussion that in the *Republic* and elsewhere in Plato are characteristic of the dialectical process. They are exemplified to some degree in Socrates' cross-questioning of Agathon and in his own speech, but these two elements taken together account for only one quarter of the work, the rest being an account of a dinner party and the speeches made there, that of Socrates being only one of seven. Indeed, the dialogue's most recent editor, Sir Kenneth Dover, declares roundly that the remaining three quarters 'are not philosophical', and is notably severe on the claims to the status of 'rigorous argument' even of the Socratic portions (1980: 5-6). However, as Kenneth Dorter pointed out more than twenty years ago, to read the bulk of the dialogue as 'padding or ornamentation' devoid of 'philosophical content' would be to bring it under the very condemnation for incoherence to which Socrates subjects the speech of Lysias in Plato's companion dialogue on love and beauty, the *Phaedrus*, even though both Socrates and his host in the *Symposium* emphasize the importance to a discourse of proper arrangement. In the *Phaedrus* (264c) Socrates declares that every discourse ought to have 'a middle and extremities composed appropriately to one another and to the whole', and Dorter (1969) argues persuasively if incompletely that such a description applies to the *Symposium*. There are dangers in reading one dialogue in terms of another, but the *Symposium*, *Republic* and *Phaedrus* are all normally classified as dialogues from Plato's middle period, and it is reasonable to treat cross-references between them as at least suggestive — though certainly not as on their own decisive.

The passage from the *Republic* with which I started characterizes dialectic as the only process of inquiry that 'destroys its hypotheses, up to the first principle itself, in order to find confirmation'. The precise interpretation to be put on this passage in its own context raises notorious problems, but in the present context it is indeed suggestive. Each of the speeches of the *Symposium* posits theses about Love (*erōs*), which turn out to be self-refuting or otherwise unsatisfactory, until Socrates recounts how his own theses had been confounded by Diotima in a way that both made sense of the inadequacies of the hypotheses proposed by his fellow symposiasts, and grounded her positive account in a vision of what looks very like an analogue of the 'unhypothesized beginning' (510b) of the *Republic*. This procedure is hardly the sort of disciplined 'discourse of reason' to which the *Republic* points as proper for its prospective Guardians, but it may very well be appropriate for the philosopher returning to the Cave who seeks to liberate its inhabitants, rather than incur their ridicule, by transforming the images in terms of which they have learnt to interpret the world. Taken in this way the dramatic movement of the whole dialogue — not merely of Dover's 'philosophical portions' — may be construed as 'dialectical', even on Plato's own terms. I shall return at the close to whether it may be so construed on other terms, and the possibility of learning from it about the proper criteria for philosophical assessment; but first it will be necessary to consider the dynamics of the dialogue.

II

The setting for the speeches is a party held 'when Agathon won the prize with his first tragedy' (173a; I have normally, as here, used the Nehamas & Woodruff translation). Agathon is the host, and among the guests is Aristophanes, the comic dramatist, who delivers one of the most powerful speeches in the whole dialogue. These facts, together with the consideration that dramatic vocabulary appears particularly apt for describing the structure of the work, point to a tempting blind alley: that of attempting to construe the coherence of the work in terms of dramatic unity and glossing that notion in terms of the conventions of Greek drama (see, for example, Randall 1970: 127). On such an account Socrates might be presented as victor over both tragic and comic poets in a dramatic form which exploits their own techniques, making sense of that notorious crux at the close of the dialogue where Socrates attempts to force Agathon and Aristophanes to agree that playwrights should be able to compose both comedy and tragedy. Even if such an intention were in Plato's mind, however, the hypothesis does not take us very far in our reading of the dialogue. For on the one hand our knowledge of the conventions of Greek Old Comedy is too sketchy to provide us with a grasp of how Plato may plausibly be said to transcend them, and on the other in so far as we try to read the work in the light of such conventions as we do understand (whether drawn from the extant plays of Aristophanes himself or from classical Greek tragedy) we find ourselves involved in some of the more vicious features of the hermeneutic circle. Perhaps the most striking such likeness emerges if we interpret Alcibiades as the leader of the Chorus, and the irruption of his party in terms of the entry of the Chorus in some of the Aristophanic comedies; but such a reading is only plausible if we have already come to see Alcibiades' speech as in some way reinforcing what Socrates has said, unless we also interpret Plato as satirizing conventional uses of Choruses — the multiplication of such *ad hoc* hypotheses soon brings diminishing returns. If we see affinities between Plato's *Symposium* and the Greek drama of the period, this should be because they have emerged through an independent reading of the text, not by reading them into the text from the start.

If a comparison of the dialogue with contemporary drama is of strictly limited usefulness, a consideration of its divergences from other Platonic dialogues of the early and middle periods may be more helpful. The most obvious difference is the already noticed absence of disciplined argument through question and answer throughout the first half of the work, and its limited role thereafter, even though the various speakers often disagree with each other. A connected point is the way that Socrates speaks for much of the time not in his own voice, but in that of a priestess whom he at one point describes as speaking 'in the manner of the perfect [complete, accomplished, *teleioi*] sophists' (208c). Socrates appears to endorse her words even though in other dialogues the sophists are frequently under attack, and although in this work Socrates opens his discussion with a critique of Agathon's speech, in part for its very exemplification of the rhetorical principles of the sophist Gorgias.

These two features of the work, taken together, provide an important clue to how it should be read. The differences between the various speakers about the nature and significance of love are expressed in terms of the type of encomium they are giving, a form of what Aristotle was to classify as epideictic rhetoric, where love is personified and 'his' parentage, characteristics and powers delineated (shadows, perhaps, on the wall of the Cave). The contrasts in their accounts derive from the diverse intellectual, imaginative and emotional capacities of the symposiasts, informed by their distinctive experiences; that is, from their differing sensibilities. The relations between conventionalized, playful form and idiosyncratic, often serious content can be problematic — hence (in part) Aristophanes' unease at 189b. Thus a purely elenctic demonstration of inconsistencies in such an account (of the sort Socrates employs with Agathon) is *by itself* of little value. A serious rebuttal of what is only semi-seriously intended, standing on its own, would merely expose Socrates as a clumsy and somewhat tactless philistine. What is required is an account of love which is not only intellectually coherent, but also makes sense of the imaginative and emotional pressures that underlie the less adequate formulations; and it is this which Socrates goes on to provide.

His medium is a form of discourse which employs rhetorical skills but arises out of dialectical argument with Agathon and continues, at least in the earlier part, by means of a reported dialectic between Socrates and the priestess Diotima, who appears to be both a skilled dialectician and a rhetorician. We seem to have an approximation here to that 'noble [*kalon*] rhetoric' which had been adumbrated in the *Gorgias* (503a) and was later analysed in the *Phaedrus*; a rhetoric which is under the control of dialectic and hence concerned with the truth, but is nevertheless able to adjust itself to the requirements of a particular audience in order to persuade its members by means which go beyond the strictly dialectical. Officially Diotima's 'audience' is Socrates himself, and Socrates accordingly represents himself as having been 'persuaded' (212b), rather than the truth as having been demonstrated. However, as we shall see, the conceit of Socrates as neophyte is not to be taken too seriously; the whole speech of Socrates, whether or not purporting to report Diotima, is constructed with an eye to what we have already heard from his fellow symposiasts. The relevant audience is neither the 'one' of strict dialectical interchange, nor the ignorant and hence rationally inert 'many', but the intelligent 'few' (194b); one notes Diotima's insistence (202a) on the importance of the intermediate and the latter's association with 'correct judgement' (*orthē doxa*). In the final part of the dialogue Plato extends this technique further with the introduction of an Alcibiades who has refused the Socratic invitation to the ascent, and indeed resisted that 'turning round' which in the *Republic* (515c) was the precondition of liberation from the Cave, thereby rendering himself unfitted to grasp the significance of Socrates' activity; he provides, as it were, an account of it from the perspective of the Cave-dwellers — which is, of course, that of the readers of the dialogue, ourselves. We, however, can compare this perspective with the Socratic one and find that Alcibiades' uncomprehending and 'Cave-like' insistence on down to earth particularity serves with Platonic irony to reinforce Diotima's otherwise inordinately high-flown conclusions.

In short, the *Symposium* presents us with a clash of sensibilities. Each speaker provides an account of love which derives from his own sensibility until Socrates, after first dissociating himself from what he sees as unacceptable elements in most standard encomia, develops an account which — while distinctive and far-reaching — nevertheless takes seriously and reinterprets in its own terms the strongest points of what has gone before. By thus relating his account to those of his predecessors, Socrates strengthens the case for taking it seriously, and its significance is pointed up by the concluding irruption of Alcibiades.

III

The dialogue begins with a series of distancing devices whose cumulative effect is to focus attention on the figure of Socrates as a man of at once great moral authority and somewhat otherworldly tendencies; his disciple professes to despise wealth and Socrates himself characteristically becomes so absorbed by his own thoughts that he is unaware of the world around him. But together with what Aristotle was to classify as the establishing of the *ēthos* of the main speaker, the complex opening appears to interweave at least two other rhetorical features.

The more obvious is the way in which the sequence of nested reports — whereby Apollodorus, in conversation with a non-philosophical friend, reports a previous conversation in which he recalled an account by Aristodemus of speeches he heard at a banquet 'when we were still children' — prepares the way for the continuation of the sequence when Socrates in the climactic speech 'reports a speech of Diotima, who reports the secrets of the mysteries' (Nussbaum 1986: 168). We are, that is, still in the Cave; our own distance even from the report of Diotima's vision, let alone its reality, is emphasized. Nevertheless this does not make the dialogue, as Martha Nussbaum half suggests (168), 'the speech of Alcibiades'; it is the speech of Apollodorus, that uncharismatic, fierce and (according to *Phaedo* 117d) over-emotional individual who nevertheless, unlike Alcibiades, has allowed himself to be 'turned round' by Socrates (173a), and so even if still in the Cave has opened his eyes towards the light. To the extent that we identify more with the 'friend' than with the philosophical 'mania' of Apollodorus, we recognize that part of our distance from Diotima's vision is of our own making. That it is the unconverted Alcibiades, not the avowed disciple of Socrates (save in his role as narrator), who conveys to us most powerfully the fascination of the figure of Socrates is an instructive irony.

Less obvious, to those who are not Plato's contemporaries, is the weight the opening (as well, of course, as the end) appears to give to the figure of Alcibiades. Glaucon, the initiator of the previous conversation which Apollodorus reports, enquires about 'a gathering at Agathon's when Socrates, Alcibiades and their friends had dinner together'. Agathon is mentioned to identify the meeting in question and Socrates because he is the friend of Apollodorus; Alcibiades is the unexplained name — and, as it turns out, the one who did not share the dinner. Martha Nussbaum has provided plausible reasons for seeing this setting as that of the Alcibiades frenzy of 404 BC and

Glaucon, who wrongly believes the dinner to be recent (its dramatic date, of course, is 416 BC), as concerned to discover whether Alcibiades has returned to Athens; he is, in fact, close to death in Phrygia. If we accept her suggestion that in the two-day gap between the conversations report of Alcibiades' death has reached Athens, whence the friend's interest in Apollodorus' story, this only strengthens our sense that the mortality of Alcibiades looms over the dialogue. The urgent concerns he passionately declares in his unstable mixture of praise for and accusation of Socrates represent, from the perspective of one who has made the ascent, 'great nonsense of mortality' (211e). We are not only invited to compare the speeches of Socrates and Alcibiades in their own terms, and in those of the other speeches of the dialogue, but in the light of what has passed since — not least the very different deaths of Socrates and Alcibiades. Much of this, admittedly, is conjectural, but if it is reasonable to suppose that such a reading might be available to a contemporary, it is just possible that this may not be the first time Plato used such a device. E. R. Dodds long ago suggested that the death of a historical Callicles might play an analogous dramatic role in the *Gorgias* (Dodds 1959: 12-15); the proposal has not found much favour, but Nussbaum's reading of the *Symposium* may be thought to increase, if marginally, its plausibility.

However this may be, the start of Apollodorus' narrative proper prepares us for what is to come. His informant, Aristodemus, has already been characterized as 'obsessed with Socrates' and, almost in the same breath, as one 'who always went barefoot'; now he meets Socrates 'who had just bathed and put on his fancy sandals — both very unusual events' (174a). The juxtaposition leads us to suppose that the events that will follow will also be unusual, and so it proves. At the close of the dialogue Aristodemus reports that the following day Socrates spent 'just as he always did', but this is not how he spends the evening in question; instead of the usual mode of philosophical questioning in public, we have a series of rhetorical speeches at a private dinner party. On the way to it Socrates twice modifies well-known sayings, twisting them to his purposes, thereby providing us with a sceptical context for the reception of received wisdom and allegedly authoritative quotations in the speeches which follow. Such urbane lightness of touch helps offset the distancing effect of some of the other opening features as well as functioning as an efficient narrative device. He compares, for example, the beauty of his best sandals with that of his host ('... so that I may go *kalos* to a *kalon*; 174a), thereby introducing a notion crucial to the subsequent speeches.

These, it is decided, are to be in the form of encomia to *erōs*. Socrates endorses this with the remark that the things of *erōs* are the only matters with regard to which he has *epistēmē* (177e). In other dialogues Plato uses this word as a technical term for 'knowledge', but we have been prepared to countenance the possibility that Socrates may not speak technically in this company and the ambiguities of the term (which covers 'acquaintance', 'experience' and 'skill' as well as 'knowledge') remain unresolved until Socrates recalls his remark half-way through the dialogue (198d) and interprets it as a claim to be *deinos* ('skilful') in love matters — a contention to which Alcibiades lends support at the close. For Socrates to claim knowledge, however ambiguously, is of course highly unusual; and thus we are alerted from the start to the possibility that what Socrates will have to say will be more closely bound up with his own experience and personality than elsewhere.

The word 'love' is, of course, both inevitable and unsatisfactory as a translation of *erōs*; there is no better English equivalent but it is too broad. *Erōs* is normally love of a thing in that sense which involves strong desire for it, hence it is particularly associated with sexual love though not limited to it; purely disinterested love, whether contemplative or altruistic, is not normally covered by the term. The close connection between *erōs* and desire is important for a proper understanding of the way Socrates' speech develops. The other key word that raises translation problems is *kalos*, for which the usual translation, 'beautiful', is too narrow, for the beauty in question can be not only physical but also moral, where a word like 'noble' or 'fine' would be more in place; indeed, the word can be used in certain contexts even more generally to mean 'admirable' or even 'good'. Since in certain respects *erōs* and *to kalon* are treated in the dialogue as correlatives (the desire associated with *erōs* should properly be directed at that which is *kalos*), the possible range of significance of *kalos* becomes important when the notion of *erōs* is given progressively wider application by Diotima.

After dispensing with the services of the girl-piper, and agreeing to Eryximachus' proposal that they take up a long-standing concern of Phaedrus and attempt to fill the gap left by the poets and sophists by constructing encomia to Love, Phaedrus is the first to speak. He invokes ancient authorities to the effect that Love is among the oldest and greatest of the gods — being the first to be born, together with Earth, after Chaos. This hint, that love provides the intelligible principles which differentiate the earth from the formlessness of the gaping void, is later to be taken up — demythologized — in Socrates' speech, as is also Phaedrus' further claim that Love is the cause of all our highest blessings. This latter contention Phaedrus supports by reference to the way lovers inspire each other to 'great and beautiful [*kala*] deeds' and honourable ways of life (178c-d) transcending their ordinary self-concerns, even for life itself, so that 'if only there were a way to start a city or an army made up of lovers and the boys they love ... even a few of them, in battle side by side, would conquer all the world' (178e-179a). Phaedrus is exaggerating, of course, but about the time the *Symposium* was written the Theban 'sacred band' was organized on just this principle and soon proved its worth. Phaedrus' phrasing is often taken to indicate that the dialogue was written before the band's formation around 379 (e.g. Dover 1965: 15); if so, the passage is evidence that the idea of such a band was current at the time. But it is at least equally plausible to read Phaedrus' contention as pointing the other way, with Plato expecting his readers to recognize that at least part of it had been borne out by experience. In terms of the dialogue itself, the thesis that love inspires the military virtues is supported by Alcibiades' account of Socrates (the 'skilled in love') in war — thereby reinforcing the impression that the love of which Socrates tells, although different from that which concerns Phaedrus, nevertheless takes up into itself all that is valid in that lesser conception of love of which his companion has spoken.

The speech of Phaedrus, in fact, betrays no first-hand experience of love; in this sense the treatment is purely 'external'. One notes that Phaedrus is reported as having complained that others have composed nothing in praise of that 'ancient and powerful' god but, until prompted by the present occasion, has apparently done nothing about it himself. The nature of love is deduced from ancient traditions, as is the somewhat 'Socratic' claim towards the end that love brings a man close to the divine (180b). The insistence on Love's great age is later rejected by Agathon for whom he is 'the youngest of the gods' (195a), thereby positioning the two of them on opposite sides of the perennial 'Ancients' *versus* 'Moderns' divide. Beyond this, the sensibility which reveals itself in this speech is one dominated not so much by love as by ideals of military honour, in particular of 'great and beautiful deeds'. Only given this perspective could the examples adduced support the claim that Love is the cause of all our highest blessings, as they are supposed to do, and it is fully in accord with this approach that in his only revealing aside Phaedrus is made to express contempt for musicians on account of their lack of heroic qualities (179d). Given this 'external' understanding of love, it is not surprising that he can make no serious connections between the nature of Love, as he has expounded it, and the benefits he sees Love as bestowing; and given any richer set of values than his own, such as are held by all the subsequent speakers, the evidence he adduces is not commensurate with the claims for Love he wishes to make. In his own speech Socrates is to develop an understanding of love in terms by means of which, with reservations, the claims may be endorsed — especially that of the self-transcending dynamic of love — and the examples accepted, but both are placed in an integrated perspective which relates them to other values and to the nature of love itself, an understanding which is not just 'external' but integrated with a wide-ranging experience of life (the testimony of Alcibiades is of importance here).

This provides the pattern for the treatment of the subsequent speeches. In each there are claims which must be taken seriously in any adequate account of love, but equally in each there are loose ends and other weaknesses which prevent us from accepting it as in itself adequate — in each case, that is, until we come to the speech of Socrates which attempts to integrate all the symposiasts' claims in a comprehensive account which frees itself from their flaws by going beyond them. In each case the purported superiority of the Socratic account is open to rational appraisal. It is worth noting, for example, that Alcibiades is presented as finding his own life unsatisfactory in the light of the precepts and example of Socrates, even though he (at least at this time) triumphantly fulfils the ideals of Phaedrus. To the extent that we find this credible we recognize the comparative poverty of Phaedrus' sensibility compared with that of Socrates.

The most obvious objection to Phaedrus' account of love is that it is undiscriminating; love may have the desirable effects it speaks of but it can also be a corrupting influence, and this is the point immediately made by Pausanias — the next speaker. No activity, he insists, is of itself either noble or base, and 'exactly this principle applies to being in love: Love is not in himself noble (*kalos*) and worthy of praise — that depends on whether the sentiments he produces in us are themselves noble' (181a); sentiments and deeds are beautiful and noble if they are in accordance with unwritten law or justice (181e) which demands that love should have concern for the goodness and wisdom of the soul rather than the fleeting bloom of a youthful body. Pausanias is presented as Agathon's lover so we may take it that he is speaking out of his own experience, with an eye to the effect his speech will have on his host. But though his speech represents an advance on that of Phaedrus it has a number of weaknesses. No attempt is made to trace the connections between the noble and base types of love, nor between sexual loves, however noble, and other desires. Socrates attempts to meet these difficulties but it is Eryximachus, the next speaker, who first takes up the issue.

Unlike Pausanias he has a systematizing mind, and Plato carries this to the point of caricature. A doctor by profession, Eryximachus has a scientific sensibility and attempts to interpret all phenomena in his own scientific terms. He takes up the implicit suggestion of Phaedrus that love provides the intelligible principle underlying the world, glosses it with Pausanias' doctrine of the two sorts of love which is reinterpreted in terms of health and its opposite, and then uses this distinction as a metaphor to analyse first medicine — in its attempts to reconcile opposed elements in the body — and then all other phenomena. As Socrates is himself to present a systematic and all-embracing account of love there is a danger that his approach will be confused with that of contemporary scientists, as Aristophanes had himself confused it in the *Clouds*. Thus great pains are taken to distance Socrates from Eryximachus; the latter is presented as pompous and insensitive, with no apparent first-hand experience of love, and without a clear grasp of the issues in question. His criterion of health leaves no room for the value of the transcendence of self-concern exemplified in the self-sacrifice praised by Phaedrus; in his list of virtues, dominated by temperance, courage is conspicuous by its absence. Further, he misinterprets Heraclitus in a way that indicates he has no conception of how different elements may be combined harmoniously without compromising their natures (see Dorter 1969: 226-8), a harmony Socrates will later seek to achieve; his only conception of mediation is imaged by his cure of Aristophanes' hiccups through use of its medical opposite, sneezing. Again, his theory is presented as being virtually vacuous.

It would appear from the *Phaedo* (96a-99c) that Plato at this time held all such scientific theories to be lacking in explanatory power, which suggests that he may here be attempting to make clear through his presentation of Eryximachus the ultimately circular nature of contemporary natural science. However this may be, the speech plays a significant part in the economy of the entire dialogue. Apart from its useful purpose in providing a shift of tone, it draws our attention to the need for any account of love to 'place' it in relation to other aspects of life, but shows how barren such placing can be if developed in a purely schematic fashion without reference to first-hand experience.

But Aristophanes, who speaks next, has no such concern for the proper placing of phenomena. His parody of scientists in the *Clouds* gives point to the short way he dismisses Eryximachus here. If the doctor's account of love has been almost wholly 'external', at least as much so as that of Phaedrus, the poet appears to speak from the heart beneath his comic mask. He is impatient of a purely moralizing approach to love, as represented by the noble/base distinction of Pausanias and Eryximachus, and prefers rather to speak of it as meeting our deepest needs. From this point of view, he tells us, *Erōs* is the most philanthropic of the gods, providing that tenderness which can ennoble desire. While his story of man's origins is not to be taken literally, his notion of love as a desire for completeness, without which we are bound to spend our days frustrated in our isolation, has great resonance. The conviction that loss is part of the human condition has dominated our culture, whether as the Christian doctrine of the Fall, the intense longings of the Romantic movement, or the more modern concern with 'alienation'; and here it is presented in memorable form. Our deepest desire is to be one again with our other half, since in life with that other lies our true good, even though a total re-melding of that broken unity is for ever impossible. Phaedrus has taken courage as his standard of value, Pausanias the unwritten law, or justice, and Eryximachus temperance; Aristophanes looks to the remaining virtue, piety, as the means to our nature's true end: '*Erōs* promises the greatest hope of all: if we treat the gods with due reverence, he will restore to us our original nature, and by healing us, he will make us blessed and happy' (the word used is *eudaimonia*; 193d). The ultimate ground of our hope is thus not in our own nature, the standard of Eryximachus, but in what transcends it.

In this speech we have a genuine depth of feeling which is only matched by Socrates and, in a very different fashion, by Alcibiades. Aristophanes and Socrates are presented as the two great masters dominating the dialogue. If Socrates is to improve on Aristophanes he must match the latter's sensibility with an account that cuts at least as deep into human psychology. But Aristophanes' weakness, in the dialogue as in real life, is at the theoretical level. Perhaps our experience of love is such (sometimes at least) that it feels as if his story were true, but plainly it is false — indeed laughable (*geloion*) as he had warned at the start (189b). The challenge, therefore, is to provide an account which takes with full seriousness Aristophanes' insights, but weaves them into an explanation we can take seriously.

Agathon, who speaks next, is not equal to the task. He has just won the prize with his first tragedy, so he is a mere beginner beside the master of comedy who has preceded him, and he borrows the principles of eloquence developed by Gorgias rather than simply trust his own voice. Nevertheless, through the highly mannered conceits a distinctive sensibility emerges, one to which love is perceived as a state of happiness and beauty and its attendant emotions tender, insinuating and ephemeral as a flower's bloom. From the nature of love Agathon goes on to consider its benefits, for Love, as well as being beautiful, is good, having and bestowing all the virtues: courage, justice, temperance and wisdom — wisdom taking the place of Aristophanes' piety as its secular equivalent which, as Dorter (1969: 223) points out, reinstates 'the element of striving and transcendence which Aristophanes was forced to renounce'. Further, it was Love — 'love of beauty ... because love is not drawn to ugliness' (197b) — which inspired the other gods to wisdom and concord. The speech concludes with a *tour de force* composed in short, parallel and somewhat euphuistic phrases, composed in accordance with the principles of balance of the best oratorical models.

Studded with quotations from the poets, clear in structure and modelled on the most modern rhetorical principles, the speech is a highly accomplished piece of work, but its inadequacies are glaringly apparent. Its conception of love is shallow — it neither distinguishes between types of love nor reckons with Aristophanes' sense of the loss at the heart of it — the account of love's benefits is only tenuously connected with that of its nature, and some of those benefits are ascribed on the basis of verbal quibbles. Further, as Socrates soon brings out, the account is inconsistent. Rhetorical devices may stun the critical intellect for a time, and Socrates uses a pun to suggest that his is in danger of being turned to stone (198c), but the adequacy of an account is to be assessed not by such considerations but rather by its coherence and correspondence with what facts are available. There is, indeed, one important thesis highlighted by Agathon which Socrates wishes to take seriously — the thesis that the object of love is beauty — and Socrates uses this as the launching pad for a dialectical reply which eventually develops into his own positive account of love.

His first move is to make use of the close connection between *erōs* and desire, together with Agathon's admission that one only desires what one lacks (or fears one may lose), to establish that if the object of love is beauty love cannot itself be beautiful. Strictly speaking, the conclusion does not follow; love might possess present beauty and desire future beauty, like the healthy man health. Michael Stokes (1986: 128-9) has argued that Socrates is using as an implicit premise the thesis, extractable from Agathon's speech, that 'Love's beauty is *neces-*

sarily permanent', but in terms of the dialogue such a premise is rhetorically redundant. To insist that the essence of love is reflexive — that love is always desire for the continuance of its own properties rather than for anything beyond itself — would be grotesque, ignoring all that has gone before. The essential Socratic point is that in love there is a sense of desire for what is not yet attained or fulfilled, that love of its very nature impels us to seek the beautiful. The obvious objection that love might possess one type of beauty and the object of love another is met at the conclusion of Socrates' speech with the claim, not just that the beauty of all bodies is 'one and the same' (210b) but that all instances of beauty are exemplifications of that which 'is not beautiful this way and ugly that way' (211a); that all beauty is ultimately of the same type.

Socrates tempers the criticism of his host by telling how he had himself once thought like Agathon but had been led through the same dialectical steps by the priestess Diotima (the name, one notes, suggests giving honour to the divine) to a deeper understanding, and he purports to give an account of the ensuing conversation. The fiction, however, is transparent, for the conversation not only adverts to Aristophanes' own tale (as the latter himself appears to note at 212c) but takes up the conceptions of the nature of *erōs* developed in the other speeches. As is argued by Kenneth Dorter (1969), it provides critiques, implicit or explicit, in ascending order of quality of the views in question: of Phaedrus' conception of love in terms of beauty seeking beauty, like for like; Eryximachus' contrary conception of the noblest love as that which unites opposites through equalizing differences; Pausanias' richer conception of that unification through 'friendship'; Aristophanes' deepening of this friendship in terms of completion and its association with goodness; and finally Phaedrus' perception of it as transcending self-concern in pursuit of a good for which one might sacrifice one's life. The use of Diotima enables Socrates to present his preferred question-and-answer mode of discourse in the form of continuous speech — a form which fits the conventions of the dinner party. As the speech progresses the question-and-answer mode is virtually abandoned until towards the end, as we have noticed, Diotima speaks 'in the manner of the perfect sophists' (208c), though the rhetoric (as is prescribed for 'noble rhetoric' in the *Phaedrus*) remains rooted in what has already been established. This mode of discourse enables Socrates tactfully to present himself in the role of seeker rather than teacher, while weaving together and transforming what the others have said in terms of a coherent sensibility.

It is not my concern here to repeat the familiar exercise of analysing Socrates' speech, with Diotima's account of the ascent to beauty itself and thereby to the engendering of true virtue. Terence Irwin provides a sympathetically illuminating summary:

> Plato ... tries to show how the desire for something as an end in itself can be a rational desire formed by deliberation.... The progress is elenctic. At each stage the pupil tests his aspiration against his present objects of admiration, and though he was not previously aware of it, finds the objects inadequate to the aspiration, in discovering that the reason he offers for choosing this object really justifies the choice of something else.... This process ... allows a conception of the final good to emerge from rational reflection ... [which is] both cognitive and affective.
> (Irwin 1977: 170-1)

I have argued elsewhere (Warner 1979) that the edge of several of the standard criticisms of Plato's representation of this 'ascent' can be blunted, and that the conception of love as directed towards a quality (beauty) rather than to what Gregory Vlastos (1973a: 31) terms 'the individual, in the uniqueness and integrity of his or her individuality' is a function of the distinctive, and surprisingly modern, conception of the self deployed by Diotima. But it is worth noting that this rival conception of love as essentially directed towards individuals is not only at the heart of Aristophanes' vision but also the theme of Alcibiades' self-styled 'encomium to Socrates' (rather than to love).

This case has been forcibly deployed by Martha Nussbaum (1986: ch. 6) who sees the final speech as putting in question Diotima's vision. In terms of the dialogue, however, the alliance of Alcibiades with Aristophanes undermines the latter's credibility. The girl-piper is excluded as the speeches start, but Alcibiades returns with another and speaks of Socrates as a Marsyas whose speech is his piping, while his untransformative though emotional response to Socrates precisely echoes that of the pipes on the Corybantes. As Andrew Barker (1993) has argued, 'a person who sees Socrates as a piper has misunderstood the nature of his activity, and cannot benefit from it'. His testimony to the outward appearance and activity of Socrates as a unique individual is not weakened by this; he shows us how one who has been transformed by Diotima's ascent might live. But it is a view from the Cave, and by one who has resisted the attempt to turn him from shadows to the light; the story he tells, taken together with his subsequent career and death, certainly encourage us to reconsider Diotima's conclusions, but in order 'to face squarely what is involved in their rejection or misinterpretation'.

IV

How, then, should we assess this dialectical drama? In my 1979 paper I pointed out that if we had independent reasons for accepting as central to our evaluative scheme a form or forms of love other or richer than that of Greek *erōs* (at least as understood by Plato) this would 'cast doubt on contemporary Diotima-like doctrines concerning personal identity' (339), but of course if we had such reasons they would also undermine the whole dialectical movement of the *Symposium*.

Here the perspective provided by our cultural distance from Plato's world may be revealing. Unchallenged by any of the participants (with the possible exception of Aristophanes) are certain conventions governing those erotic relationships which the speakers in the dialogue regard as most important, in particular those determining the proper roles of the lover (*erastēs*) and the beloved (*erōmenos*). The asymmetry between them allows for no proper mutuality in the relationship — Aristophanes, as we have seen, admits that his story may prove *geloion* — and this perspective undergirds the vision of 'the beautiful itself' as *erōmenon*. It is worth noting that the vision is in this respect wholly different from that which we find in Dante's *Divine Comedy*, the closest Christian equivalent to the *Symposium*. In Dante God is at once lover and beloved, and the mutuality of Trinitarian love incorporates '*la nostra effige*' (*Paradiso* XXX 131;the image of Christ, who, in the words of the Athanasian Creed, has taken 'the Manhood into God'); further, in *Purgatorio* IX Dante can dream of himself as Ganymede, as *erōmenos* to the divine *erastēs*. The Christian conception of love at its deepest involving mutuality is grounded in the New Testament vision of God as love as well as beloved; in Plato the proper object of love cannot itself love, the roles of *erastēs* and *erōmenos* are at their deepest incompatible. In the *Symposium* the pattern is complicated from the outset by *Phaedrus'* casting of the female Alcestis in the role of *erastēs* and allowing the *erōmenos* Achilles to sacrifice himself for his *erastēs*. However at 208d Diotima reinterprets these examples in terms of the underlying asymmetric perspective which is preserved, and indeed plays a key role, in the final speech where Alcibiades tells of his discomfiture as he discovers that the roles he had casually assumed of himself as *erōmenos* and

Socrates as *erastēs* were in fact reversed. This is not the place to consider whether contemporary Christian and post-Christian conceptions of mutuality at the heart of love are richer, or otherwise more adequate, than that of the Platonic asymmetry; but the possibility throws an instructive light on the potential for disruption of the Aristophanic vision presented in the *Symposium*, of which Plato himself may have been only partially aware.

Considerations such as these, however, constitute only one strand in recent critiques of the *Symposium*. Significantly more influential has been the recent — negative — judgment of Sir Kenneth Dover (1980), a judgement which focusses on Socrates' speech and dialogue with his host and is grounded both in the detail of his scholarly edition, and in more general considerations.

At the level of detail he identifies a number of fallacious inferences and implausible assumptions, notes that neither Agathon in discussion with Socrates nor Socrates in dialogue with Diotima criticizes them, and remarks tartly:

> A dialogue in which one speaker agrees at every step with the other, never offering serious resistance or making serious criticisms, differs in form from the type of continuous, authoritative exposition which Socrates decries in *Prt* 328d-329b, 335a-336d, and differs (at least on a cursory reading) in the impression which it conveys, but does not differ in substance. (Dover 1980: 133)

Against this attack Michael Stokes has argued that many of the alleged weaknesses in the Socratic dialectic turn on incoherences in the speech of Agathon itself which provide crucial terms of reference for the discussion with Diotima; Agathon is, after all, the host. Given that context, the Socratic arguments are less easily faulted. But this raises, as Stokes is well aware, the objection that it is Plato himself who has constructed those very terms of reference. Stokes's response to this difficulty is weak. He suggests that it may be that 'Plato thought he had shown that if you speak as Agathon in this dialogue speaks, and are the sort of person Agathon is, then you will in the end be forced in the name of consistency to accept sundry Platonic propositions' (Stokes 1986: 178). He adds that 'It is not clear that he believed it possible to produce an objectively convincing proof of his views' (182).

The obvious question, however, still remains: Why is Agathon's sensibility so important? The account I have given may begin to suggest an answer. His speech takes account of much that has gone before providing, as Dorter has argued, a standard for judging the goodness of love which improves on those of his predecessors. When one considers the points at which Stokes uses Agathon's perspectives to rebut Dover's attempted diagnoses of Socratic fallacy, one soon notices that these perspectives are not just those of Agathon. Stokes (114-29) argues that Agathon's speech contains the conception of *erōs* as a desire to possess that which is beautiful and which itself produces that which is good, a running together of love for a person with desire for impersonal items, and the conception of *erōs* as necessarily and permanently beautiful; also (140) the treatment of an abstract item as an instance of itself. But Phaedrus has maintained (178c) that *erōs* is the cause of all our highest blessings and he is seconded by Eryximachus (188d). Pausanias (182-4) sees the noble form of *erōs* as inspiring the desire for the 'capture' (*helein*) of that which is beautiful and virtuous, the true lover being less attracted by the fleeting bloom of the body than by abiding qualities of the soul with which he seeks to be 'fused' (*suntakeis*); while Aristophanes enriches the model of possession in terms of capture and submission with the ideal of becoming permanently one with the beloved — Hephaistos offering (192d) not only to 'fuse them together' (*suntēxai*) but also to 'make them grow together' (*sumphusēsai*), adding to a metaphor from craftsmanship one from nature. Eryximachus, as we have seen, insists on viewing personal love as an exemplification of impersonal principles, and Pausanias attributes to his two forms of love — themselves abstracted from concrete instances — the qualities of those instances. The only item in Stokes's list which has no counterpart or analogue before the speech of Agathon is that concerning the necessary beauty of love, and of course it is this claim that Socrates immediately sets out to demolish.

Plato may indeed doubt the possibility of 'objectively convincing proof' if by this is meant a form of demonstration independent of our subjectivities, but may well regard as reasonably reliable argument tested against a range of varying and credible sensibilities (compare Socrates' exchanges with Polus and Callicles in the *Gorgias*) — hence, in part, the familiar question-and-answer method. It is worth remembering that it is characteristic of Plato's Socrates to work with premisses provided by others.

This brings us to Dover's more general charge against Plato, that he nowhere gives a comprehensive account of his philosophy 'declaring its axioms, explaining its methods systematically and offering proof of its conclusions' (5). Instead of axioms which might be 'replaced' by 'reasoned reflection on experience', Dover attributes to Plato 'a kind of craving' for 'something more' than 'indefinitely adjustable generalisations and pragmatic definitions' can give us (6). The charge, however, is double edged. The notion of axioms being tested by experience is logically odd, but is characteristic of a certain pragmatist school of thought (well exemplified by Richard Rorty), which despairs of geometric reasoning about substantive philosophical matters, cannot conceive of an alternative, and resorts to the inconclusive and indefinite play of 'pragmatic definitions'; in Rorty, indeed, this leads to the dropping of the notions of argument and even truth (1980: chaps. 7-8), to what the Socrates of the *Phaedo* (89d) calls 'misology'.

In that dialogue Socrates proposes an alternative to the Dover mathematical model, a picture of the philosophical activity which, though according to method, is not probative. Its aim is rational persuasiveness, but ultimately the only test of this is the actual persuasion of those who are fitted to judge and have argued rationally. It has clear affinities with that model of dialectic later sketched by Aristotle (*Topics* 100a-b) which reasons from plausible opinions (*endoxa*) which it subjects to criticism, 'wherein lies the path to the principles of all inquiries' (see Warner 1989: chaps. 2-3). On Aristotelian principles, too, it appears, the dramatic movement of the *Symposium* may be characterized as 'dialectical'; in Plato's Cave we can have no axioms, but only criticizable *endoxa* — and we have seen how Plato has set about criticizing these. Instead of objecting that Plato does not argue axiomatically in the *Symposium*, and makes remarkably limited use of that characteristic geometric form the elenchus, we might do better to consider how the procedures he does use might be generalized and defended. But that would be another story.

Bibliography

Adam, J. ed. 1963. *The Republic of Plato*, 2nd edn., intro. D.A. Rees (Cambridge, Cambridge University Press).

Allen, R.E. 1961-2. 'The Argument from Opposites in Republic V', *Review of Metaphysics* 15, 325-35.

Anderson, G. 1986. *Philostratus: Biography and Belles lettres in the Second Century AD*, (London, Sydney and Dover, New Hampshire: Croom Helm).

Annas, Julia 1981. *An Introduction to Plato's Republic* (Oxford: Clarendon Press).

_____ 1982a. 'Plato's Myths of Judgment', *Phronesis* 27, 119-43.

_____ 1982b. 'Plato on the Triviality of Literature', in Moravcsik and Temko, 1-28.

_____ 1982c. 'Aristotle on Inefficient Causes', *Philosophical Quarterly* 32, 311-26.

Annas, Julia and Grimm, R.H. eds. 1988. *Oxford Studies in Ancient Philosophy: Supplementary Volume*, (Oxford: Clarendon Press).

Barker, Andrew ed. 1984. *Greek Musical Writings: Volume I, The Musician and his Art* (Cambridge: Cambridge University Press).

_____ 1993. 'The Daughters of Memory', *Musica e Storia* 2 (forthcoming).

Berg, G.O. 1904. *Metaphor and Comparison in the Dialogues of Plato* (Berlin).

Berman, Scott 1991. 'Socrates and Callicles on Pleasure', *Phronesis* 36, 117-140.

Blank, D.L. 1986. 'Socrates' Instructions to Cebes: Plato, *Phaedo* 101d-e', *Hermes* 114, 146-63.

Bowra, C.M. 1961. *Greek Lyric Poetry*, 2nd edn. (Oxford: Clarendon Press).

Bramble, J.C. 1974. *Persius and the Programmatic Satire* (Cambridge: Cambridge University Press).

Brandwood, L. 1976. *Index to Plato* (Leeds: Mahey).

Burnet, J. ed. 1911. *Plato's Phaedo* (Oxford: Clarendon Press).

Burnyeat, Myles 1984. 'Aristotle on Understanding Knowledge' in E. Berti, ed., *Aristotle on Science* (Padua).

_____ 1990. *The Theaetetus of Plato* (Indianapolis: Hackett).

Cooper, N. 1986. 'Between Knowledge and Ignorance', *Phronesis* 31, 229-42.

Crombie, I.M. 1969. *An Examination of Plato's Doctrines*, 3rd impr., (London: Routledge).

Delatte, A. 1934. *Les Conceptions de l'Enthousiasme chez les Philosophes Présocratiques* (Paris).

De Romilly, J. 1973. 'Gorgias et le Pouvoir de la Posie', *Journal of Hellenic Studies* 93, 155-62.

_____ 1975. *Magic and Rhetoric in Ancient Greece* (Cambridge, Mass.: Harvard University Press).

de Ste. Croix, G.E M. 1972. *The Origins of the Peloponnesian War* (London: Duckworth).

Dixsaut, M. 1991. *Platon: Phédon* (Paris: GF - Flammarion).

Dodds, E.R. 1951. *The Greeks and the Irrational* (Berkeley: University of California Press).

_____ ed. 1959. *Plato: Gorgias* (Oxford: Clarendon Press).

Dorter, Kenneth 1969. 'The Significance of the Speeches in Plato's *Symposium*', *Philosophy and Rhetoric* 2, 215-34.

Dover, K.J. 1965. 'The Date of Plato's Symposium', *Phronesis* X, 2-20.

_____ 1974. *Greek Popular Morality in the Time of Plato and Aristotle* (Oxford: Blackwell).

_____ ed. 1980. *Plato: Symposium* (Cambridge: Cambridge University Press).

Farrar, C. 1988. *The Origins of Democratic Thinking* (Cambridge: Cambridge University Press).

Ferrari, G.R.F. 1987. *Listening to the Cicadas: a Study of Plato's* Phaedrus (Cambridge: Cambridge University Press).

_____ 1989. 'Plato and Poetry', in G.A. Kennedy, ed., *The Cambridge History of Literary Criticism*, vol. 1 (Cambridge: Cambridge University Press), 92-148.

Fine, Gail 1978. 'Knowledge and Belief in Republic V', *Archiv für Geschichte der Philosophie* 60, 121-39.

_____ 1990. 'Knowledge and Belief in *Republic* V-VII', in Stephen Everson, ed., *Epistemology (Companions to Ancient Thought 1)* (Cambridge, Cambridge University Press), 85-115.

Flashar, H. 1958. *Der Dialog 'Ion' als Zeugnis platonischer Philosophie* (Berlin).

Frede, D. 1978. 'The Final Proof of the Immortality of the Soul in Plato's *Phaedo* 102a-107a', *Phronesis* 23, 24-41.

Frede, Michael 1980. 'The Original Notion of Cause', in M. Schofield et al.,(eds.), *Doubt and Dogmatism: Studies in Hellenistic Epistemology* (Oxford: Clarendon Press).

_____ 1988. 'Being and Becoming in Plato', in Annas and Grimm, 37-52.

Friedlaender, P. 1958-1969. *Plato*, i-iii, tr. H. Meyerhoff (London: Routledge).

Gallop, David tr. 1975. *Plato: Phaedo* (Oxford: Clarendon Press).

Genette, Gérard 1980. *Narrative Discourse: an Essay in Method*, tr. J.E. Lewin (Oxford: Blackwell)

Gill, Christopher and McCabe, Mary Margaret forthcoming. *Form and Content in Plato's Later Dialogues* (Oxford: Clarendon Press).

Goldschmidt, V. 1947. *Le Paradigme dans la dialectique Platonicienne* (Paris).

Goodwin, W.W. 1875, repr. 1965. *Syntax of the Moods and Tenses of the Greek Verb* (repr. London/New York: Macmillan).

Gosling, J.C.B. 1960. '*Republic* V: *Ta Polla Kala*', *Phronesis* 5, 116-28.

_____ 1968. '*Doxa* and *Dunamis* in Plato's *Republic*, *Phronesis* 13, 119-30.

_____ 1977. 'Reply to [F.C.] White', *Canadian Journal of Philosophy* 7, 307-14.

Gosling, J.C.B. and Taylor, C.C.W. 1982. *The Greeks on Pleasure* (Oxford: Clarendon Press).

Grenet, P. 1948. *Les origines de l'analogie philosophique dans les dialogues de Platon* (Paris).

Gould, T. 1964. 'Plato's Hostility to Art', *Arion* 3, 70-91.

Guthrie, W.K.C. 1962-1981. *A History of Greek Philosophy*, i-vi (Cambridge: Cambridge University Press).

Hackforth, R. tr. 1952. *Plato's Phaedrus* (Cambridge: Cambridge University Press).

Halliwell, S. 1988. *Plato: Republic 10* (Wiltshire: Aris and Phillips).

Halperin, David M. 1992. 'Plato and the Erotics of Narrativity', in Klagge and Smith, 93-129.

Havelock, E.A. 1963. *Preface to Plato* (Oxford: Blackwell).

Hintikka, Jaakko 1973. 'Knowledge and its Objects in Plato', in Moravcsik, 1-30.

Hudson-Williams, H. 1950. 'Conventional Forms of Debate and the Melian Dialogue', *American Journal of Philology* 71, 156ff.

Irwin, Terence 1977. *Plato's Moral Theory: the Early and Middle Dialogues* (Oxford: Clarendon Press).

Jowett, B. and Ostwald, M. trs. 1956. *Plato: Protagoras*, intro. Gregory Vlastos (Indianapolis: Library of Liberal Arts).

Kahn, C.H. 1981. 'Some Philosophical Uses of "to be" in Plato', *Phronesis* 26, 119-127.

Kerferd, G.B. 1981. *The Sophistic Movement* (Cambridge: Cambridge University Press).

Klagge, James C. and Smith, Nicholas D. 1992. *Methods of Interpreting Plato and his Dialogues, Oxford Studies in Ancient Philosophy: Supplementary Volume* (Oxford: Clarendon Press).

Kneale, W. and M. 1962. *The Development of Logic* (Oxford: Clarendon Press).

Krämer, H.J. 1990. *Plato and the Foundations of Metaphysics*, tr. J.R. Catan (New York: State University of New York Press; English translation of *Platone e i fondamenti della metafisica*, Milan, 1982).

Laborderie, J. 1978. *Le dialogue platonicien de la maturité* (Paris).

Lattimore, R. 1960. *Greek Lyrics*, 2nd edn. (Chicago: University of Chicago Press).

Lee, Desmond tr. 1987. *Plato: The Republic*, 2nd edn. (Harmondsworth: Penguin).

Linforth, I.M. 1946. 'The Corybantic Rites in Plato', *University of California Publications in Classical Philology* 13, 121-62.

Lloyd, G.E.R. 1966. *Polarity and Analogy, Two Types of Argumentation in Early Greek Thought* (Cambridge: Cambridge University Press).

____ 1979. *Magic, Reason and Experience* (Cambridge: Cambridge University Press).

LSJ 1943 Liddell, H.G., Scott, R. and Jones, H.S. *Greek-English Lexicon*, 9th edn. (Oxford: Clarendon Press).

MacDowell, D.M. 1982. *Gorgias: Encomium of Helen* (Bristol: Bristol Classical Press).

Mackenzie, Mary Margaret 1981. *Plato on Punishment* (Berkeley: University of California Press).

____ 1982. 'Paradox in Plato's *Phaedrus*', *Proceedings of the Cambridge Philological Society* 208, 64-76.

____ 1988. 'Impasse and Explanation: from the *Lysis* to the *Phaedo*', *Archiv für Geschichte der Philosophie* 70, 15-45.

MacNeice, Louis 1964. *Selected Poems* (London: Faber and Faber).

Malcolm, J. 1991. *Plato on the Self-predication of Forms: Early and Middle Dialogues* (Oxford: Clarendon Press).

McCabe, Mary Margaret 1993a. 'Arguments in Context: Aristotle's response to the Platonic challenge', in D.J. Furley and A. Nehamas, eds., *Proceedings of the Symposium Aristotelicum* (Princeton: Princeton University Press; forthcoming).

____ 1993b. *Plato's Individuals* (Princeton: Princeton University Press; forthcoming).

Moline, J. 1981. *Plato's Theory of Understanding* (Madison: Wisconsin).

Moravcsik, J.M.E. ed. 1973. *Patterns in Plato's Thought: Papers arising out of the 1971 West Coast Greek Philosophy Conference* (Dordrecht and Boston: Reidel).

Moravcsik, J.M.E. and Temko, P. eds. 1982. *Plato on Beauty. Wisdom, and the Arts* (New Jersey: Rowman and Allanheld).

Morrison, J.S. 1941. 'The Place of Protagoras in Athenian Public Life (460-415 B.C)', *Classical Quarterly* 35, 1-16.

Murdoch, Iris 1977. *The Fire and the Sun: Why Plato Banished the Artists* (Oxford: Clarendon Press).

Murray, P. 1981. 'Poetic Inspiration in Early Greece', *Journal of Hellenic Studies* 101, 87-100.

Nagy, N. 1989. 'Early Greek Views of Poets and Poetry', in G.A. Kennedy, ed., *The Cambridge History of Literary Criticism*, vol.1 (Cambridge: Cambridge University Press), 1-77.

Nehamas, Alexander 1982. 'Plato on Imitation and Poetry in *Republic* 10', in Moravscik and Temko, 47-78.

Nehamas, Alexander and Woodruff, Paul trs. 1989. *Plato: Symposium* (Indianapolis: Hackett).

Nettleship, Richard Lewis 1901. *Lectures on the Republic of Plato*, 2nd edn. (London: Macmillan).

Nietzsche, Friedrich 1966. *Beyond Good and Evil: Prelude to a Philosophy of the Future*, tr. W. Kaufmann (New York: Vintage Books).

Nussbaum, Martha C. 1982. '"This story isn't true": Poetry, Goodness, and Understanding in Plato's *Phaedrus*', in Moravcsik and Temko, 79-124.

_____ 1986. *The Fragility of Goodness: Luck and Ethics in Greek Tragedy and Philosophy* (Cambridge: Cambridge University Press).

Orwell, George 1950. 'Lear, Tolstoy and the Fool', in his *Shooting an Elephant and Other Essays* (London: Secker and Warburg), 33-56.

Osborne, Catherine 1988. 'Topography in the *Timaeus*', *Proceedings of the Cambridge Philological Society* 214, 104-14.

_____ forthcoming. 'Space, Time, Shape and Direction: Creative Discourse in the *Timaeus*' in Gill and McCabe.

Owen, G.E.L. 1960. 'Eleatic Questions', *Classical Quarterly* NS 10, 84-102.

Page, D.L. ed. 1962. *Poetae Melici Graeci* (Oxford: Clarendon Press).

Patterson, R. 1985. *Image and Reality in Plato's Metaphysics* (Indianapolis: Hackett).

Penner, Terry 1987. *The Ascent from Nominalism* (Dordrecht: Reidel).

Pesce, D. 1990. *Il Platone di Tubinga* (Brescia: Paideia Editrice).

Pfeiffer, R. 1968. *History of Classical Scholarship*, vol. 1 (Oxford: Clarendon Press).

Pohlenz, M. 1920. 'Die Anfänge der griechischen Poetik', *Nachrichten von der Gesellschaft der Wissenschaften zu Göttingen*, Phil.- hist. Klasse, 142-178; reprinted in his *Kleine Schriften* ii (Hildesheim 1965) 436 ff.

Pöhlmann, E. 1976. 'Enthusiasmus und Mimesis: zum platonischen Ion', *Gymnasium* 83, 191-208.

Randall, John Herman Jr. 1970. *Plato: Dramatist of the Life of Reason* (New York and London: Columbia University Press).

Robinson, Richard 1953. *Plato's Earlier Dialectic*, 2nd edn. (Oxford: Clarendon Press).

Rorty, Richard 1980. *Philosophy and the Mirror of Nature* (Oxford: Blackwell).

Rosen, S.H. 1959. 'Collingwood and Greek Aesthetics', *Phronesis* 4, 135-48.

Rowe, C.J. tr. 1986. *Plato: Phaedrus* (Wiltshire: Aris and Phillips).

_____ 1993a. Plato: *Phaedo* (Cambridge: Cambridge University Press; forthcoming).

_____ 1993b. 'Explanation in Phaedo 99c6-102a8', *Oxford Studies in Ancient Philosophy* 11 (forthcoming).

Santas, G.X. 1973. 'Hintikka on Knowledge and Its Objects In Plato', in Moravcsik, 31-51.

_____ 1990. 'Knowledge and Belief in Plato's *Republic*', in P. Nicolacopoulos, ed., *Greek Studies in the Philosophy and History of Science, Boston Studies in the Philosophy of Science*, vol. 121 (Dordrecht and Boston: Reidel), 45-59.

Schaper, E. 1968. *Prelude to Aesthetics* (London: Allen & Unwin).

Scheinberg, S. 1979. 'The Bee Maidens of the Homeric Hymn to Hermes', *Harvard Studies in Classical Philology* 83, 1-28.

Sedley, David, 1991. 'Teleology and Myth in the *Phaedo*', in J. Cleary and D. Shartin, eds., *Proceedings of the Boston Colloquium in Ancient Philosophy* (Lanham, MD: University Press of America), 359-83.

Segal, C.P. 1962. 'Gorgias and the Psychology of the Logos', *Harvard Studies in Classical Philology* 66, 99-155.

Seligman, P. 1974. *Being and Not-Being: an Introduction to Plato's Sophist* (The Hague: Nijhoff).

Sharples, R. tr. 1985. *Plato: Meno* (Wiltshire, Aris and Phillips).

Shorey, Paul tr. 1930. *Plato: The Republic*, 2 vols. (London and Cambridge, Mass.: Loeb Classical Library).

Sperber, D. 1975. *Rethinking Symbolism* (Cambridge: Cambridge University Press).

Stadter, P.A. 1991. 'Pericles Among the Intellectuals', *Illinois Classical Studies* 16, 111-124.

Stokes, Michael C. 1986. *Plato's Socratic Conversations* (London and Baltimore: Athlone Press and Johns Hopkins University Press).

Sullivan, J.P. 1967. 'The Hedonism in Plato's *Protagoras*', *Phronesis* 6, 10-28.

Taylor, C.C.W. tr. 1976. *Plato: Protagoras* (Oxford: Clarendon Press).

Tigerstedt, E.N. 1969. 'Plato's Idea of Poetical Inspiration', *Commentationes Humanarum Litterarum* 44, 2, 5-76.

_____ 1970. '*Furor Poeticus*: Poetic Inspiration in Greek Literature before Democritus and Plato', *Journal of the History of Ideas* 31, 163-78.

Tolstoy, Leo nd. 'Shakespeare and the Drama', tr. V. Tchertkoff, in *Tolstoy on Shakespeare* (Christchurch, Hants and London: Free Age Press and Everett), 7-81.

_____ 1930. *What is Art?*, trans. A. Maude (London: Oxford University Press).

Turnbull, R.G. 1988. 'Response to Professor Fine's Critique', in Annas and Grimm, 29-36.

Velardi, R. 1989. *Enthousiasmos: Possessione Rituale e Teoria della Communicazione Poetica in Platone* (Rome, Edizione dell'Ateneo).

Verdenius, W.J. 1943. 'L'Ion de Platon', *Mnemosyne* 11, 233-62.

_____ 1962. 'Der Begriff der Mania in Platons Phaidros', *Archiv für Geschichte der Philosophie* 44, 132-50.

_____ 1983. 'The Principles of Greek Literary Criticism', *Mnemosyne* 36, 14-59.

Vicaire, P. 1960. *Platon: Critique Litteraire* (Paris).

Vlastos, Gregory 1956. Introduction to Jowett and Ostwald.

_____ 1973a. 'The Individual as an Object of Love in Plato', in his *Platonic Studies* (Princeton: Princeton University Press), 1-34.

_____ 1973b. 'Reasons and Causes in the *Phaedo*', in his *Platonic Studies* (Princeton: Princeton University Press), 76-109; reprinted, with corrections and additions, from *The Philosophical Review* 78 (1969).

_____ 1991. *Socrates: Ironist and Philosopher* (Cambridge: Cambridge University Press).

Warner, Martin 1979. 'Love, Self and Plato's *Symposium*', *The Philosophical Quarterly* 29, 329-39.

_____ 1989. *Philosophical Finesse: Studies in the Art of Rational Persuasion* (Oxford: Clarendon Press).

White, F.C. 1977. 'The "Many" in *Republic* 475e-480a', *Canadian Journal of Philosophy* 7, 291-306

_____ 1981. *Plato's Theory of Particulars* (New York: Arno Press).

_____ 1984. 'The Scope of Knowledge in *Republic* V', *Australasian Journal of Philosophy* 62, 339-54.

White, N.P. 1979. *A Companion to Plato's* Republic, (Oxford: Blackwell).

Wiggins, D. 1986. 'Teleology and the Good in the *Phaedo*', *Oxford Studies in Ancient Philosophy* 4, 1-18.

Woodruff, P. 1982a. 'What Could Go Wrong with Inspiration? Why Plato's Poets Fail', in Moravcsik and Temko, eds, 137-50.

_____ tr. 1982b. *Plato: Hippias Major* (Oxford: Blackwell).

Notes on Contributors

Andrew Barker was until recently Senior Lecturer in Philosophy at the University of Warwick and is now Senior Lecturer in Classics at the University of Otago. His publications include the two volumes of *Greek Musical Writings* (Cambridge University Press 1984 & 1989) and articles on Greek music, philosophy, literature and science. He is a Fellow of the Institute for Research in Classical Philosophy and Science at Princeton.

John Gould is Emeritus Professor of Greek at the University of Bristol. His publications include *The Development of Plato's Ethics* (Cambridge University Press 1955; reprinted 1972), *Herodotus* (Weidenfeld and Nicolson 1989) and articles on Greek poetry, drama, religion and society.

Mary Margaret McCabe is Reader in Philosophy at King's College, London. Her publications include *Plato on Punishment* (University of California 1981), *Plato's Individuals* (Princeton University Press, forthcoming) and numerous articles on ancient philosophy.

Penelope Murray is Lecturer in Classics at the University of Warwick. Her publications include (as editor) *Genius: the History of an Idea* (Blackwell 1989), and she is working on a Commentary on Plato's *Ion*.

Christopher Rowe is Henry Overton Wills Professor of Greek at the University of Bristol. He has translated and commented on Plato's *Phaedrus* (Aris and Phillips 1986) and has just completed a commentary on the *Phaedo*, to be published by Cambridge University Press in the *Greek and Latin Classics* series in 1993. He was Chairman of the International Plato Society from 1989-92.

Richard Rutherford is Tutor in Greek and Latin Literature at Christ Church, Oxford. His publications include *The Meditations of Marcus Aurelius: A Study* (Oxford University Press 1989), a Commentary on Books 19 and 20 of Homer's *Odyssey* (Cambridge University Press 1992) and a number of articles, especially on Homer. He is currently working on a general book on the interpretation of Plato's dialogues.

Michael C. Stokes is Professor of Greek at the University of Durham. His publications include *One and Many in Presocratic Philosophy* (Harvard 1971), *Plato's Socratic Conversations* (Athlone 1986) and (edited jointly with Barry S. Gower) *Socratic Questions* (Routledge 1992).

Manuela Tecuşan is Junior Research Fellow at Selwyn College, Cambridge. Her publications include a Romanian Introduction and Commentary to Plato's *Phaedo* and work on the *sumposion* in Plato.

Martin Warner is Senior Lecturer and Director of Graduate Studies in Philosophy at the University of Warwick. His publications include *Philosophical Finesse: Studies in the Art of Rational Persuasion* (Clarendon Press 1989) and (as editor) *The Bible as Rhetoric: Studies in Biblical Persuasion and Credibility* (Routledge 1990).

Index locorum Platonicus

General Index

Adam, J., 106
Aeschylus, 19, 33
Alcibiades, 15, 137, 149, 152, 159, 161, 162-3, 165, 166, 168, 171, 172
allegory, 1, 4, 7, 8, 47, 48-9, 50, 53, 60, 62, 64
Allen, M.J.B., 44n
Allen, R.E., 125
Anaxagoras, 54, 64, 65, 90, 91, 92, 94, 101
Anderson, G., 142n
Annas, J., 41, 43, 44, 60n, 111n, 112n, 130n
Archelaus, 138
Aristophanes, 18-19, 31, 32, 34, 55, 138, 141n, 151n, 159, 160, 167-9, 170, 172, 173, 174
Aristotle, 9, 47, 50, 51, 53, 55-7, 63, 70, 72n, 75, 121, 122, 160, 162, 175
art, 7, 13-15, 17, 20, 21, 22, 24, 25, 27n, 31, 41, 42, 45, 83, 86

Barker, A.D., 1, 30n, 155n, 157n, 171
Battersby, C., 157n

beauty, 9, 10, 11, 35, 44, 52, 53, 64, 79, 92, 93, 96, 99, 100, 104-5, 106-7, 108, 110, 111-12, 115, 118, 125-31, 136-7, 157-8, 163-5, 169-71, 172, 174
belief (and opinion), 9, 48, 56-8, 60, 62-3, 79, 83, 85, 108-9, 115-19, 122, 123-32, 145, 152, 153n
Berman, S., 131-2
Bowra, C.M., 150n
Bramble, J.C., 149
Brandwood, L., 107n
Burnet, J., 90n
Burnyeat, M., 55n

Cave, 4, 6, 8, 9, 10-11, 20, 48, 69, 80-2, 89, 95-6, 100, 103, 132, 156, 157-8, 160-1, 162, 171, 175
Chadwick, H.M. and H.K., 33n
Cicero, 32n, 39
concept, 3, 7, 11, 35, 46, 80, 134
Cooper, N., 109n, 112n, 124
Crombie, I.M., 119n

Dante, 172
deconstruction, 10-11
Delatte, A., 32n
Democritus, 32n
De Romilly, J., 38n, 145n
de Ste. Croix, G.E.M., 143n